Innovation, Startups and Intellectual Property Management

Ignacio De Leon • Jose Fernandez Donoso

Innovation, Startups and Intellectual Property Management

Strategies and Evidence from Latin America and other Regions

Springer

Ignacio De Leon
Competitiveness and Innovation Division
Inter-American Development Bank
Washington, DC, USA

Jose Fernandez Donoso
Facultad de Economía y Negocios
Universidad del Desarrollo
Las Condes, Santiago, Chile

ISBN 978-3-319-54905-7 ISBN 978-3-319-54906-4 (eBook)
DOI 10.1007/978-3-319-54906-4

Library of Congress Control Number: 2017933680

Printed on acid-free paper

This Springer imprint is published by Springer Nature
The registered company is Springer International Publishing AG
The registered company address is: Gewerbestrasse 11, 6330 Cham, Switzerland

Acronyms

AIPLA	American Intellectual Property Law Association
BD	The U.S. Bayh-Dole Act of 1980
DPA	Defensive Patent Aggregator
FRAND	Fair Reasonable and Non-Discriminatory Royalties
IDB	Inter-American Development Bank
IEPI	Instituto Ecuatoriano de la Propiedad Intelectual
IMPI	Instituto Mexicano de la Propiedad Industrial
INAPI	Instituto Nacional de la Propiedad Industrial de Chile
INDECOPI	Instituto de Defensa del Consumidor y de la Propiedad Intelectual del Peru
IP	Intellectual Property
IPR	Intellectual Property Right
IPXI	Intellectual Property Exchange International, Inc.
NPE	Non-practicing Entity
OAS	Organization American States
OECD	Organization of Economic Cooperation and Development
R&D	Research and Development
SEP	Standard-Essential Patent
SME	Small and Medium Enterprise
SMIE	Small and Medium Innovative Enterprises
SSIPEX	Shanghai Silicon Intellectual Property Exchange
TTO	Technology Transfer Office
WSJ	Wall Street Journal

Acknowledgements

We extend our sincerest thanks and appreciation to those patient souls who helped us accomplish this study. In particular, special thanks to the Inter-American Development Bank for financially supporting our preliminary research on the Costs of Use of Intellectual Property in Latin America, which ultimately led us to expand our conclusions into this book.

This work would have not been completed without the support received from the Intellectual Property Offices of Mexico, Colombia, Chile, Peru, Ecuador and Costa Rica. Out special thanks to Mr. Jose Luis Londoño, Adjunct Superintendent of the Superintendencia de Industria y Comercio of Colombia; Mr. Miguel Angel Margáin, Executive Director of the Instituto Mexicano de la Propiedad Industrial; Mr. Herbert Tassano, Chairman of INDECOPI of Peru; Mr. Maximiliano Santa Cruz, National Director of the Instituto National de la Propiedad Industrial of Chile; and Santiago Pelaez, from Ruta N of Medellin, who gave us a thorough overview of their IP management program.

Finally, we would like to thank our wives and sons for all the time we stole from them to write this book.

Contents

Preface

In 1986, biochemist Fernando Fischmann bought 60 hectares (almost 150 thousand acres) in the Chilean Pacific coast to build a vacation resort. A south current in the Pacific, known as the Humboldt current, makes the Chilean and Peruvian coastline cold, with murky waters in most of their harbors, including the Valparaiso Region, where Fischmann had decided to buy his land. His dream was to build an artificial lagoon for the resort, with crystal, warm waters, so that vacationers felt as though they were spending their summers in an idyllic beach paradise. That seemed to be beyond his means, however, because of the natural conditions of the place.

Yet, after several years of research and frustrating results, in 1997 Fischmann succeeded in developing an eco-friendly system around a large crystal-clear lagoon. The technology developed by Fischmann maintains large bodies of crystalline fresh salt or brackish water at a low cost. It is an automated process based on pulses and ultra-sonic filtration. The use of large quantities of chlorine for purification is avoided and the energy usage of the filtration systems used in the lagoons' technology are the equivalent of 2% of the energy consumed by traditional pools with standard filtration systems.

The first lagoon to use such technology was in the holiday complex of San Alfonso del Mar, and in 2007 the lagoon was identified by Guinness World Records as the largest crystal lagoon in the world—covering 8 ha and containing 250,000,000 l of water drawn from the Pacific Ocean. During the summer the lagoon is maintained at a temperature of 26 °C, nine degrees warmer than the adjacent sea.

Once he finished his resort, Fischmann used the resources gained to start a new venture in 2007, to commercialize the technology internationally. He named the company Crystal Lagoons. In 2008, only one year after the company's foundation, Boston Consulting Group calculated the firm's value at US$1.8 billion. Fischmann now has his technology patented in 160 countries, and Crystal Lagoon has commercialized its technology to more than 300 projects in 60 countries. In the United States, the company has plans for an estimated value of US$30 billion. The firm's industrial technology is claimed to be applicable for industrial cooling for thermoelectric power plants, data centers, concentrating photovoltaic plants, mining, purification of great volumes of water, infiltration of high-quality water into underground aquifers to prepare for droughts, drinking water production for reverse osmosis processes, among others. Fischmann has been awarded several international recognitions for his innovative capacity.[1]

Unfortunately, Fischmann's story of a successful intellectual property (IP)–driven startup is exceedingly rare in Latin America. In fact, most small and medium enterprises around the world display a significant lack of knowledge about how to monetize their intellectual assets. Indeed, stories about failures of IP management abound, and certainly, they are not limited to Latin America or even the developing world.

Contrast that story with that of Belize's Marie Sharp. Anyone who is from or has ever been to Belize knows about Marie Sharp's hot sauce. It's like ketchup at a Mc Donalds—in other words, you can't get away from it. Marie Sharp's famous sauces grace every dining table in the land. Even if you opt to eat out, you will find it, sitting expectantly next to the ketchup or the fine wine, omnipresent in the Belizean consciousness and omnipotent in its fieriness. No lunch, dinner or even breakfast is complete without a little habanero.

However, unlike Fishmann's successful startup experience, this story begins with a dark twist. The first successfully commercial agricultural export from Belize was Melinda's Hot Sauce, started by a Belizean woman working with an importer in the United States who is a Belizean American. However, she neglected to get the American trademark on the name. She thought that he had done that for her, but he had taken it out in his name.

Once the brand was well established, the importer got the recipe, found somebody to make it more cheaply in Costa Rica, and cut Ms. Sharp out of the business completely. So after spending years and years building the business up and exporting, her marketer basically stole the business from her by taking the trademark. The brand was the valuable thing in that case, and it took her 20 years to build it back up. As for the owners of the Melinda brand, in mid-2016 they achieved sales of $5 million (Sada 2016).

These two contrasting lessons that raise the issue of why some entrepreneurs perceive the relevance of doing IP management, whereas others simply don't.

[1] These recognitions include, among others, the Gold Stevie® Award "Innovator of the Year" and "Energy Industry Innovation of the Year"; the Green Apple Award "Environmental Best Practice for Sustainable Cooling Technology"; the London Business School "Real Innovation Award"; the Greater Miami Chamber of Commerce "Best New Business"; the Avonni "Best Innovator Award"; the Ernst & Young "Best Entrepreneur Award"; the National Environmental Award and the Best Real Estate Reputation Award.

The Problem: Why Startups Choose to Undercapitalize Their Intellectual Assets?

Regretfully, Marie Sharp's story highlights very eloquently the attitude of most SMIEs entrepreneurs towards IP, i.e., a disastrous combination of naïveté and unawareness about how they can avail from IP, or more importantly, how IP can be used against them.

The relevance of IP today is enormous; yet SMIEs hardly take into account the strategic value of their IP. In the European Union, the Office for Harmonization in the Internal Market (OHIM) released a study in 2015 that shows a meager 9% of European SMEs being IP owners; however, on average, such IP owners generate 32% more revenue per employee than those that do not. The problem is not even the limited use of IP but the failure to commercialize technologies even when IP was actually protected. According to Walker (2014), "Of today's 2.1 million active patents, 95% fail to be licensed or commercialized. These unlicensed patents include over 50,000 high-quality patented inventions developed by universities. More than $5 trillion has been spent in the U.S. alone on research and development over the past 20 years, much of which went to create the very patents that remain unlicensed. According to Forrester Research, "U.S. firms annually waste $1 trillion in underused intellectual property assets by failing to extract the full value of that property through partnerships." In a similar fashion, the UN (2011: 11) notes the following:

> [...] all available studies confirm that the [patent] value distribution is highly skewed, i.e. that there is a small number of very valuable patents, while the vast majority of patents turn out to have little or no value. As a result, most patents are allowed to expire long before their statutory maximum lifetime, simply because their holders consider the renewal fees too high compared to the value of the patent.

This process is expensive and usually not assumed by most entrepreneurs, due to its sophisticated nature.

Yet at the same time, there is wide recognition of the relevance of intellectual assets as a source of wealth in today's economy. The intangible asset value of the S&P 500 grew to an average 84% by January 1, 2015; that is, an increase of 4 percentage points over 10 years (Ocean Tomo 2016). In the U.S., according to the USPTO (2016) IP-intensive industries contributed more than $6 trillion dollars in 2014, up more than $1.5 trillion (30%) from $5.06 trillion in 2010. The share of total U.S. GDP related to IP-intensive industries increased from 34.8% in 2010 to 38.2% in 2014. Finally, in 2011 the International Chamber of Commerce commissioned from Frontier Economics an assessment on the value of global trade in counterfeit goods. The report stated that this cost would reach the astronomical amount of $1.77 trillion by 2015. This value is stolen or lost to the market, a foregone source of wealth very much like $100 bills left unnoticed on the pavement.

"Knowledge" as Francis Bacon observed "is power." 500 years later, in today's technology-led economy, Bacon's observation is truer than ever. Study after study has demonstrated that companies that create and successfully leverage knowledge and innovation (intellectual property) consistently and significantly outperform their competitors and create lasting shareholder value. Yet, for all its importance, entrepreneurs often are unaware of their IP's worth in the critical launch phase of a startup. According to a 2010 awareness survey conducted by the UK Intellectual Property Office, SMIEs know very little about why knowledge of IP is relevant to their business. Only 21% of companies with 50–250 employees were conscious that publication of an invention would prevent them obtaining a patent for it; companies with less than 50 employees ranked even worse (just 14%). Also, 77% of enterprises did not know that a contractor would retain copyright in a website created for a company unless they negotiated specific contractual provisions to the contrary. IP is money, but few people seem to notice it.

Firms that fail to utilize IP effectively inevitably face increasing competition, declining margins and tolling from companies that own key industry innovations. Further, in the last 5 years increased litigation activity by IP owners now means Boards which fail to manage IP risk also leave their company exposed to damaging IP infringement actions including legal injunctions, major damages awards or product recalls.

So, yes, knowledge is power; but what is knowledge? To Loasby (2005), it means "making connections." Like the hubs of a network, individuals create knowledge once they connect to each other with information that otherwise would remain fragmented, scattered and useless. Information is useful if it can be connected to something else, and this 'something else' is a pattern of relationships – how things fit together. Knowledge is a set of connections; information is a single element which becomes information only if it can be linked into such a set. We can also define knowledge as a structure, in the form of categories into which phenomena may be grouped or in the form of relationships between such categories.

Our cognition gives us the means to make connections; to build structures, or 'connecting principles,' to put it in Adam Smith's terms. Awareness or cognition are human traits that result from a long evolutionary process. Loasby (2005) explains how this evolutionary process came about as an accumulative process where human beings developed capacity to vary their behavior by forming new linkages in their brains that replaced generically programmed behaviors, by giving priority to performance over logical processing and neurological coding over explicit codification. The resulting consciousness helped human beings conceive ideas about the future by making conjectures about new categories and relationships yet unknown, through definition of new 'connecting principles'. Hence, rather than bounded rationality, which is usually interpreted as a particular limitation in processing knowledge, it is better to begin with bounded cognition. This has the advantage of corresponding with current ideas about the development of human cognitive abilities.

Tomas Sowell expressed in his 1980 book "Knowledge and Decisions" that "ideas are everywhere, but knowledge is rare"; they only become knowledge once we have transformed them through a validation set of rules or system. Information is not inherent in an isolated message, but the product of an interpretation derived from supposedly relevant knowledge. It follows that the contextual knowledge against which information is interpreted, is as important as the information itself. Information that is derived from a message may differ substantially according to the knowledge by which it is interpreted. In addition, knowledge emerges as the result of a filtering mechanism that verifies how viable or sound ideas are (Sowell 1980). Verification may lead to different levels of "knowledge"; some knowledge may seem unchallengeable, some highly reliable, some plausible within limits (which are rarely well-defined), some speculative, and some once accepted but now discarded (Loasby 2005).

In our case, new insights that generate ideas about new possible solutions become valuable intellectual assets once they have undergone a process of transformation through validation protocols that include IP legislation, but also other rules emerging from the way the ecosystem is structured: case law, technical standards, professional guidelines, and IP auditing and valuation to name a few. Devising and managing these rules is the purpose of IP management.

We will explore in this book the relevance of such cognitive abilities in developing "institutional awareness," as the conceptual bedrock explaining why most startups choose undervalued IP management strategies, by not presenting their assets into the market through patent registration, but instead relying on less visible and more difficult means of commercializing assets, such as trade and industrial secrets. In doing so, they fail to obtain the maximum possible benefit the IP system can deliver them, and their monetization possibilities vanish. In our view, the explanation of this has roots in structural flaws of the IP systems around the world to allow SMIEs grasp, organize, and process information they need to capitalize their intellectual assets.

In essence, the question is whether the very structure of the patent system undermines the possibilities that IP management offers. This problem is relevant because the empirical evidence is increasingly showing a significant fracture in the very structure of the patent system. For example, Jaffe and Lerner (2004: 12–13) contend that the patent explosion of the 1990s in the U.S. is the consequence of patent awards of dubious merit (i.e. are not new or are trivially obvious). Granting patents without clear evidence of invalidity in the form of prior art is the result of the USPTO being overtaxed, working under skewed incentives so that the tests for novelty and non-obviousness it applies to assess new inventions have mostly become non-operative. From the users' perspective, the system delivers lots of uncertainty. It is this issue that we structure the thesis of this book, namely, an exploration of the impact of awareness upon the practical use of the IP system.

However, before we explain the importance of awareness upon the effectiveness of intellectual property management, we need to explain first what intellectual property is, and its role in the generation of innovations.

IP integrates a bundle of rights and legal concessions that protect different aspects of the intellectual creation. This distinction is critical from the viewpoint of legal effects. The United Nations (2011: 7) defines intellectual property rights (IPRs) as: "the rights to use and sell (or otherwise dispose of) creations of the mind: inventions, literary and artistic works, and symbols, names, images, and designs used in commerce for the firms owning them. They form part of their intangible assets (as opposed to tangible goods such as machinery or buildings), together with customer goodwill, the firm-specific skills of their workforces, knowledge embedded in the organization, or good management practices.[2]"

This definition, possibly brought from the experience of countries where IPRs are taken for granted, assumes that institutions are "givens" and also, that the business community is aware of them and willing to act upon them. However, this assumption is far from the truth. Culture is a central factor that one has to consider in explaining why some countries make better use of their IP than others. Bader et al. (2012) note that culture plays a central role in the expansion and use of the IP system: "IP culture can be observed on an inventor, company or country level. It reflects the attitude and beliefs towards IP and related issues."

But "culture" is a very broad term that may lose meaning in the context of public policy. Thus the question treated in this book pertains not only to the overall state of cultural awareness enabling SMEs to develop their activities as the impact of such knowledge in the strategies they develop to position themselves competitively, and why they have a comparatively poorer capacity to manage intellectual assets.

In this book, instead of vaguely speaking of "societal culture" in favor or against IP, we take a different, micro look into the perception of individuals (inventors, venture capitalists, entrepreneurs, and IP attorneys) about the possibility and purpose of using IP as a competitive strategy.

Specifically, this book connects intellectual assets trading with the subjective perceptions of those who participate in the innovation process. We pay attention to the impact of this phenomenon on Small and Medium Innovative Enterprises, or SMIEs.[3] We examine how the weak entrepreneurial perception of "official" intellectual property undermines the institutional role of these instruments, intended to help firms capitalize their intellectual assets in technology markets through IP management.

Therefore, in this book we focus on that "additional" ingredient needed for transforming brilliant ideas into commercially useful knowledge, and on IP institutions, as something more than merely established protocols for granting patent or copyright ownership. Our focus is on the "marketing" element required to bring the IP into the full view of potential investors interested in the knowledge embedded in these rights. Innovators need a marketing strategy to commercialize and monetize their IP. That means clearing two stages: the first one focuses on obtaining the high-

[2] Technically patents and copyrights are not property rights that remain in the hands of the titleholder until they are surrendered or sold to a third party; instead, they are legal concessions that enable their titleholders to use them for a limited amount of time. From the viewpoint of their legal effects, though, they comprise a bundle of entitlements with impact on the expectations of market agents, or to be more precise, innovators. Notice that the legal definition implicitly assumes IP's impact upon entrepreneurs' expectations; therefore, this definition is silent about whether IP institutions convey this effect or whether they are in fact "dead letter."

[3] Our definition of SMIEs prioritizes how recently the firm has introduced innovation in products or processes in the market, as opposed to measuring their "size," because of the particular distributive connotations that small and medium enterprises usually have under public policy. In this book, instead, we focus our attention on how fast or recently have these firms been able to innovate in the market. We rely on the literature (Haltiwanger et al. 2013; cited in IDB 2014).

est degree of legal protection afforded by the particular government where innovators seek IP protection. IP management transforms IP legal titles into valuable intellectual assets. It takes innovative ideas arising out of research and product development and turns them into legally enforceable IP through applications, prosecution, and maintenance. Obviously, the degree of legal protection depends on the particular capacity of the governments where innovators submit their respective petitions. The second phase is IP trading. Trading involves creating economic benefits through portfolio management through the management of IP portfolio assets, integrating IP into business strategy and maximizing its value. A fundamental consideration of any IP strategy is to always balance any short-term gain against any potential long-term pain about the company business goals. In short, IP management is much more than filing for obtaining patents or other alternative ways of protecting technology.

From the old days of the Industrial Revolution, featuring individual inventors like Bell, Edison, Ford, De Forest or Scott de Martinsville, the epicenter of innovation shifted in the twentieth Century to the big corporations like AT&Ts, Intel, Krupp, Omega Monsanto and university labs of the Ivy League in the United States. Today, however, we are entering the dawn of a new era featured by inter-firm collaboration and spin-offs offering new outsourcing possibilities through open innovation. For these reasons, knowledge of IP management is more relevant than ever.

Let us elaborate on this.

The Fourth Industrial Revolution, Intangible Assets' Value, and IP Management

In 1946, the first electronic general-purpose computer, known as ENIAC, was formally dedicated at the University of Pennsylvania. This was the first Turing machine (a machine theoretically invented 10 years earlier) able to perform complex calculations. Thomas Watson, president of IBM, predicted in 1943: "I think there is a world market for maybe five computers." Indeed, for approximately 20 years, computers would be thought of as machines able to perform complex calculations, only useful for a handful of laboratories, universities, and R&D companies. The relationship between humans and computers was "one computer for many users."

The ENIAC patent was applied for in 1947 and granted in 1964, but was voided in 1973 in a decision by the landmark federal court case Honeywell v. Sperry Rand, putting the invention in the public domain. This decision of putting the ENIAC in the public domain coincided with a trend in the 1970s of computer companies beginning to form R&D partnerships (Clodt et al. 2006). By the early 1970s, researchers in academic or research institutions had access to single-person use of a computer system, but these systems were still too expensive to be owned by single users. The decision to put the invention in public domain and the expansion of the global computer industry allowed developing personal computers at costs affordable for single-users' ownership.

The third industrial revolution started in the early 1970s, and was characterized by electronics and information technologies' production. Cyber systems and massive access to computers have transformed how we organize production, consumption, transportation, and even war. Over the last 70 years, we have seen how the relation has turned from "one computer and many users" to "many computers and one user". Indeed, the number of personal computers and smartphones combined surpassed four billion in 2016. The number is near ten billion, when all computers are taken into account (e.g. embedded computers). Moreover, the relation between humans and computers has changed dramatically in the last decades. Computers are increasingly becoming part of almost every aspect of our routine life. Internet has changed how (and sometimes who!) we date, how we choose a restaurant, or the destination of our next vacation.

In the very near future, internet will tell us if we forgot to brush our teeth in the morning, or if we are running out of milk in our refrigerators. Concepts such as "the internet of things" or "smart cities" have increased their value on Google trends from values of 6 and 2, respectively, in 2012, to 75 and 100 in 2016.[4] Over the next decades, part of the world's population will see their cities, grid, energy, and even appliances become smarter. Computers will be embedded almost everywhere in our daily life. The era of "industrial internet", a term by General Electric to describe how "digital technology will ultimately be added to all machines and all devices". According to the World Economic Forum, this integration between cyber and physical systems is the beginning of a new technological revolution, the fourth industrial revolution (Schwab 2016).

The integration of physical and cyber systems raises several concerns: individual privacy, the substitution of labor, security, etc. In the last 10 years, we have experienced a drastic change from "one computer to one user" to "many computers to one user". The revolution of physical and cyber systems also means a radical change in organizations. Smart factories, with thousands of sensors in the production line, and big data analysis for cost efficiency, are replacing twentieth century factories. This also means that labor will be replaced. According to the World Economic Forum (2016), by 2020, over five million jobs will be lost in 15 major developed and emerging economies.[5]

As for startups and companies' value, we know that intangible assets account for an important share of firm's total asset value, and that these assets generate important benefits in productivity (Brynjolfsson et al. 2002). Ocean Tomo, LLC, an intellectual capital merchant firm, in its annual study of intangible asset market value, estimated that in 2015, 87% of the assets' market value listed in the S&P 500 was intangible.[6] Furthermore, as our grids, factories, energy, cities, and appliances become smarter, we expect the share of intangible assets' value for startups and corporations to increase even more.

[4] The index is a normalized metric (between 0 and 100) of the number of searches of the term of interest over the total number of searches in Google.

[5] The Future of Jobs. Employment, Skills and Workforce Strategy for the Fourth Industrial Revolution. World Economic Forum (January 2016). Available at: http://reports.weforum.org/future-of-jobs-2016/

[6] Available at: http://www.oceantomo.com/blog/2015/

Table 1 Innovation rankings with technological complexity

Country	Innovation	Innov. per-capita
United States	1	3
China	2	30
Japan	3	9
Germany	4	7
France	5	6
Great Britain	6	10
Korea (Rep.)	7	13
Canada	8	11
Netherland	9	4
Italy	10	24
Switzerland	11	5
Belgium	12	12
Austria	13	8
Singapore	14	1
Sweden	15	14
Spain	16	26
Finland	17	2

Source: Fernandez Donoso (2017)

Intangible assets are not physical in nature. These assets account for more than 80% of the asset value of S&P 500 listed companies, and we expect this value to increase in the future. Can secrecy be the optimal IP strategy for appropriation of these non-physical assets? Another method to explore this question is looking at the global innovation output by countries. Measuring innovation is a difficult task, as many innovations are kept outside of the formal IP system and since patents differ considerably in quality, inventive steps, or market impact. Using quantitative information theory, Fernandez Donoso (2017) proposed an index of innovation output that takes into account both patented and non-patented innovations, as well as considering the technological complexity of each technology (Table 1).

According to this metric, Singapore, Finland, and the United States are the most innovative countries per inhabitant. If we consider total output, the United States, China and Japan are generating most of the technologically complex innovation. Indeed, China, a country with significant remaining challenges in IPR, has become the second most important player in global innovation output (Amcham China 2016).[7] Moreover, when splitting the innovation output by patented (formal IP) and non-patented (informal IP), China's informal innovation output metric is more than 30 times its formal innovation output value, while Japan's informal value is less than three times the formal value. That is, innovative output in China happens out-

[7] In the 2016 China Business Climate Report, by The American Chamber of Commerce in the People's Republic of China, over 500 of its members doing business in the country were surveyed. The report concludes with respect to IPR, data security environment and anti-corruption: "These areas continue to be pressing concerns for many survey respondents, but trends are positive."

side the patenting system much larger proportions than its next competitor in the rankings (Table 2).

The landscape is certainly surprising: we are living the fourth industrial revolution, an era characterized by intangible value, complex technologies, and non-patented innovation. Hence, what factors are influencing the decision of not using intellectual property or deciding to develop a reliable IP management strategy?

Table 2 Formal and informal innovation metrics

Country	Formal	Informal
Armenia	4.74e-06	0
Australia	1.04e-02	5.42e-03
Austria	8.77e-03	5.99e-02
Belarus	5.64e-05	3.31e-07
Belgium	5.69e-03	6.51e-02
Bosnia and H.	3.97e-05	0
Brazil	3.23e-03	5.86e-03
Bulgaria	2.81e-04	7.06e-05
Canada	2.40e-02	1.95e-01
Chile	2.63e-04	1.53e-05
China	2.70e-02	8.53e-01
Colombia	9.32e-05	1.26e-03
Croatia	5.16e-04	5.45e-06
Czech R.	2.15e-03	1.62e-02
Denmark	6.42e-03	1.28e-02
Dominican R.	2.22e-05	0
Ecuador	2.69e-04	4.41e-07
Egypt	2.11e-04	3.95e-06
Estonia	2.90e-04	5.34e-05
Finland	2.22e-02	8.58e-03
France	1.87e-01	1.18e-01
Georgia	5.60e-05	0
Germany	1.12e-01	5.09e-01
Great Britain	1.34e-01	1.24e-01
Greece	6.37e-04	2.09e-04
Hong Kong	1.84e-04	7.08e-03
Hungary	3.41e-03	8.63e-03
Iceland	2.74e-04	4.71e-07
India	5.52e-03	1.35e-02
Indonesia	8.21e-05	1.60e-04
Ireland	1.62e-03	1.78e-02
Israel	1.04e-02	1.32e-02

(continued)

Table 2 (continued)

Country	Formal	Informal
Italy	6.66e-03	7.75e-02
Japan	1.96e-01	4.95e-01
Kazakhstan	9.42e-05	1.08e-07
Korea (Rep.)	5.76e-02	1.67e-01
Latvia	1.31e-04	1.55e-06
Lithuania	1.92e-06	1.18e-07
Luxembourg	1.04e-03	1.50e-04
Malaysia	1.04e-03	7.76e-03
Mexico	6.42e-04	2.59e-02
Morocco	1.74e-04	5.04e-05
Netherland	2.49e-02	1.39e-01
New Zealand	1.59e-03	2.56e-04
Norway	4.97e-03	3.46e-03
Philippines	2.06e-04	6.03e-04
Poland	2.35e-03	9.61e-03
Portugal	8.45e-04	3.06e-04
Romania	6.82e-05	2.26e-04
Russia	2.55e-03	1.39e-03
Serbia	9.98e-05	2.53e-07
Singapore	3.08e-03	6.27e-02
Slovakia	2.29e-04	7.12e-04
Slovenia	9.35e-04	3.76e-04
South Africa	4.55e-04	9.63e-05
Spain	1.25e-02	2.22e-02
Sweden	1.09e-02	2.86e-02
Switzerland	7.58e-03	6.43e-02
Thailand	2.76e-04	3.78e-03
Tunisia	4.29e-05	7.95e-10
Turkey	2.51e-03	6.78e-04
Ukraine	4.59e-04	2.92e-04
United States	1	1

Source: Fernandez Donoso (2017)

What Is IP Management and Why It Matters?

Contrary to what people commonly think, IP management is most helpful to SMIEs at their earliest stage of development; that is, before the firm gains traction and starts making revenues. Indeed, during this period, IP is the only real asset available to these companies, which in some cases conditions their business model.

Entrepreneurs increasingly recognize IP as a key business asset. IP is the basis for a significant portion of venture capital investments. For technology-based companies, IP is the essential element in obtaining venture capital funding. Investors seek to maximize returns and look to determine whether the target company has proprietary inventions and innovations that bring her an advantage over competitors and, of equal importance, whether that advantage over competitors is sustainable.

IPRs management, including funding business activities, is now said to be "a pillar of corporate strategy." Also, there is an increasing desire on the part of most IP owners to turn them from being a cost to a profit center.

IP management is essential to enhance business's competitiveness. Companies focus on developing core capabilities while acquiring accessory ones from others. Strategically, businesses do this by developing new knowledge around their core, patenting that knowledge, and licensing incidental knowledge from others. Making products or services can be daunting, particularly in the high-tech industries, where a single product can embody thousands of patents and other IP. Due to the knowledge fragmentation that features products and services in these sectors, where productive capabilities to make them are scattered among different firms, usually IP ownership is not centralized either. Therefore, businesses may find it hard to identify and obtain useful IP protecting those complementary capabilities.

IP management seeks to develop a thicket around core technologies protected by patents. Building patent portfolios around the core capabilities allows businesses to control sectors of technology, adding increasing value through new products and services associated with it. At the same time, such strategy prevents competitors from developing parallel technologies. This is critical for a startup, as the competitor may be better positioned to exploit his incumbent market position, or his cost-advantage (attained through imitation, rather than R&D), thereby displacing the pioneering firm, if the latter has his core unprotected.

Besides patents, other IPRs guard the inventor's core capabilities by protecting specific attributes of the product, the process used to develop it, or the identity of the business trading with it. Trademarks give the developer means to build his commercial reputation through differentiating external signs, sounds, symbols, words and even smells representing the company or the product. Copyrights protect the written words, sounds or signs used to describe the ideas, concepts, or methods sustaining the underlying technology. Registered designs protect the external shape of the product, so people can clearly distinguish it from others. Trade secrets help developers protect their know-how through confidentiality, in case these are easily replicable through reverse engineering either because of the simple technology involved or because the legal institutions are ineffective to protect it. Other IPRs such as geographical indicators, plant varieties or integrated circuits protect specific attributes of origin, nature or complexity. In all cases, IPRs are intended to differentiate whoever develops a novelty from other competitors.

Getting the right mix of IP protection, therefore, involves not only an assessment of how much protection the institutional setting provides to IP owners, it also includes selecting the right mix of IPRs that best suits the entrepreneur. Every IP asset is unique; therefore, companies need to individualize their approach for each asset in their portfolios. IP management is not only about whether IP is important to the enterprise, but also about the type of IP that optimizes the corporate strategy. Patents may not be the most valuable assets for some companies, but know-how and reputation (Levin et al. 1987; Cohen et al. 2000; Cimoli and Primi 2008: 33). In many situations, these other IP assets are neither well understood nor managed effectively. Thus IP management is about tailoring the strategy best suited to accommodate the nature of the particular IP asset. This unique craft is often forgotten, as people tend to assimilate IP with patents exclusively. Clearly, management is far from simple.

Also, one can clearly see how IP management is relevant to increase businesses' turnover. IP valuations are necessary to negotiations involving selling or licensing intellectual assets; to carry out M&A activity involving those assets; or to use these as collateral for secured loans.

Despite the importance of IP management, SMIEs fail to develop IP strategies integrated with their broader business strategy. In particular, companies often fail to identify when it would be more lucrative to engage in either licensing or joint ventures to maximize the value of their IP, rather than using it merely to prevent competition. This book argues that such failure is associated with the complexity of the intellectual property system, which many SMIEs perceive as a nuisance, not an opportunity to make profits.

The question then is why is IP management relevant at all?

On April 20, 2015, Joe Kiani, founder, CEO and chairman of the Board of Masimo won the 2015 IP Champion Award. There were good reasons why the U.S. Chamber's Global IP Center elected him for this prize. Mr. Kiani has more than 65 patents issued in his name and more than 575 patents issued or filed by Masimo in medical technologies related to noninvasive patient monitoring.

The UN (2011: 8) expresses the relevance of IPRs as a mechanism helping entrepreneurs like Mr. Kiani develop their capacity to monetize their intellectual assets: "being intangible assets, IPRs can in principle be bought and sold or licensed out just like other assets. In this way, IPRs underpin a market for innovations, which is significant because brilliant inventors are not always brilliant entrepreneurs and vice versa. Markets for innovations allow inventors and entrepreneurs to match their talents in successfully bringing innovations to market."

Under closer inspection, it is interesting to learn about Mr. Kiani's own perception concerning the relevance he attached to the IP system in bringing about his creative endeavors. To him, the relevance of IP goes beyond the mere existence of IP regulations. He said, 'Without the promise of a strong IP system to defend our innovation, we wouldn't have been able to raise the more than $90 million in venture capital financing we needed to break even. However, to be a champion of innovation means so much more to me. In the middle of more than 100 billion galaxies each with billions of stars and all of the forces around us, innovation is crucial for the survival of the human race. To be on the side of a strong and deliberate IP system that fosters innovation is to be on the right side of history.' (Marketwired 2015)

The critical word here to understand is "promise". Promises rest on the expectation of someone else's probabilistic behavior. They involve a subjective state of mind, not an objective reality. Usually, institutions such as legal rules are presented to us like objective givens that are "there" waiting for us to use them. In reality, however, there is nothing that guarantees they will be used unless people are aware of their existence and utility. Innovation ecosystems like those where Mr. Kiani successfully built his $90 million worth intellectual assets are particularly hard to make because they entirely rest upon perceptions about the activities of their members.

Cognitive perceptions affect entrepreneur's behavior across the board; they affect different phases of the corporate's development, not only their startup beginning. Many lost opportunities arising from IP mismanagement involve successful firms in developed countries. Take the case of Morgan Confections Company, a successful candy company whose total sales had increased by 2004 to more than $15 million annually, with nearly 10,000 stores across America. This company was brought into bankruptcy and sale of its assets a mere year later, just because its management could not leverage its intellectual assets to compensate the weight of increasing debt resulting from its growth. No one thought about the value of the company's IP and other intangible assets, including research, recipe refinements, marketing materials, public relations, customer lists, trade dress, trademark registrations, and contracts with major retailers such as Kmart and Wal-Mart. As the turnaround management failed to market these assets before the company was forced to close operations, its value virtually vanished in just 6 months. Then, these assets appeared unsaleable (Anson 2010).

This book explores the impact of entrepreneurial cognition over the use of the IP system, and how these perceptions influence the design of IP strategies. We all know that assets are valuable to a business because they allow a potential stream of cash to their holders. However, in principle these assets convey no value until entrepreneurs perceive value in them; this awareness is what induces them to trade. Once entrepreneurs become "aware" of the existence and use of institutions in support of IP exchanges, trading of intellectual assets will take place. It is only then that entrepreneurs can establish whether the legal means available do help them create a competitive strategy to outdo a competitor. For example, patents give their owners a legal monopoly over the underlying intellectual assets, but in return, they must disclose these assets in full, so they can be publicly known and thus enjoy legal protection.

However, entrepreneurs may find it more convenient not to reveal their knowledge (as patent filing requires them to do) if the legal means are ineffective to protect them, or if there are alternative and more efficient ways to protection, given the nature of the technology involved. Entrepreneurs might find it more useful and less costly to keep their knowledge secret if it was cumbersome to replicate, for example. The UK Intellectual Property Office (2012) referred to a study conducted by Hargreaves (2011), which found that many SMIEs find it difficult to identify the best source of advice for their business needs, because of the presence of multiple sources of information. Most importantly, however, the study found that SMIEs said that what they needed most was access to basic, low-cost advice to help them make informed decisions about their IP. Further, SMIEs wanted that help to be integrated with wider business information, and not as an isolated issue, to allow them to make decisions on IP as part of their overall business strategy. Hargreaves recommends that: "The IPO should draw up plans to improve the accessibility of the IP system to smaller companies who will benefit from it. This should involve access to lower cost providers of integrated IP legal and commercial advice."

It is reasonable to expect that IP management problems are comparatively less relevant for SMIEs because priorities for these smaller firms are usually other more "immediate" concerns affecting growth, such as production organization, logistics, and finding venture capital. Of course, the incubation of a flawed IP management strategy is not to accrue immediately, but affects the business's long-term performance, usually with disastrous results. After all, for SMIEs, intellectual assets embodied in their IP portfolio are often the only assets they can rely on: the value of their own intellect.

The economics literature on IP usually does not emphasize the capacity of SMIEs to be aware and ready to act upon their IP portfolio, because it takes IPs as entitlements that create incentives upon individuals to act in a certain way. For example, this view emphasizes the value that IP creates upon patentees because it allows them to wield a legal monopoly that gives them a capacity to establish an exclusive market and to exclude competitors. This monopoly ensures the firm an exclusive strategic position at a particular stage of the production process. This exclusivity translates into a competitive advantage that could prevent other competitors from seizing a critical beachhead over the pioneering technology. The market measures these "valuable" ends by giving the IPR a particular value. This value allows IP holders to trade their IPRs either by selling or licensing them. IP is thus a mechanism that businesses can wield as a competitive advantage tool; they can leverage value by using it strategically, to position themselves in exclusivity over resources that can be essential in positioning themselves ahead of their competitors in the wave of technological evolution of the industry concerned.

While we do not contradict this "incentives" view, we perceive it conveys an incomplete explanation about why entrepreneurs build intellectual assets out of their creative process. IP adds value to a business insofar that it serves a particular business purpose. Yes, IP is useful because it helps the title owner to build a monopoly over a particular market, but that monopoly has meaning only in the context of subjective options that the entrepreneur assesses in his mind. If he does not perceive the comparative value of the alternatives, or if his uncertainty about possible outcomes is extreme, it is very unlikely that he or she will take action and ideas will not become valuable knowledge. Intellectual assets will remain idle.

Awareness about the existence and use of relevant IP is the hallmark of this book. The conventional economic theory of IP, however, is not attuned with this problem. Instead, it perceives IP as a set of incentives that bring about innovation. This assumption, however, is debatable, as we will explain in the next section. More importantly, it has little connection with the practical use of IP management.

Let us explain this critical point in more detail.

Our Hypothesis: IP Management Rests on Cognitive Perceptions

The history of innovation is full of disappointed creators who could not or would not protect their intellectual assets. Consider the story of Edwin Armstrong, inventor of the Radio FM, and creator of the first network of nicer-sounding FM radio stations. His invention reduced interference across radio bands in the 1910s. Soon afterwards, however, he would face the mighty lobby of Radio Corporation of America (RCA) and AT&T who did not stop until bringing Armstrong out of the market, and to suicide in 1954.

How about the story of Bob Kearns, who patented a windshield wiper technology? After he used his knowledge of electronics to develop an intermittent windshield wiper mechanism, which was useful in light rain or mist, he was misled into a deceiving licensing negotiation with Ford Company, who seized the technology through reverse engineering after it had been shared by Kearns, and immediately dismissed him, regardless of his heaving investments in producing inputs intended to fulfill his contract with Ford. Kearns was forced into years of despair, including a divorce and a nervous breakdown before litigation restituted him part of his lost life.

Drama comes hand in hand with uncertainty and that, in turn, is closely linked to institutional breakdown. When these circumstances arise, people hide their assets to prevent a future loss. Yet, in the case of intellectual assets, this is somewhat of a paradox, because hiding is exactly what prevents these assets from becoming valuable. Hence, something deeper than mere fear of being taken advantage is what underlies these stories. That something is ignoring the consequences arising from ignoring how the IP rules can work to our advantage. This is what underlies the three stories told earlier: Armstrong's lack of knowledge about radio spectrum regulations; Kearns naïveté by surrendering his equipment without ensuring the licensing contract first; and Disney's lack of knowledge about IP contracts and copyrights.

These stories, as well as several others that we will explore throughout this book, tell us a great lesson: that *awareness* about the rules governing IP transactions is as important as the existence of rules themselves. How do entrepreneurs interpret these rules and why it is so important for entrepreneurs to be aware of their existence?

IP management, also known as "technology transfer", does more than simply devise rules that "protect" intellectual property. They use these rules strategically to develop competitive capabilities, by exerting market power where possible, and yielding to cooperation and sharing where the owner's position vis-à-vis his competitors is untenable. However, such market power and such cooperation are limited by the extent of the participants' cognitive capabilities.

Our view emphasizes how such capabilities actively filter random scientific ideas ("pure science") and transform them into applied scientific knowledge that they can monetize. But here, the role of the entrepreneur is critical to decide whether the filtering mechanism is correct and supports his hypothesis about the possible outcomes he can expect from investing in a new gadget or process. Is the entrepreneur conscious about the possibilities that the new technology has in bringing about a profit opportunity? Is our entrepreneur correct about the potential use he expects to draw at the end of the period from the R&D process he embarks on at the beginning of the period? His cognitive capability about the marketability of his IPRs is critical to make the connection between investment and expectation of rewards.

In this cognitive approach, finding adequate technologies results from a trial-and-error finding process in which firms test their capabilities with those of other firms, to find complementarities that add value to the production process (Richardson 1972). Building these capabilities is expertise that takes time to be incubated through a learning process, and it implies internalizing knowledge that most likely than not is hard to codify (Hayek 1948; Polanyi 1958; Arrow 1962).

This is a radical shift from the conventional IP approach, which perceives entrepreneurs, whether large firms or startups, merely reacting to the external stimulus staged by the IPRs framework where they happen to be. In our view, entrepreneurs actively seek to develop internal capabilities that help them produce useful and valuable knowledge, that is, innovations that let them seize market opportunities. IPRs in this understanding is not merely a formal set of incentives but instead, a capability to exert market power which is conditioned by cognitive limitations resulting from the institutional flaws of the innovation ecosystem, that is, from the lack of reliable protocols enabling the validation of ideas. Those flaws limit entrepreneurs' capacity to transform mere ideas ("information", as economists usually refer to), into valuable knowledge, either internally or in collaboration with other entrepreneurs. By linking the entrepreneurial knowledge building process to the value it creates through IP management validation mechanisms, our cognitive perspective explains the source of technological value, which is the foundation of the innovation ecosystem.

IP management is thus the mechanism that coordinates diverse, and complementary entrepreneurial capabilities owned by different firms through alternative strategies that include the patent sale and licensing commercialization; litigation of unassigned rights; or strategically withdrawing from the IP market assets whose value lies on the know-how, to negotiate them on a bilateral basis. In all these cases, to be effective, IP management options need to be understood by their users; if not, they will allow IP market failures to endure.[8]

Therefore, cognitive awareness is critical in our assessment. The essential discussion here is not so much "who owns what" as is the problem of "how well aware" are firms of coordination possibilities in the IP system, and how easy it is for them to exploit them through their current provision of entrepreneurial capabilities or by outsourcing these to other entrepreneurs.

Our cognitive hypothesis rests on the set of priorities that startups have during the early stages of their corporate life. Under this scenario, SMIEs find it hard to be aware of the importance of developing IP competitive strategies, because they believe that other business decisions are more critical to their corporate survival in

[8] IP management is often confused with technology transfer because it usually refers to the commercialization of patent rights. However, in our view, IP management has a broader meaning. We use this term to cover all possibilities of rights' transfer that may or may not occur through widespread commercialization (sale and licensing) in IP markets, but also through litigation, and even from the bilateral negotiation of trade secrets and know-how.

the early years. Startups prefer to devote their scarce resources to other activities different from learning about IP. They fail to see how bringing innovations successfully into the market ultimately rests on how competitively entrepreneurs treat their IP assets in the market, that is, how they perceive these legal holdings have strategic value for them to increase their company's net present value.

To develop our hypothesis we borrowed the notion that expectations drive decisions (Richardson 1960). SMIEs' perception about the irrelevance of learning how to use IP is not only a problem of personal sheer ignorance, or lack of acumen, but stems from the institutional milieu where they operate. Latin American SMIEs show that there is also a component of misunderstanding and logical distrust on the purpose of the IP system. They perceive IP to be at the behest of government bureaucracies willing to extort rents from them; at best, they are indifferent towards these rules, which they fail to connect to their productive endeavors.

These perceptions undermine the use of the IP system, as they tend to reinforce the problem of widespread confirmatory bias that affects the startups' negative perception towards the innovation ecosystem. Confirmation bias, also called confirmatory bias or "my side" bias, is a tendency to search for or interpret information in a way that confirms one's preconceptions, leading to statistical errors. Entrepreneurs think of the IP system as a hurdle, rather than as an opportunity; therefore, they abstain from using the system strategically, which leaves the IP system useless, i.e., a plain obstacle.

As a result of their cognitive limitations, entrepreneurs weaken their capacity to use the intellectual property system to monetize their ideas, and very likely decide not to invest resources in seeking higher forms of IP assets (such as patents or utility models), but prefer to resort to lower ones, such as trade secrets. Naturally, this is not to say that entrepreneurs choose trade secrets over patents due to a cognitive reason alone; indeed, building a competitive advantage may involve other factors.

Trade secrets are less valuable forms of asset capitalization since their liquidity in the IP market is lower compared to that of patents or utility models: secrecy withdraws information about the technology from the market, which would otherwise attract investors. Cognitive problems on an IP system also raise the financial risk of technology-based operations because the value reduction on underlying assets (innovative technology) ensuing from uncertainty impairs their use as collateral for bank loans. At the societal level, lower liquidity reduces the number of transactions on intellectual assets, thus undermines the deal flow that makes the innovation ecosystem sustainable.

In short, this book emphasizes why the value of intellectual assets rests not only on their scientific or innovative value but most importantly, on their commercial viability or, put it differently, on their likelihood to hit the market. Pure science, though potentially beneficial, does not translate into tangible value if the industry fails to see the use of it. For this to happen, it is essential not only to lay down the rules of the IP commercialization but also, to make sure that users know how to use them well.

Structure of This Book

The thesis of this book emphasizes the relevance of the cognitive foundations of IP, and how awareness flaws negatively underpin startup's lack of use of IP institutions thus systematically undervaluating their intellectual assets. We have structured this thesis in seven chapters.

Chapter 1 sets forth the theoretical background supporting our cognitive interpretation of the IP institutions. This chapter explores how market agents undertake their innovation endeavors by experimenting with successive hypotheses about potential opportunities to reap rewards, and why this is inevitable within uncertain institutional settings. Entrepreneurial experimentation is essential to building dynamic capabilities that change over time and are necessary to seize a competitive position. However, entrepreneurial probing takes place amidst institutional uncertainty, which in the context of building up intellectual assets is particularly high, because of the convoluted layered structure of the IP system. Under this system, concurring patent claims collide, and only a vaporous 'state of the art' provides some benchmark guiding judges and IP offices in their endeavors to allocate entitlements over IP contenders.

Naturally, entrepreneurs react to the IP institutional uncertainty they live under by devising alternative IP management strategies. Depending on how stable or reliable the system is they will resort to either voluntarily accommodating the concurring claims over patents through a contractual framework, or to litigate unassigned rights over these allegations if they fail to reach an agreement. Sometimes they will even use the threat of litigation to pressure reluctant parties to reach an agreement. At times, they will focus on inventing around or making key knowledge public, to preempt competitors from gaining a knowledge-based competitive advantage. Finally, if the system is particularly haphazard or unreliable, their instinct will drive them to withdraw their intellectual assets from the market. These strategies are presented successively in the following chapters.

Chapter 2 explores the extent to which entrepreneurs may impose market power by using IPRs. This chapter elaborates on the reasons why their strategy of imposing market power upon consumers and competitors may take different use of alternative forms of IP, depending on the degree of law enforcement, as well as on the type of intellectual asset, particularly on how difficult it is for their owners to protect the underlying knowledge. Furthermore, increasing market power in the context of complex technology wars may require businesses to expand their patent portfolio, so to ensure that competitors remain away from critical areas of competitive advantage. Finally, this chapter explores three strategies aimed at impeding competitors to develop market power, these include developing alternative technologies, rapidly disseminating critical knowledge and donating patents.

Chapter 3 examines the contractual nature of patent licensing and selling, as an IP management strategy focused on sharing critical IP. It highlights the aspects that usually contracting parties consider when negotiating a licensing deal; these are elements intended to cover all possible contingencies arising out of potentially conflictive competing patent claims. Strategies increasingly used to support patent negotiations include patent pools. This strategy is becoming popular among companies interested in acquiring complementary – yet complex capabilities they need to develop products with added value. In this chapter we focus on the role of patent traders or brokers in structuring deals in the IP market. Finally, this chapter explores why measuring IP value is critical to eliminating systemic uncertainty, and why it is so difficult to accomplish.

Chapter 4 analyzes litigation as a strategy designed to seize complementary capabilities by extra-contractual means. Litigation is particularly popular among Patent Assertion Entities (PAE), also known as "patent trolls." PAE identify attractive technologies and pressure patentees, sometimes by forcing them into extrajudicial settlements to avoid pesky litigation, which delayed responses of the IP system create to settle claims efficiently. Finally, this chapter examines the failed experience of building a "rational" IP market; this experience shows how litigation may prevail over any attempt to "organize" the IP market if the price of market uncertainty is such that it becomes cheaper to litigate than to trade.

Chapter 5 explores an IP management strategy that prevails among SMIEs, namely, abstaining from trading their intellectual property. Our findings are based on the observation of 352 SMIEs located in 6 different Latin American countries. Our explanation about cognitive causes being primary drivers of businesses' decision to use or not to use intellectual property does not focus on the corporate culture of Latin American firms; it focuses instead on the set of operational priorities that SMIEs have during in the early stages of their corporate life. We take the Latin American merely as a backdrop where innovative startups are born and quickly die due to the adverse setting where they are forced to operate; where confirmatory bias induces them to see how pointless it is to rely on the IP system.

This chapter examines the underlying reasons for SMIEs to undervalue their intellectual assets by not registering them under the IP system. These reasons are associated with their cognitive bias about the use and role of the IP system, which they perceive as an obstacle rather than as a mechanism to add value to their assets. By focusing our attention on this cognitive problem we ground our explanation in the alternative understanding of the role of IP.

Chapter 6 examines the risk management strategies that businesses use to reduce their exposure to the unpredictability of the IP system. These strategies are important because they all converge in the positive reduction of market friction that otherwise limits the interest of innovators to bring their new technologies into the market. We identify IP valuation as the main problem generating the need of risk management; its solution could induce companies to trade their IP in the market confidently. On the other hand, businesses deploy large and diversified portfolios, as a means to protect themselves from the volatility of unpredictable outcomes resulting from the IP market. Finally, we explore two mechanisms designed to counteract the adverse effects of systemic IP risk: the first one is insurance, which eliminates risk ex ante, and the second one is securitization, which creates the conditions for compensation ex post in case of an IP failure.

Chapter 7 analyzes the scope and depth of the IP market in Latin America, and initiatives that have emerged to support it, particularly, the intensity of use of technology transfer mechanisms across the region. In the light of undervalued intellectual property traded in Latin America, we explore the consequences of this phenomenon in the production of fewer transactions of lower value. This chapter analyzes the impact of legal rules in defining the scope of the intellectual property market.

We focus our attention into the Bayh-Dole Act of 1980 which revolutionized the technology transfer office in the U.S. by giving universities, the major producers of patented IP in that country, the capacity to commercialize technology owned and funded through federal funds. Similarly, we analyze if a similar body of legislation would work under the conditions prevailing in the patchy innovation ecosystem of Latin American countries. Does it make sense to transform universities in Latin America as the center of the tech transfer revolution or should governments in the region consider alternative options?

This chapter ends with an examination of the role of governments in creating institutional stability and a higher awareness through the more intensive strategic use of technology transfer. Our focus is to highlight strategies for the government to create a stable market setting for intellectual assets. We propose some government measures that could enhance the predictability of market transactions in this field. Similarly, we analyze some of the current trends with potential stirring effects on this market.

Last, we summarize the conclusions of this book. We include here some reflections about the future of intellectual property strategies in the region.

Chapter 1
Why Do We Need Intellectual Property Rules?

The scientific story of Charles Babbage (1791–1871) highlights the pitfalls of an invention that was brilliant yet could never be commercialized. In 1837, this English mathematician and computer pioneer developed what he called the "analytical engine," a mechanical general-purpose computer that could carry out a variety of different operations based on programming instructions given to it. This machine incorporated an arithmetic logic unit, control flow in the form of conditional branching and loops, and integrated memory, making it the first design for a general-purpose computer. Also, it could perform one task, then switch and perform another. This device could be described in modern terms as Turing-complete.[1]

Nevertheless, for all its brilliance, Babbage's engine did not attract the attention of anyone. Isaacson (2014) indicates that "few people saw the beauty of Babbage's proposed new machine (…). Try as he might, Babbage could generate little notice in either the popular press or scientific journals." The lack of investors' interest doomed his invention; Babbage was never able to complete construction of any of his machines because he could get no one to fund it.

One wonders what would have happened if the opposite had happened; perhaps British science would have leapfrogged ahead several decades.[2] Yet another interesting question is why the British scientists and venture capital were so unable to understand the brilliance of Babbage's analytical engine?

The answer seems to suggest a breakdown of the protocols by which the British innovation ecosystem turned ideas into valuable knowledge or perhaps, to be more accurate, an underdevelopment of such protocols. Well-functioning social systems

[1] In laymen's terms, a Turing-complete system is a system in which a program can be written that will find an answer to a problem (although with no guarantees regarding runtime or memory). In other words, it means that it could be used to solve any computation problem.

[2] Turing's machine, which is considered to be the first modern computer, was invented in 1936 by Alan Turing. It was an abstract machine that manipulates symbols on a strip of tape according to a table of rules; to be more exact, it is a mathematical model of computation that defines such a device.

I. De Leon, J. Fernandez Donoso, *Innovation, Startups and Intellectual Property Management*, DOI 10.1007/978-3-319-54906-4_1

require some mechanism giving their members the analytical tools for discarding senseless ideas and approving sound ones. Also, implicitly, such protocols allow parties to fix good solutions into rules, until changing circumstances force their revision. Hence, in the field of innovation intellectual property (IP) rules help entrepreneurs to filter their hypotheses about what ought to be considered as 'new', 'original' or 'unique', and distinguish them from the 'prior art', or, to put it differently, to test their ideas, and verify whether they are original. Trust in the capacity of such rules to account for verification means is as critical as the existence of the rules themselves. If entrepreneurs do not perceive their relevance, or are not aware, the economic consequences on their innovative activity are as decisive as if there were no rules at all.

Babbage's failure shows us that innovation depends on the organic emergence of a set of social rules, which extends beyond legal reforms aimed at modernizing IP legislation and its enforcing mechanisms. It is a multilayered ecosystem of complex rules, traditions, and protocols—of which only some are decreed—that transforms information into valuable knowledge. What is the essence of this ecosystem of rules? How do these protocols, rules and conventions emerge?

1.1 Innovating Amidst Institutional Uncertainty

Suggesting that innovation is consubstantial to uncertainty may seem somewhat counterintuitive. After all, our genes, evolved out of countless strategies aimed at ensuring self-preservation, should induce us to act defensively, telling us not to change the status quo, but we obviously know better. Yet, this idea oversimplifies the nature of what innovation is really about, and how entrepreneurs are anything but conformist risk avoiders.

The very purpose of innovation is to produce new knowledge with which to confront emerging new circumstances constantly challenging entrepreneurs. Know-how, either embedded in a product or in a set of instructions or protocol, helps produce new solutions to recurrent problems. But innovation is more than an epiphany or coming to the 'eureka' moment with which we usually associate inventors. It is about bringing these new solutions into the market, that is, framing them into the problems that society (the market) considers important to obtain solutions. Innovation is above all cooperation of the different actors bringing their capabilities, ingenuity and resources to make these ideas flourish and place them at the disposal of those valuing them; they are not isolated moments of inspiration (Hill 2015).

This process requires creating a web of stable expectations that help everyone align their conduct with the minimum chance of disruption. So, the process of innovation is one of tension between the need for new problems to arise, triggering the interest of finding solutions, and the need to align the relevant parties' conduct, so as to make innovation happen.

Therefore, it is necessary to understand the way these expectations evolve, and how they grow steadily, so we can understand the mechanics underlying the way investment decisions on innovation activities take place. The underlying purpose behind IP rules is to bring about the stability of these activities that otherwise would be halted by a fog of ignorance.

To make sense of how IP rules emerge, we need to understand the innovation process that they regulate. Unfortunately, conventional explanations are unclear on this issue, as they focus on assumed incentives that rules set on entrepreneurs. Yet such understanding takes entrepreneurs to be well-informed about the choices these incentives available to them. Thus, the theories of innovation based on the notion of incentives neglect the important role of business failure and oversight that is inherent to the status of entrepreneurship, as anyone who has been an entrepreneur could certify. Business failures are a reality that no incentive can overcome.

Innovation works in a different way. Entrepreneurs predict future outcomes, but that does not mean that success is warranted. They take action in the present with the expectation of favorable future outcomes, which may well fail. Market expectations are thus *working hypotheses* that an entrepreneur postulates about future outcomes associated with their activity (Lachmann 1943; Harper 1994), which may or may not turn out to be correct. These hypotheses are tentative predictions about possible solutions to given problems. When Adam Smith (1776) explained the nature of labor division he emphasized how the factory worker learns from the new division of tasks, furthering his productivity, not only by increasing his 'dexterity' in addressing these problems each time but, more importantly, in developing machines (i.e., innovating) to solve them consistently.[3] Smith did not address business failure, possibly because he felt that it was a premise of his notion of learning. Experience tells us that for every successful new capital good invented, ten attempts had to go wrong.

Business history tells us that Jack Dorsey, the founder of Twitter, spent years of experimentation before he finally came up with the Twitter social network that we know today. Likewise, Starbuck's CEO Howard Schultz had to overcome his first try, before the American consumers acknowledged his great foresight of bringing into the United States a real European communal coffee experience. His first store opened in Seattle in 1986, played non-stop opera music, had no chairs, and offered menus in Italian. Finally, Perez de Anton notes (2002: 37–39) recounts the story of failed attempts of Central America's most successful food franchise, Pollo Campero, to come up with a novel fried chicken recipe. He notes how many failed attempts the product development team had to undergo in the early years before they would find the right cooking temperature and pressure for frying the Pollo Campero chicken that people of 11 countries enjoy today, even in Bahrain.

[3] In his words: "the invention of all those machines by which labour is so much facilitated and abridged, seems to have been originally owing to the division of labour. Men are much more likely to discover easier and readier methods of attaining any object, when the whole attention of their minds is directed towards that single object, than when it is dissipated among a great variety of things. But in consequence of the division of labour, the whole of every man's attention comes naturally to be directed towards some one very simple object. It is naturally to be expected, therefore, that some one or other of those who are employed in each particular branch of labour should soon find out easier and readier methods of performing their own particular work, wherever the nature of it admits of such improvement" (Smith 1776, I.1.8).

One can realize the real experience of becoming an innovative entrepreneur by the number of business mistakes or successes they make. Entrepreneurship is not so much about succeeding as it is about avoiding mistakes. We all know Thomas Edison's dictum, "genius is 1% inspiration, 99% perspiration.[4]" Pundits (Relan 2012; Zimmerman 2013; Tavoletti 2013) agree that stories of business incubation failure are probably more resilient and important for entrepreneurial learning than successful ones. After all, trial-and-error marks the awareness of entrepreneurs, thereby inducing them to postulate hypotheses about future outcomes arising from investing resources in the midst of uncertainty. New circumstances never stop from rising, and the entrepreneur has to adapt permanently through a learning process that never ends; the unexpected is an integral part of the innovation process.[5]

Clearly, the possibility of failure is inherent in the speculative activity of entrepreneurs. Reciprocal speculation between entrepreneurs takes the form of 'expectations,' that is, subjective and speculative hypotheses that are contingent to personal interpretations of how likely uncertain outcomes will be. Lachmann (1943, 1994: 122–123) notes the speculative nature of market expectations: "The subjective nature of expectations, due, in the first place, to divergences in individual interpretations of identical observable events, is thus seen to derive ultimately from divergent judgments on the strength of the economic forces believed to have caused them."

If we assume the market system to be truly decentralized—its participants act independently and don't communicate—then market expectations are inherently uncertain because they rest on the participants' reciprocal speculations about the behavior of other participants of the innovation ecosystem, which in the absence of communication is unfathomable.[6]

Endless stories about scientific serendipity account for the nonlinearity of innovation: Thomas Edison saw the phonograph as an answering machine, not as a helping device to record artists' voices that would trigger the emergence of the large music recording industry. Propecia was originally marketed as Proscar, a drug to treat the benign enlargement of the prostate until patients began to notice hair growing effects that would make this drug more attractive to treat male-pattern baldness. Play-Doh, the kids' clay, was invented by Joseph and Noah McVicker while trying

[4] The statement in a press conference (1929), as quoted in Newton (1987: 24).

[5] Innovation results in the production of a novel product or service whose acceptance by the market analysts cannot ascertain with the help statistical data (Taleb 2007). In the language of Industrial Organization, the introduction in the market of an innovative product or services flattens the industry's demand curve, but no one can anticipate by how much; it all depends on the public's acceptance, whose endorsement will remain unknown even for the innovator until the launch of the innovation.

[6] Keynes (1936); Lekachman and Keynes (1964) demonstrated in his "Beauty Contest example" how mutual expectations lead to absolute uncertainty, this is the common trait that pervades markets and explains the emergence of institutions as connecting mechanisms that transform scattered ideas into meaningful, linked knowledge. Richardson (1960) explored in depth how entrepreneurs overcome the uncertainty of decentralized market systems by developing connections, or links, either as competitors or as suppliers or clients.

to make wallpaper cleaner; Listerine was invented as a surgical antiseptic and a cure for gonorrhea. The list is endless. The entrepreneurial uncertainty stems from the fact that real life is multidimensional, in the sense that it contains many multiple elements that interact in a non-simple (i.e. linear) way (Simon 1962: 468); some factor influences on another, which in turn creates a feedback on the former.

The role of rules is to stabilize expectations, by providing a framework within which certain 'proven' routines or 'solutions' evolve into rules of thumb that provide entrepreneurs with cognitive boundaries to what otherwise would be unfathomable. These boundaries help them to focus their attention on the novel elements that the evolving reality brings about. Given the speculation that innovators engage in due to their endeavors to forecast future consumer needs, it clearly follows that the rules have a key role in eliminating all possible sources of noise arising from speculation that is not strictly associated with the innovation or creation process, but rather from the activity of other economic agents with effects on the creative process, including the government. For this reason, entrepreneurial expectations are also constitutive of the system of rules, in the sense that these speculative interactions shape the set of rules that govern them; in other words, these rules are not external constraints imposed on their learning process, but rather the outcome of it.[7] They create a filtering mechanism that conveys verified knowledge, thereby helping them to 'frame' their decision-making process.

In other words, confirmation of these entrepreneurial expectations generates stability on the knowledge they need to induce them to invest time and thought into the innovation process and to overcome what would otherwise generate paralyzing uncertainty. Ultimately, the innovative process is based on bounded expectations on the predicted outcomes resulting from R&D investments and generally, the entrepreneurial creative effort. Exploring the nature of these guesses or expectations, and learning how they emerge and are stabilized is a critical source of learning.

Building coalescing expectations is at the core of the innovation process, because innovation is, to a large extent, collaboration among innovators that possess complementary aptitudes to combine and recombine knowledge and produce endless combinations. Empirical evidence shows that firms from high-tech industries place greater value on cooperation partners in the innovation process. These firms seek cooperating actively with other businesses, while they also have higher innovation investment levels, and absorptive capacity; they give importance to incoming spillovers management and collaborate with businesses from the same group or with suppliers (De Faria et al. 2010; Un et al. 2010). Thus, cooperation yields innovation.

Market expectations are subjective, because they revolve around entrepreneurial cognition, which develops from their interpretation of their entourage; therefore,

[7] In his 1952 book The Sensory Order, F.A. Hayek noted that human perception and human action is a purely subjective phenomenon. The mind does not represent physical or external events but is an interpretation of these events that we call reality.

their knowledge is subject to cognitive biases.[8] Economic science, groomed in the concept of rationality and forecasting, usually plays down the importance of cognitive biases. After all, these are systematic deviations from norm or rationality in judgment, leading to illogical inferences about other people and situations. Yet, cognitive biases are ever present in the appraisal that entrepreneurs make towards the operating rules within which they construe their innovative endeavors; therefore, it is essential to understand how these biases influence their innovative activity. The presence of such biases distorts the entrepreneurs' perceptions about the use and value of such rules.

Innovators may sometime misjudge the meaning of the rules developed in support of their inventive activities. In extreme conditions, the misperception is so big that they abstain from using them. Instead, they follow alternative protocols that give them more certainty about their control over the intellectual assets they develop, but at the expense of renouncing to use protocols or rules widely accepted by everyone else. In doing so, they lose capacity to access to 'packed' and standardized information, thus raising transaction costs, by undermining their capacity to use such rules to their advantage. Entrepreneurs manage their IP because they need to develop strategies to fill gaps of knowledge left by gaps on the operating rules of the innovation ecosystem that undermine their expected turnover.

In short, IP rules 'pack' and standardize the information needed for innovation markets to develop quicker and with fewer transaction costs because they separate the grain from the shaft, by providing rules of thumb that ease entrepreneurial endeavors finding genuinely new solutions to perceived problems. That filtering mechanism simplifies the complexity of the landscape for the entrepreneur. Such rules simplify transactions as they coordinate different participants to the innovation ecosystem into coalescing expectations that induce them to seek new solutions that the existing rules do not offer. For example, the parties to a licensing agreement will not need to check that the technology licensed belongs to whoever claims to hold a patent grant, but will be able to focus on fewer collateral issues, such as conditions for sublicensing, or its geographical scope. Cognitive biases constantly undermine entrepreneurs' capacity to rationalize their actions; therefore, they need rules of thumb that we call 'intellectual property.'

[8] Cognitive biases are thinking errors that individuals make in processing information. Some of these have been verified empirically in the realm of psychology, while others are considered general categories of bias. These thinking errors prevent one from accurately understanding reality, even when confronted with all the needed data and evidence to form an accurate view. Cognitive biases are inherent to human thought, and therefore, any systematic method of acquiring knowledge must control bias; otherwise it is inherently invalid. They include a list of more than 35 identified forms of decision-making and behavioral biases; 25 forms of biases in probability and belief; 25 forms of social biases; and 10 forms of memory errors.

1.2 Conventional IP Theory Does Not Explain IP Management

Attention to the way entrepreneurial expectations are coordinated in the innovation process is not the emphasis that the conventional economic theory gives to the role of IP. In fact, the outlook that the theory gives to the role of intellectual property blurs the role of IP management, as a mechanism that helps firms to build alternative responses to cope with problems emerging from uncoordinated expectations.

Innovation, in the conventional 'incentives' view, focuses on its alleged 'public good' nature, namely, when the incentives between IP developers and the public are aligned. These incentives collide because IP developers expect to get a monopoly over the knowledge they develop to commercialize it exclusively, whereas the public good involves breaking the monopoly to get open access to the knowledge as fast as possible. Government intervention is required to find an optimal balance between these two opposing interests by drafting IP rules that equilibrate these contradictory interests through incentives. The United Nations (2011: 7) put it succinctly as follows: "From an economic point of view, IPRs are a policy tool to align the private returns to innovative activity with its social return, i.e. its benefit to society and thus to generate socially optimal incentives for innovative private-sector activity."

IP is intended to help entrepreneurs align their incentives towards the 'public good,' namely, the production of more innovation, by rewarding innovators' efforts. Innovator companies often fail to obtain significant economic returns from innovation, while customers, imitators, and competitors benefit from the endeavors of innovators because of flawed legal or contractual incentives (Teece 1986). Seizing financial returns out of innovation depends on the degree of integration or collaboration that entrepreneurs are willing to have with other market participants, and this, in turn, rests upon the set of legal rules in place. When imitation is legally permitted markets do not reward the developer of the intellectual asset; instead, the profits may accrue to the owners of certain complementary assets (e.g. manufacturers). Therefore, it may be necessary for the innovating firm to establish a former position in these matched assets. Consequently, the innovators may be ill-positioned in the market to seize economic returns out of their innovations, because they are not in control of the critical assets they need to do so. Licensing and outsourcing complementary capabilities may be required for innovators to put their technologies out in the market. However, under closer inspection, IP management is entirely at odds with the role of IP, because the former aims at obtaining market power to exploit information advantages in its favor, whereas the latter seeks to eliminate such asymmetries.

Another formulation of the incentives view links innovation to the size of SMIEs on the one hand, and on the other hand, to the complexity of the industry that usually makes use of the patent system. Under this structural thesis, Cho et al. (2015) argue that causal paths vary not only by industry but also by firm size. Stronger IPR are beneficial to R&D-intensive industries where large domestic enterprises have high R&D and IPR capabilities but have little impact on globalized sectors. On the other hand, stronger IPR are detrimental to industries and to startups, which are characterized by limited resources. These authors conclude that the use of IPR is customized to industries as well as startups. Universally high IPR policies are likely to discourage innovation and growth, causing some industries populated by startups to suffer. Interestingly, this explanation turns the incentives view upside down. Here, IPRs are perceived as a 'disincentive' to SMIEs innovation activities, since their small size will always play out against them. Under this light, Latin America's economic structure, where SMIEs operate in non-R&D intensive industries and there is seldom use of patents, but rather a preference for trade secrets and trademarks, seems to validate this theory. We believe this structural explanation conflates cause and effect. In our view, large R&D-industries have strong R&D and IPR capabilities as a consequence of their previous awareness that these activities are valuable within their productive process, and they can only reach that conclusion once they have undergone the transformative process that IP management represents.

Finally, Harper (2014) presents us with an interesting theory of 'modular rights.' He envisions IP as a 'modular' mechanism that allows entrepreneurs to adapt to their business milieu, thereby arranging the pieces of 'ownership' over the expected returns, once that innovation accrues in the market. But in fact, the static modular view overlooks the important role that entrepreneurial awareness plays in making such adaptation possible. While it is true that the IP system features a kaleidoscopic layout, its uncertainty ultimately has to do with the failure of entrepreneurs to weave changing perceptions about new knowledge introduced as a result of the innovation activity.

Both the conventional incentive-based and the structural-based explanations portray intellectual property rules as 'givens' towards which entrepreneurs merely react to. These theories do not consider the transformative process of ideas into valuable intellectual assets that active entrepreneurs engage in through IP management. Rather, they postulate a closed-ended view of economic relations, where startups automatically respond to 'systemic incentives' or to the 'structure' of the market where they operate that implicitly rejects the very idea of an entrepreneurial search for novelty, implicit in the innovation process.

Despite their widespread use in economic models, the conventional literature on the economics of IP (Machlup 1958; Kitch 1977; Besen and Raskind 1991; Besen 1998) is unsuited to explain why firms choose specific IP strategies. Instead, it takes entrepreneurial behavior in this area as guided by a set of undifferentiated 'incentives,' inducing him or her to carry out innovation activities. The incentives view takes technology as a homogeneous input that leads production closer to the optimal production 'frontier.' It focuses on the intangible nature and complexity technology level of the invention, as opposed to the particular perception of the trading parties involved in the technology market. Therefore, all the information about the interaction of such markets is centralized around wise administering policymakers who can administer incentives to tap on any potential opportunities or to prevent flaws from reducing the potential opportunities for optimal market functioning. Innovation under this blackboard economics approach is perceived as a 'good' whose existence is brewing in the incentives that the institutional system established to organize incentives between consumers and innovative technologies. This widely reported incentive approach is not interested in the institutional milieu that shapes the awareness of the entrepreneur, to discover profit opportunities needed to create innovations. This approach overlooks the coalescing expectations of both innovators and technology market traders that sustain the innovation ecosystem. Indeed, in this perspective, the construction of positive expectations for inducing effort is even outside the field of economics. Innovation in this view is assumed a matter of efforts, rather than creativity.

Viewing IP as a set of incentives runs at odds with the human nature of flesh-and-bone entrepreneurs, that is, if one accepts that nine out ten times business ventures fail because of oversights, hastiness, poor judgment and many other factors associated to business failure. It is not surprising that empirical evidence shows that regardless of increased incentives, i.e., expected rewards through harsher laws condemning piracy, better functioning IP institutions, and other promotions, entrepreneurs do not show equivalent increases in their productivity outputs (Ip 2016).

The entrepreneurial function is not merely triggered by the promise of rewards, real or fictitious. Awareness of opportunities around is as important as their actual existence, because it is their expectation of becoming that triggers on economic agents a need of change, i.e., to act.

More recent empirical evidence challenges the assumption of innovation being driven by incentives (Mercurio 2014: 4). The 'incentives' theory of IP does not explain why despite the stronger IP regulations issued between 2003 and 2013 not only resident firms still lagged behind in their levels of patent applications compared to other regions (2.5% of the world total), but actually the margin decreased in the period (from 2.9%).

Table 1.1 shows that the average share of patent applications from Latin American resident firms decreased in the decade between 2003 (13.8%) and 2013 (12.2%). This evidence contradicts the assumption that the creation of an efficient IP system lies on 'incentives.' If there are more incentives to seek IP protection why do patent filing remains low? Despite the reduced costs of enforcing IPRs, there has been no

Table 1.1 Patent applications by region

	Number of applications		Resident share (%)		Share of world total (%)		Average growth (%)
	2003	2013	2003	2013	2003	2013	2003–2013
World total	1,490,300	2,567,900	62.5	66.5	100	100	5.6
Africa	9200	14,900	18.5	15.4	0.6	0.6	4.9
Asia	705,600	1,500,400	74.3	78.8	47.3	58.4	7.8
Europe	324,500	346,400	62.2	63.3	21.8	13.5	0.7
Latin America & the Caribbean	42,800	63,300	13.8	12.2	2.9	2.5	4.0
North America	379,700	606,300	50.8	48.2	25.5	23.6	4.8
Oceania	28,500	36,600	15.1	12.8	1.9	1.4	2.5

Source: World Intellectual Property Organization (2014)

significant increase in the volume of applications; in fact, the opposite is true. This situation is not confined to Latin America, as a recent Wall Street Journal report indicates (Ip 2016).

Scholars note that 'high' patent protection results from innovative development, not the other way around (Teece 2000). Moreover, IP only increases innovation if accompanied by high levels of development, educational attainment, and economic freedom (Quian 2007). Also, IP effects are uneven. Therefore one cannot construe a general theory based on incentives created but note their differential effects (Cho et al. 2015); indeed, it does not have uniform effects on innovation across countries, particularly in developing ones (Kim et al. 2011). For example, evidence shows that IP has mixed results in attracting foreign investment because it largely depends on the recipient industry. Strong patent protection does not necessarily increase productivity (Boldrin and Levine 2012).

While we believe that innovation is not about random ideas, but about ideas that connect with the innovation ecosystem, thus producing knowledge, inputs are not sufficient to produce innovation outputs. In other words, creativity entails something more than mere monetary rewards. Monetary incentives alone cannot trigger creativity because the human mind is complex, non-linear and evolutionary. Thus, finding new solutions to old problems does not follow predictable patterns, as one could infer from the mechanic, physical, rational and linear approach of the incentives-based theories.

One can see that innovation has to do with creativity to develop inventions that provide new socially valuable solutions. Naturally, the only way to learn whether society values an invention is through the IP market. Put differently, creativity includes a capacity to anticipate the positive reaction of the market towards the new idea embedded in a product or a process. Here, no outcome is ever assured, because even shrewd entrepreneurs often fail to foresee all the upshots of their inventions on society. Even with a positive encouragement to develop a product, their imagination could very well fail.

In a Lecture given in 2004 at the University of Milan, Brian Loasby noted the relevance of what he termed the 'psychology of wealth' in economic science. Analyzing Carlo Cattaneo's 1861 work, 'Del Pensiero come Principia d'Economia Publica', Loasby refers to the author's emphasis on the role of 'intelligence and will' as drivers of the different productivity levels among countries. This emphasis of the psychology determinants of wealth was implicit in Adam Smith's recognition that the division of labor generates improved skills and better practice. Unfortunately, he notes, economists diverted their science towards emphasizing the 'physics of wealth'—the contribution to production of natural resources, the work of man, and capital—as opposed to the assessment of the 'opportunity cost of intelligence' or put it differently, the application of human cognitive powers. This research agenda was emphasized by a minority—even if a formidable group of economists that included Smith, Marshall and Hayek; the way human cognition interprets reality, and interprets the environment, is critical to understand how creativity emerges and how innovators connect with the innovation ecosystem.

In contrast with the incentives-based analysis of incentives inducing the activity of rational agents, we underline the relevance of cognitive analysis to understand why entrepreneurs sometimes fail to seize business opportunities in IP markets. In this we follow Cattaneo's proposition (1861: 59) whereby "there is no work no capital which does not start with some act of intelligence", because as Loasby (2004: 3) notes "if all actions are rationally chosen then 'intelligence', like 'utility', has no analytical content."

Indeed, deploying intelligence in the design of IP management strategies requires awareness of the possibilities that IP rules give to their owners, so they can use it strategically. If an entrepreneur ignores the value of a patent, because he does not know that the legal system can enforce a patent protection effectively, or simply because he does not know what a patent is for, then it is unlikely that he or she will realize the value accruing from using such instrument to obtain income. Cognition biases limit IP management strategy's effectiveness.

IP rules emerge out of a trust-building process between members of the innovation ecosystem. Their role is to encapsulate knowledge resulting from verification protocols that these put into place to build knowledge about possible new ideas, discoveries, solutions to problems, in a word, innovations that change the landscape of received science. In this view, IP management comprises alternative strategies that help entrepreneurs to gauge how much real market power they yield and how much are their competitors. Entrepreneurs attach IPRs varying enforcement probabilities that allow them different levels of exclusive control over their assets, therefore, possibilities to impose market power. The probabilities' set encapsulates the vetting process that entrepreneurs do over what ideas are original, thus valuable, and what ideas are not.

One can see this by looking at cases where entrepreneurs made mistakes because their cognition bias led them into conducting a faulty IP management strategy. Several business stories highlight what happens when the corporate management fails to anticipate how innovation will happen, because of these biases, and the devastating effects that this creates upon their intellectual assets value.

Take the case of Xerox. This company (Xerox PARC) developed several technologies including graphical user interfaces, Ethernet networking, and bit mapping, as part of the technology that went into the production of Xerox's 914 photocopiers. However, Xerox's corporate managers had little idea of their IP portfolio value, particularly in connection with the evolution of the personal computing industry, which they perceived unrelated. Their cognition was limited to the realm of their own industry, so they were not aware of the increasing threads connecting their industry to the personal computing industry, particularly in the development of the latter's critical competitive factor, the Graphic interphase that allowed a huge potential market of untrained consumers to get a familiar use of the – then – personal personal computers' industry.

Therefore, Xerox's managers did not bother to protect it; they merely focused on the photocopier elements of their products, thus neglecting the personal computing potential of their intellectual assets. Consequently, they let companies like IBM and Apple take advantage of market opportunities much later. They did not see the future value of their technology being embedded in personal computing; therefore they missed the chance to jump on the wagon of the new market they had helped to create.

To summarize, IP management has little to do with finding "right" incentives that encourage innovators to commercialize their intellectual assets. Instead, IP management is about supporting entrepreneurs' market power, through strategies that help them seize gaps of knowledge stemming from the uncertainties of the IP system. To put it differently, it is about enabling entrepreneurs to verify the information they receive from the innovation process and turn it into valuable, i.e., tradable, knowledge[9] by connecting scattered bits of information and thus gaining valuable knowledge and competitive capabilities which ensure their market power.

In our view, instead, startups' low awareness of the benefits accruing from the IPR system is primarily responsible for the breakdown of IP management. In other words, the capacity of the IP system to bring about coordination among individuals involved in the creation and dissemination of knowledge is what marks its inner economic role.

How does the IP system create a structure that allows coordination among the different parties involved? The next section examines the patent claims structure, which is the legal mechanism used to allocate businesses allegations of developing innovative technologies.

1.3 Establishing Priority over the Creative Work or Discovery

Before the enactment of IP laws, authors and scientists had a hard time showing their authorship over literary and scientific discoveries as they relied entirely on their fame and reputation. The situation was hard for those scientists introducing disruptive theories, for pioneering ideas often generated multiple independent discoveries[10] (Merton 1963), thus generating several contending candidates for peer recognition. This situation naturally tended to stir embittered quarrelling among them.

[9] This conclusion is now new. Loasby (2005) notes that Adam Smith found more relevant for his analysis to focus on how people come to accept some propositions as true, as opposed to attempting to establish the truth of any general empirical proposition by logic or evidence, which is impossible. The 'discomfort' produced by the failure of existing patterns of knowledge to account for newly-observed phenomena leads individuals to invent new 'connecting principles' that will impose a new understanding of things. But new 'connecting principles' lead to new expectations, new activities and new observations; thereby giving rise to its their anomalies and consequent stimuli to imagination. Thus, Smith transferred to economics his emphasis on knowledge about knowledge.

[10] Merton (1963) indicates "sometimes the discoveries are simultaneous or almost so; sometimes a scientist will make a new discovery which, unknown to him, somebody else has made years before." Johnson (2010) explains this phenomenon as a result of the similar technological departing ground from which new discoveries are developed, which he calls "the adjacent possible." In other words, both evolution and innovation tend to happen within the bounds of possibilities available at any given moment.

In the field of science Robert Merton (1957) gives us a full historical account of how scientific giants in physics and chemistry claimed priority over scientific discoveries, sometimes very bitterly.[11] At times, these claims of priority existed even when the scientists themselves act collegially, such as the controversy between Darwin and Wallace over their respective theories of natural selection as a driving force of natural evolution, or the dispute between Heisenberg and Bohr over the notion of Quantum Mechanisms, which was lumped together as "the Copenhagen interpretation" (Faye 2014).

Sometimes that forced them to publish articles, not to explain their discoveries as to lambast their competitors' claims. In the field of literary works, it is hard not to recall the unusual, yet very effective, way by which Miguel de Cervantes claimed ownership of his character Don Quixote in the fact of plagiarism by Alonso Fernandez de Avellaneda. Miguel Cervantes's Second Part of Don Quixote had to be published hurriedly in 1615, since a year earlier another author Alonso Fernandez de Avellaneda published a *Second Book of the Ingenious Knight Don Quixote of La Mancha*, an unauthorized and unofficial sequel of Cervantes' famous novel. Cervantes was still writing the second part of his Don Quixote when Avellaneda's unofficial sequel was released, but he did not seek legal relief from a court.[12] Instead, Cervantes wittingly used the popular Don Quixote to mock Avellaneda.[13] Cervantes' strategy worked so

---

[11] With or without reason, sometimes these battles turned these towering figures into ungraceful advocates of their own causes. Take the case of Galileo's "Defense against the Calumnies and Impostures of Baldassar Capar," where he showed how his invention of the "geometric and military compass" had been taken from him; or his 1623 work *The Assayer*, which speaks of a villain who "attempted to rob me of that glory which is mine, pretending not to have seen my writings and trying to represent themselves as the original discoverer of these marvels." Isaac Newton's dispute with Robert Hooke over the discovery of optics and celestial mechanics seems to have become so sour that some accuse Newton, as President of the Royal Society, of doing much to obscure Hooke, including destroying (or failing to preserve) the only known portrait at the Society.

[12] The "*Act for the Encouragement of Learning, by Vesting the Copies of Printed Books in the Authors or Purchasers of such Copies, during the Times therein mentioned*," (short named as Statute of Anne, after the name of the Queen of England) is considered the first modern copyright law. It would not see the light until 1710, and would be signed in England. The first copyright statute in Cervantes' Spain was the Royal Order of 1764. So his options to protect his creation from plagiarism were fairly limited.

[13] So, in Chapter 59 Don Quixote becomes outraged when he learns of Avellaneda's book and the way he is portrayed in it. Then, he avoids attending a jousting because it took place in the Avellaneda edition. In another chapter he uses Don Alfaro Tarfe, a character from Avellaneda's work, to get him to sign an affidavit that he and Don Quixote have never met before. However, the funniest reference of all is found in Chapter 70, where Cervantes had the character Altisodora recount her journey to the gates of hell, and there she observed a group of devils playing tennis with books, instead of balls; one of these books being Avellaneda's Quixote. The story is worth of recount in full. As Altisodora was viewing the game with books, she notices one of them, a brand-new, well-bound one. To this book, the devils "gave such a stroke that they knocked the guts out of it and scattered the leaves about." "Look what book that is," said one devil to another, and the other replied, "It is 'Second Part of the History of Don Quixote of La Mancha,' not by Cid Hamet [the metafictional historian of *Don Quixote*], the original author, but by an Aragonese who by his own account is of Tordesillas." "Out of this with it," said the first, "and into the depths of hell with it out of my sight." "Is it so bad?" said the other. "So bad is it," said the first, "that if I had set myself deliberately to make a worse, I could not have done it."

effectively that it may have given underserved recognition to Avellaneda's work, which is still remembered today, even if as *the False Don Quixote.*

It is natural that policymakers felt necessary to end such uncertainty, as the progress of the Industrial Revolution increasingly multiplied the number of inventions over which pioneering scientists and authors claimed priority. Not surprisingly, the first IP modern statutes emerged in this period, even though the first patents date as far back as 1450.[14] The previous inorganic priority claim system increasingly was addressed by these new laws. Although some authors like Merton (1957) claim them to be fundamentally different in purpose and effect,[15] the logic of patents and copyrights is traceable to the flaws of the previous system of peer acknowledgement over authors' and scientists' claim of priority.

Although the patent system (and to a lesser extent the copyright system) was an improvement over the previous system, it is not free from complications. In this section we will focus our attention in the patent system, to highlight its complexity. In particular, we shall examine how the uncertainty found in the IP system, in general, is particularly visible in the patent system.

Patents comprise the hallmark of the IP system. Compared to other IPRs these assets are highly liquid, due to their structure as well as the legal monopoly they confer to the titleholder. However, no matter their liquidity, they still suffer from the very structure of the patent registration system. The patent system rests upon a network of claims that interested parties present before the patent offices to obtain exclusivity in the use of the technology or knowledge upon which they claim an inventive step and which is non-obvious.

In the context of the present discussion, it is necessary to lay out the nature of patents and the role they fulfill in the innovation process. This explanation is critical to understand the complexity of the patents system, which adds to the difficulties of use and uncertainty pervading the system.

[14] It was inevitable that the Industrial Revolution needed a legal foundation to sustain the increasing number of innovations. Patents were systematically granted in Venice as of 1450, where they issued a decree by which new and inventive devices had to be communicated to the Republic in order to obtain legal protection against potential infringers. This led to the diffusion of patent systems to other countries. However, the system was viewed as a royal monopoly granted to the privilege of subjects favored by the King. Consolidation arrived at the end of the eighteenth century, when the granting of patents began to be viewed as a form of intellectual property right. Following the new approach, several changes were introduced to patent law including requirements on those applying to a patent to supply a complete description of how the invention works, available for public access.

[15] According to Merton, the intent of a patent claim and priority of discovery are also fundamentally different. The primary goal of a patent is to stake territory as one's own and exclude others (or make them pay for using your intellectual property), thus serving a goal of commercialization. The invention only enters the public domain for free use after many years. In contrast, the disclosure of work for "priority of discovery" is intended to encourage others to make use of the discovery and expand upon it for non-commercial use. Not only is this aligned with mission of science, but the scientist's claim "priority" can only be firmly established when others validate (i.e. repeat) and affirm the importance (through further development) of the original discovery.

The conventional view of patent rights emphasizes a bundle of rights that patentees can selectively assert. Those rights carry different types of entitlements, e.g., the exclusive right to make, the sole right to sell, the right to license, etc. The notion that statutory patent law, as applied by the patent office, offers the prospect of exclusive rights over "the invention" conveys this view (Rantanen 2015: 900–901). In a similar fashion, the economic view also regards them as clear-cut entitlements enabling their titleholders to enjoy temporary economic rents (Dam 1993: 4) or as "blocks of Lego that can be mixed and matched in particular ways" (Harper 2015).

Contrary to this view, the structure of the patent rights' system comprises a subjective bundle of claims, and these claims create multiple sets of overlapping layers of rights. Moreover, the boundaries of these claims do not get fixed by the patent office at the time of registry but are contingent on the potential prosecution outcome throughout the life of the patent. Such trial outcome is the product of many factors, including the level of prosecution that exists in the country, the complexity of the technology involved, the speed of technological evolution in the industry, and the capacity of competitors and the patentee to sustain expensive prosecution trials.

To understand the kaleidoscopic structure of this system, let us explain the structure of the patent claim system. Consider the following hypothetical example of a two-sided hammer:

Claim 1 A two-sided hammer.
Claim 2 The hammer of claim 1, further comprising at least one side of aluminum.
Claim 3 The hammer of claim 2, wherein the hammer is covered by a resistant polymer.

In this example, the first claim (claim 1) comprises the basic invention; it is independent because it does not reference any other complaint; it stands alone because it has all of the details needed to define the invention. Independent claims may describe a "thing," such as a device, apparatus, machine or composition of matter. They may also represent a method of how to make a "thing." Finally, they may explain a method of using a "thing." Finally, claim 1 should always be independent. In case claim 1 is canceled or withdrawn (for example, during prosecution), the examiner would renumber the claims so that the first independent claim is once again numbered claim 1.

On the other hand, claims 2 and 3 are dependent, because they indicate another claim and are proper subsets of their respective parent claim. In the example above, claim 2 is dependent because it references claim 1; claim 3 is dependent because it references claim 2 (and implicitly, claim 1). Dependent claims include all the limitations of the referenced claim; thus, in this example claim 2 implicitly describes a hammer with two sides. To infringe claim 2 a competitor's hammer would not only have to have at least one side made of aluminum, as it expressly indicates claim 2, but also has to fulfill the condition laid down in claim 1 (i.e. two-sided). Dependent claims help ensure broad interpretation of the claims upon which they are dependent.

The complexity does not stop there. Dependent claims rely on either an independent claim or on another dependent claim. In the example above, claim 3 (covered by a polymer) is based on claim 2 (one-sided aluminum) and includes all of the limitations of claim 3, plus the limitations of claim 2, plus the limitations of claim 1 (two-sided hammer).

Now, suppose that our hypothetical example contains more subsequent claims 4, 5 and 6 such that:

Claim 4 The hammer of claim 3, wherein the hammer has a rubber grip;
Claim 5 The hammer of claim 3 wherein one side has one pointed edge;
Claim 6 The hammer of claim 3 wherein the hammer has a wooden grip.

In these cases, prosecution could reverse dependency, such that claim 2 becomes dependent of either claims 4, 5 or 6 even though these claims appear later in the listing. Assume, for example, that independent claim 1 is invalidated. In this case, the applicant could make claim 2 dependent of claim 4. The patent office will renumber the claims to put them in a logical order.

Further, claims 2 and 3 add up more specificity so that it results in a full description of the version that represents the innovator mind's eye. These claims set out the boundaries of the invention from a general level of abstraction that defines the invention in broad terms, to succeeding narrower claims. So the invention is whittled down from a more general claim to narrower ones.

Now, these claims are valid on the condition that the technology or knowledge described in them represents an inventive step and is non-obvious, i.e., that the invention is sufficiently beyond or above the state of the art. That creates a first significant problem in the way parties construe their expectations because a broader claim is more likely to be held invalid because it covers more categories of prior art; whereas a small claim is more likely valid but weaker as it is easier to design around. The solution that patent practitioners usually adopt is drafting multiple broad and narrow claims, in a way that patent applicants cover every possible gap.

To make things more complicated, the sets of claims are semi-independently structured, so the validity of one is not necessarily contingent to the others (as seen in the example above, invalidation of claim 1 does not invalidate claim 2). At the same time, however, they remain interrelated to a point where dependent claims provide assurance that the technology or knowledge described in the independent claim would still prevail (albeit in a narrower sense) through the validity of the dependent claims.[16] Strategically, too, parties at a prosecution may broaden the scope of the independent claims they make by connecting these to dependent claims.

[16] Dependent claims provide patent claimants a backup during prosecution and enforcement actions. In our case, let us assume that a court invalidates claim 1 over the prior art during litigation. If the claimant only asserted claim 1 the case would be over, and the claimant would lose. Claims 2, 3, 4, 5 and 6, however, provide him or her a fallback. Claim 2 ("The two-sided aluminum hammer") would be patentable if until then these peculiar hammers had been made of different materials but aluminum (say, plastic, or wood). Claim 3 ("two-sided aluminum hammers covered with a resistant polymer") made possible for the claimant to obtain a patent even if two-sided aluminum hammers are prior art because it may be that the only hammers found in the market had no polymer covering. The same patent approval would occur if these hammers found in the market had no rubber grips (claim 4); or if they had one pointed-edged side, (claim 5) or if they had a wooden grip. In short, the dependent claims in a patent application provide useful fallback positions during patent filing, and then later on during litigation.

All this makes determinations as to the validity of multiple patents claims independent of one another, but only to some degree. So, the outcome of this intertwined combination of overlapping claims is a structure that has little to do with the idealized notion of a bundle of rights that pervades the legal literature.

In short, as Rantanen notes (2015: 944):

> Patents end up being comprised of multiple sets of semi-independent bundles of rights that overlap with one another and that include both bundles of strong-but-narrow rights and weak-but-broad rights. Unsurprisingly, many of the paradigmatic validity disputes in patent law turn out to be over this latter set of claims: the weak-but-broad rights. The narrow-but-strong claims were likely still around, in the background, and typically protected the core embodiment of the patent holder's technology…
>
> This multi-claim structure also allows patent drafters to include both highly ambiguous (and vague) claims and those that are much more specific to the embodiments of the patent. It represents a critical difference between patent rights and any form of traditional property regime.

The way the patent system is structured forces those who want to obtain a patent to formulate them through "claims." But these claims are conditioned by the intervention of patent authorities, who review them in the light of their novelty. Thus the scope and strength of the right can be changed even after the patent is issued through a myriad of tools, allowing actors operating within the patent system the ability to alter the contours of their registered patents.

Thus, patentees can change the precise scope of this structure after the approval of the patent. They can do so through reissue proceedings and ex parte reexamination. The first mechanism enables patentees to seek modification of patent claims with certain restrictions, while the second allows another party to propose changes, albeit in very exceptional circumstances (Rantanen 2015: 945). The plasticity of patent rights follows the structure of patent claims, which overlap creating a complex layer of intertwined rights, contingent to the acknowledgment of experts who review them in the light of "prior art."

This convoluted structure naturally generates uncertainty in the way parties construe their claims regarding the technology upon which they want to gain exclusivity. Rantanen (2015: 898–900) explains how this way of constructing overlapping claims makes them "malleable," that is, the actors who interact with the issued patent can alter their formal scope.

Finally, time scalability is another decisive factor undermining the transparency of the IP market (Bader et al. 2012). The time it takes to the patent authority to process a filing and grant a patent title could impair patent filing of innovations in fast-evolving markets, such as technology markets. These radical changes, according to Gordon Moore (1965) take place every 18 months (as opposed to patent granting, which may take between 3 and 5 years, depending on the jurisdiction).

Patent decisions thus involve a complex judgment that could broaden the scope of patentability on individual cases. An example refers to claims that extend to innovations still unknown. Merges and Nelson (1990) note a 1988 U.S. Patent Office decision that granted a patent to the inventors of a transgenic mouse (U.S. Patent No. 4,736,866 issued Apr. 12, 1988, at col. 9, claim 1). The Office accepted the inventor's contention that their procedure could be used to engineer "non-human mammals." That opened the door for the claimant to claim that they could patent higher-order animals made with their procedure. This assertion brings us to the question whether such a generalization of specific results can be made consistent with what we know about this area of technology. Moreover, such a broad claim could ask whether the patent protection includes other transgenic animals, even if researchers do employ creative new ways of bringing them to life.

This broadening tendency stems from the so-called "doctrine of equivalents," used since the nineteenth century to prevent copycats from usurping inventions by making minor changes and claiming them as their own. This doctrine held that a patent can be infringed by something that is not falling within the scope of the claims because the copycat has changed a somewhat minor feature (for example, a screw with a rivet). A Federal Court challenged this doctrine in the 2002 case Festo Corp. v. Shoketsu Kinzoku Kabushiki Company Ltd. (535 U.S. 722), but later the U.S. Supreme Court reversed it. Apparently, this wavering decision making shows how the law is far from settled as far as the scope of patentability is concerned.

In sum, low patent quality, i.e., the ability of a patent to withstand a court challenge without being invalidated, is a significant deterrent of liquid IP markets. For patentees, the scope of the claim and the quality of the underlying technology can define patent quality. The broader the claims and the more valuable the underlying technology, the higher the quality of the patent is. The catch is to choose the jurisdiction with the best combination of patentability scope and enforceability that ensures the highest patent value. The nature of this decision turns into a probabilistic calculation that underlies in every litigation strategy among patent litigants.

1.4 The Malleable Nature of the IP System

Drafting open IP rules may be a deliberate policy strategy to address the complex, non-linear, organic and evolutionary features of the innovation process (Cockburn et al. 2002). These rules are "open," i.e., incomplete to address unexpected contingencies arising out of the market interaction (MacNeil 1978; Hart 1988; Pistor and Xu 2003).[17] In the field of patents, establishing a definite ruling over what constitutes

[17] MacNeil's "relational contracts" theory postulates that contracts are "relational," that is, their explicit terms merely outline the contractual boundaries of a relationship between the parties, the contours of which implicit terms and understandings arising out of their relationship fill in. Therefore, no contract can set forth all the contingencies that can emerge between two or more parties over the life of their contractual relationship. The theory emphasizes the open bounds of contractual relationships, because of the unexpected events that can arise throughout the life of the contract relation. More recently, Pistor and Xu (2003) note that the incomplete contract literature, drawn from the economics literature to explaining the boundaries of firms, also emphasize such boundless nature of contracts. Thus, a contract is complete if (and only if) all relevant contingencies and equal control rights – such as responsibilities of the parties for different aspects of the relation, rewards and punishments for certain actions, etc. – are specified unambiguously. Complete

"prior art" in a given case is costly. It requires the patent reviewer to examine a database of patent registries that is not centralized, due to the territoriality of the patent system. The same can be said in connection with other IPRs that require prior review in order to produce constitutive effects on the applicant, such as utility patent, design and trademarks. The international harmonization of IP rules has accepted certain protocols of recognition in certain cases, such as "well-known trademarks[18]" and the development of a provisional system of patent protection under the Patent Cooperation Treaty, but these are "seconds best" solutions that do not cover every instance. Furthermore, contemplating a protection system that meets all possible contingencies in the case of other IPRs involving no prior registration, such as copyrights or trade secrets would be unaffordable and incredibly complex. For this reason, the system is conceived to allow some degree of flexibility by focusing on the ex post control of any infractions. In both cases, judicial intervention may prove necessary, in view of the impossibility of defining in advance the optimal IP rule.

Flexibility is therefore in the essence of intellectual property rules. However, institutional plasticity has its limits, because it does not imply that the system is boundless (Harper 2015). Gaps in the system threaten IP owners' legitimate control over intellectual assets, because it opens the possibility of rent seeking at their expense, thus undermining the potential of the IP system to stir innovation.[19]

The IP system has to grant predictable legal rights over intellectual assets generated thanks to the innovative endeavors of entrepreneurs. It has to align their cognitive expectations around their research hypotheses, thus narrowing their predictions to certain possible scenarios. Even when serendipity plays a part in the discovery resulting from the innovation process, IP rules must credit the fortunate scientist or entrepreneur with control over the results of the innovation resulting from it.

---

contracts resolve all possible disputes between the contractual parties ex-ante. A contract is incomplete when some appropriate contingencies are missing, or some items are specified ambiguously. As a result, the contract is unenforceable and on its own cannot resolve disputes. The critical issue, then, is who has the right to decide the issues that are not contractually fleshed out. These "residual rights" have to be allocated to achieve economic efficiency, by enabling one party full control of the outcome, thus narrowing the degree of "openness" in the relationship.

[18] The TRIPS Agreement contains certain provisions on well-known marks, which supplement the protection required by Article 6bis of the Paris Convention, as incorporated by reference into the TRIPS Agreement, which obliges Members to refuse or to cancel the registration, and to prohibit the use of a mark conflicting with a mark which is well known. Yet, even here one has to note there is no commonly agreed detailed definition of what constitutes a "well-known mark." The WIPO Joint Recommendation Concerning Provisions on the Protection of Well-Known Marks provides certain guidelines, but again, the existence of these guidelines highlights the fact that the system is far from fully certain.

[19] Delays in the administration of justice and definition of rights can create opportunities for rent seeking (Bessen et al. 2012). Harper (2015) indicates that absence of appropriation over the intellectual resources resulting from the innovation process presents us with a case of the tragedy of the commons: dispute over the unowned areas. Uncertainty about the scope of IP increases the risk of abusive litigation through concurrent claims over disputed areas. This situation increases transaction costs in the ecosystem that can derail the emergence of technology markets.

In the context of the systemic uncertainty that innovation activity implies, intellectual property introduces a sense of order. Intellectual property plays a key role in enabling entrepreneurial expectations to coalesce, by setting the framework within which entrepreneurs combine and recombine their assets into innovation activities. But the way the system operates is not merely that of an "enabler" in the sense of laying down the rules that economic agents will follow. The system allows the user to interpret its use in the context of unexpected circumstances.

The uncertainty surrounding each patent is about the technological boundaries described in the patent claims, as seen in the previous section. Technological boundaries that are too broad or not detailed enough can create overlaps with other patent claims. In turn, this uncertainty could affect the perception of potential patent users about the real application of the invention, because such undefined claims may convey the impression that the invention affect others that are already "prior art."

Therefore, flexibility and uncertainty in the field of intellectual property come at a price. Marco (2005: 20) measured the value of certainty in intellectual property rights, by looking at the stock market reaction to patent litigation, and comparing them to market reactions at the time of patent award. He found that termination of a litigated case alone implied 1% return increase, which is similar in magnitude to the original patent grant. The elimination of uncertainty is as valuable to the firm as the initial patent grant. Thus, leaving uncertainty unresolved reduces the patent value and the rewards of innovation.

Now, should we brand these flexibilities as opening up opportunities for "market failures"? The answer is ambiguous because it ultimately rests on the vantage point of the reviewer. Evidently, if we take the viewpoint of an idealized "optimal" scenario of well-adjusted incentives inducing scientists, entrepreneurs, and competitors to align their conduct towards the "common good," i.e., disseminating their knowledge to the "public domain" without depriving the former from undertaking their innovative endeavors, we will arrive at the logical conclusion that any misalignment would lead the ecosystem to "fail.[20]" Obviously, such perspective is that of a closed-ended world, where one has the benefit of knowing what information is

[20] An example of these failures is asymmetric information or search costs that may retard efficient technology transfer (Gans et al. 2008). Ziedonis (2004) showed that in the semiconductor industry an aggressive patenting behavior not only depends on the level of the firm capital intensity but also on the fragmentation of patent ownerships in the industry. This phenomenon increases transaction costs in markets for technologies and the probability that firms infringe each other. Another example of failure is the murkiness that surrounds IP markets, which has made it incredibly difficult to facilitate to the public information about bilateral transactions, either sales or cross-licenses among firms. There is no efficient, transparent online platform for IP sales or license or exchange for patents; the attempts to do this by setting two-sided patent platforms have failed hopelessly (Hagiu and Yoffie 2013), as we will explore in detail later when we examine the case of IPXI. The result? When buyers and sellers do manage to find each other, they usually negotiate under enormous uncertainty: prices of similar IP differ a lot from transaction to transaction, and the terms of the transactions are often confidential (Hagiu and Yoffie 2013). Such inefficient trading mainly among big industry firms on IP markets is a welfare loss for the economy as a whole, as it delays the dissemination of useful knowledge in society.

missing (i.e. asymmetric), and what incentives are needed to bring the system into equilibrium.

By contrast, if we conceptualize the world as evolving, open-ended, generating and non-linear (in one word "innovative"), our obvious cognitive limitations make it impossible, indeed undesirable to encompass every possible unknown contingency. Also, this perspective highlights the need of intermediaries that can help produce knowledge in the system, by matching the open opportunities created by the ongoing process of change. In the close-ended view of optimality, these brokers are not welcomed, because they are assumed to introduce a "market failure" in need of policy intervention. As Hagiu and Yoffie (2013: 46) indicate "inefficient and illiquid markets, such as the one for patents, generally create profit opportunities for intermediaries."

Here one has to note the normative tension between the need for flexible IPRs and the emergence of profit opportunities arising from such flexibility, which obviously creates a competitive disadvantage upon firms that fail to see them. Intellectual property rules are flexible enough to accommodate the systemic uncertainty, but this flexibility is the very cause of possible attempts for profit opportunity at the expense of the system.

The fact that rule flexibility creates opportunities for arbitrage and profit does not imply the "failure" of the system. It means that we need to reassess our concept over business strategies that emerge in response to such changes, as mechanisms that filter information and create valuable knowledge that is transmitted across the system, so that everyone can adapt and change as quickly as possible. This is where IP management sets in.

IP management emerges as a strategy that allows innovators, businesses and entrepreneurs to seize control over intellectual capital that other entrepreneurs fail to perceive or protect because of the flaws of the legal system or because their lack of awareness about the profit potential of such assets, which a strategic use of IP rules could unlock.

Innovators understand the implications of these instruments in the light of their intended paths as innovators. This recognition is critical for them to structure their commercialization strategies around the intellectual assets (as they construe them). In other words, coordination does not mean that IP is a framework of clearly defined rules. Real life complexity indicates a non-linear, multi-causal relationship where subjective reciprocal expectations of individuals influence one another. Harper (2015) emphasizes the adaptive nature of the IP law, which allows it to create complex capital structures. The law is complex, adaptive, stratified, and knowledge is generating. Therefore, the challenge for lawmakers is to make sense of such novelty without introducing too much noise in the system that could make it unnecessarily harder for entrepreneurs to develop their innovative activities.

In the cognitive perspective that we emphasize in this book IPRs present to us as a set of probabilities defined by the multilayered interaction of those who participate in the innovation ecosystem: businesses, scientists, venture capitalists, incubators, IP judges and IP offices, and innovators. Their "awareness" of the likelihood of IPRs being tradable is thus critical in this assessment. Hence, their failure to gauge the impact of the probabilities governing the enforcement of IPRs could be called "awareness failure," as opposed to "market failure." The notion of awareness failure captures how the parties in the innovation ecosystem are bound to misapprehend the probabilities created by the convoluted IP system, due to their perceptual flaws about the technological path evolution; the position of entrepreneurs; the constraints created by the way governments dictate and enforce the law, and so on.[21]

In short, if we assume that such an ideal scenario of balanced incentives does not (and cannot) exist anywhere but in mathematical formulations of equilibrium, and that reality is evolving, non-linear, and uncertain, institutional gaps may be well portrayed under a benevolent light, as mechanisms that allow flexibility to help individuals adapt and experiment within predictable bounds. This is a recognition that the position of the entrepreneurs is radically different from that of the analyst, or policymaker, who visualizes the way the system operates concerning a "social efficiency" perspective, where the benchmark is how well resources (in this case, knowledge) are allocated among market participants. The entrepreneurial view towards intellectual property is one that discounts the costs of these "noises," and focuses on the varied forms of intermediation that occur, given the existence of alternative forms of IPRs and the alternative levels of protection by type of IPR, and by country. In this view, it may be more useful to see how the system is structured to deal with institutional uncertainty as opposed to emphasizing the misallocation resulting from the flawed set of IP rules. What actions do entrepreneurs adopt in response to these awareness failures?

In the following chapters, we explore in detail how IP management strategies address these awareness failures. Market arrangements such as patent pooling are intended to address fragmentation and overlapping of complementary technologies; while defensive patent aggregation seeks to increase the size of a patent portfolio by snatching idle patents from potential competitors. Litigation may become an interesting opportunity if the parties perceive that it would let them access to spaces that could otherwise become very expensive for them to access through organic development.

1.5 Factors Influencing the Selection of IP Instruments

Corporations do not rest their IP competitive strategy upon a single form of IP but rather they combine different forms of IP into an optimal mix or portfolio, which they continually review, given their capacity to sustain their dynamic capabilities to

[21] Paradoxically, awareness failures occur at a time where the world has the highest available number of databases of patents in history. These databases hold the entire text of all granted patents and applications published by all the most relevant patent offices. Also, they include information about the inventors, technology, backward and forward citations, prior art and ownership background. Under closer inspection, however, this phenomenon reveals that patent filing is only one of the many steps building up the ladder of certainties around the IP system, which is what nurtures the awareness of those involved in the innovation ecosystem.

compete in the market. From the perspective of the firms, probabilistic calculation of the likelihood that IPRs will be effective as a tool to develop IP competitive strategies varies according to the protection given by the IP system to the particular intellectual property right sought.

Corporations design their IP management strategy taking into account the nature of the technology, and the position it has in the company's IP stock. They organize their patent portfolios into four types of assets. First, they prioritize core patents that are central to their respective venture. Then, they select defensive patents that they need to protect core technology. Next, they focus on patents that can bring them income via selling or licensing. Last, they consider patents that were no longer of use to the organization, except for obtaining a tax write-off by donating them to non-profit or governmental entities. In the first case, ceteris paribus, legal monopolies such as patent and copyrights may be the best alternative; regarding defensive patents, litigation strategies may be an option; and last, in the case of orphan technologies, donation and defensive publishing could be the option to follow.

How do these IPRs allow the participants of the innovation ecosystem to match their talents given the complexity of such set of rules? IP helps them to combine and recombine their assets at multiple levels. The combination of different forms of IP is contingent to their awareness about the purpose these assets serve in their profit-making calculus. For instance, the costs of registering patent claim may induce firms to look for more affordable forms of IP protection. Also, the problems of keeping trade secrets confidential may persuade them to not choose this mechanism, and prefer instead to display their knowledge through patent filing.

Cognitive awareness determines the intensity of IP use. However, can we say anything about the particular mix of IP instruments that innovations will choose? One rule of thumb tells us that, ceteris paribus, one should expect innovators to prefer trade secrecy where the institutional setting is uncertain and prefer patents where certainty is warranted. However, this conclusion only begs the question of what settings are certain or not.

The choice of alternative forms of IP, however, does not solve the inherent uncertainty affecting the integrity of these entitlements to carry out market power but does influence the relative preference for either instrument chosen. In other words, managers should not be too hasty in assuming that these options enable them an unlimited capacity to eliminate competitors from the market. In the end, it all depends on the certainty that institutions afford in the sense of enforcing these entitlements. The market power these instruments provide ultimately rests on the perception of entrepreneurs about their relative costs and the efficacy that the legal system vests upon them.

Entrepreneurs select their IP portfolio mix taking into account the costs and benefits of the intellectual property spectrum available. They will find it convenient to select trade secrets over patents if the costs of patenting do not justify the protection or the know-how protected under the trade secret is more valuable and technologically-specific than the operating written instructions laid out in a patent filing. There are several factors they consider. We can divide the protection methods into two broad categories: legal protection methods and accurate protection methods.

The legal protection methods can be further divided into registrable and non-registrable legal rights. Patents belong to the registrable rights. Registrable means that the invention must be applied for at a national or international institution.

Let us start by assessing patents. The main reason for SMIEs not to use patents is the costs. These costs include both patent application costs and the costs of defending a patent. Especially the second argument, the costs for defending a patent seems to be important for SMIEs. WIPO estimates that obtaining and maintaining a patent for the full term normally exceeds $500,000 in the 50 largest countries in the world. These costs include filing, translation, prosecution, and maintenance fees. Not all firms can afford to pay such expenses, much less SMIEs. Colson (2007) indicates: "Average legal fees to file one patent application in the U.S. are in the range of $12,000–$15,000. Multiply that by three or four to file applications in key locations throughout the world. Then add over $100,000 to maintain each patent in those locations throughout its life. All that cost for one invention. The problem grows when you consider that for most companies, the number of inventive ideas exceeds the number of budgeted patent applications by at least ten times." Patent registration is very expensive because its valuation, patent search, patent drafting and strategic market assessment are valuable skills that few businesses can afford.

In addition to patents, there is in many countries the utility patent, also called the petty patent. It differs from the patent regarding examination, protection time and costs. Whereas in most countries a patent application is examined for novelty before being granted, the utility patent is not examined. Due to the lower effort, the filing costs for obtaining a utility patent is lower than for a patent. As to the protection time, patents are protected for 20 years, utility patents for 10 years.

The fear of patent infringement and litigation costs has a significant impact on the SMIEs' decision on patenting because they often do not have the financial means for such efforts (University of Dublin 2001). The next reason not to patent is the disclosure of information (Arundel 2003; Moulin, Lie 2005; Harabi 1995; Blind and Thumm 2006). A lot of firms view disclosing information to be a high risk, particularly the way that only specialists can do to reproduce the technology. Further, the Derwent study (Derwent 2000) reveals that an important reason for SMIEs not to patent is that patents are considered not to be relevant in their business sector.

So, the costs are not easy to assess because they are multidimensional, that is, they not only refer to the official registry but may refer to the unofficial control of the intellectual assets, which depends on various factors. These factors include the nature of the technology underlying the asset, how much does the IP instrument allow the party to commercialize the asset, and how much liquidity does the IP instrument offers to the party.

Cost-benefit considerations are also determined by how easy it is for the technology to be commercialized. This capacity is contingent on the nature of the product embodying the innovation, and of the market where the innovation is expected to have an impact. Here, patent and copyright registration offers the advantage of being the most liquid form of IP.

Factual protection methods also play a major role, especially for SMIEs. As patents are often considered to be too expensive, SMIEs are likely to choose protection methods with low additional costs. Non-legal means of protection like secrecy or lead time advantage do not implicate direct additional protection costs. Hence, for SMIEs, factual protection methods are often considered to be more adequate than legal ones. The University of Dublin (2001) discovered that SMIEs rather rely on secrecy and lead time advantage than on patents. The findings are confirmed by Harabi (1995), Arundel (2003) and Blind et al. (2006) who all show that lead time advantage is the most effective means of protection. Arundel (2003) found out in his investigation that 50% of his sample firms consider lead time advantage as the most important protection method. Secrecy ranked second with 18%, followed by complexity (17%) and patents (9%). Kitching and Blackburn (1999) reveal in their study that SMEs prefer factual protection methods to juridical ones. Trust relationship was considered as the most important protection method. It has been used by 76% of the firms, followed by lead time advantage with 66%.

On the other hand, there are important motives for patent applications. The major reason for a patent application is the protection of innovation. This argument is followed by the blockade of competitors (Blind et al. 2006). Besides this, there are further arguments why firms chose patenting as a means of protecting intellectual property. Especially for SMIEs, Blind et al. (2006) discovered a high emphasis on improving its position about cooperation partners by holding patents. This finding is also presented by Harabi (1995). According to his results, patents play an important role regarding enforcing the firm's negotiating position towards other firms or governmental agencies.

The Derwent study (Derwent 2000) discovered that only 30% of the sample SMEs have ever applied for a patent. In a survey conducted with UK SMEs, half of the firms did not apply for patents even if they assessed the inventions to be patentable (McDonald 2003). The University of Dublin (2001) reveals in its examination for the European Commission that patenting is considered not to be cost-effective for SMEs. According to Kitching and Blackburn (1999), the registrable rights—patents, trademarks and industrial designs—are used less than nonregistrable ones. Their results show that trademarks and patents were applied by 52% (trademarks) and 30% (patents) of the firms. In comparison, contractual confidentiality clauses as non-registrable rights are used by 75% of the SMEs and 60% rely on copyright protection.

The level of costs may change unexpectedly as a result of legal change. In Common Law jurisdictions, even a single case can change the law significantly. To illustrate how much patent rules are subject to possible changes in the case law, one has to look at the effects of *Alice Corp. Pty V. CLS Bank*. This case stands out as an example of how judicial decisions can impact patent eligibility, patent validity and patent value. The case involved claims about a computerized electronic escrow service which covered abstract ideas ineligible for patent protection. The service helped banks mitigate settlement risk, i.e., the risk that one party will fulfill its obligation to an agreed-upon financial transaction. Alice patented any computer implementation of this process as well as any computer systems containing program code that could carry out the method. The U.S. Supreme Court unanimously invalidated the patents because they claimed abstract ideas, a claim that violated Section 101 of the

U.S. Patent Act. Commentators indicate that as result of this decision, many existing, granted software and business method patents are "at great risk" of being invalidated. In fact, the Alice decision is already taking toll, both in the reduced number of patents granted to software and business method patents, which have declined significantly, as well as the favorable reception of motions to invalidate patents by competitors. As a result, "any company that has a software or business method patent that it believes is protecting its right to exclude others from competing, is producing licensing revenue or is the basis for infringement, may no longer have a patent that provides such benefits" (Weingust 2016). Clearly, legal amendments like these change the relative value of patents with respect to other IPRs; therefore, they may encourage firms to seek alternative ways of protecting their IP.

In short, the level of certainty very much depends on the particular institutional context and relative price (i.e., cost-benefit relationship) that a particular IPR offers. Also, Gans et al. (2008) showed that in those environments where productive efficiency is important (e.g., where the technology lifecycle is short), or when alternative mechanisms such as copyright protection, reputation, or brokers are available, the impact of patent allowances on licensing is reduced. The findings suggest that imperfections in the market for ideas may be important and that formal IP rights may facilitate gains from technological trade. They conclude that the impact of the patent system depends on the strategic and institutional environment in which firms operate.

What about the strategy followed by SMIEs from Latin America? The evidence also shows that Latin American firms prefer to use the trademark and trade secret protection as a defense mechanism of its intangible assets, as opposed to patent and utility model registration. In a study in the case of Brazil, Zucoloto (2013) indicates that only 6.7% of small companies (10–29 employees) and 38.8% of large companies (over 500 employees) use patents and industrial designs. This finding confirms a general trend in the region. Thus, while in 2013 the resident companies claimed approximately 61% of the registered brands in the region, they requested 8.2% of total patents in the region in process (an even smaller number corresponds to granted patents), as evidenced in Fig. 4.1 ("Intellectual property right used, by region").

This evidence suggests that in the absence of an expedient legal enforcement mechanism, Latin American entrepreneurs favor legal instruments that are harder to replicate, such as trade secrets or trademarks as means of appropriating intangible assets, because in the context of weak institutions (as they perceive these), these are instruments harder to replicate. Patents, on the other hand, embody information easy to classify and to pass on through manuals and written coding; therefore, they are also easy to be replicated through reverse engineering, which is particularly risky if the business has a small capacity to launch a prosecution, due to high costs of accessing justice.

In the next chapters, we will examine the commercialization strategies that SMIEs could use to deploy their intellectual assets strategically. In doing so, we shall refer to an international comparative perspective that attempts to highlight the strategies already taking place in countries with more IP management experience, and how SMIEs in countries with less experience (particularly in Latin America) are reacting to them.

Chapter 2
Exercising Market Power Through IP

In the previous chapter, we explored how the underlying kaleidoscopic structure of the patent system in particular, and of the intellectual property rights (IPRs) in general, stir uncertainty over the scope and duration of patent awards. The convoluted nature of the patent claim system is bound to produce a lax interpretation of patent claims under the light of broad technical notions such as 'novelty' and 'non-obviousness.' The lax interpretation of what is subject to patentability adds further imprecision to an already incomplete set of legal rules.

In an attempt to redress this situation, patent and copyright laws concede IP owners a legal monopoly to exploit their intellectual assets. These provisions are intended to give title holders an exclusive title that seemingly reduces their uncertainty over their effective control of these assets. Exclusivity ensures that, at least on a formal level, no one else but them will control the intellectual asset. On closer inspection, however, the market power arising from such legal monopoly is qualified by the market context within which the patent owner intends to enforce it. These contextual circumstances impair the patent holders' cognitive certainty about the precise extent to which they control such assets.

2.1 The Elusive Market Power of IP Monopolies

Businesses succeed in the market when they develop specialized, dynamic capabilities that give them the capacity to shape, reshape, configure, and reconfigure assets so as to respond to changing technologies and markets and escape the zero-profit condition (of the perfect competition model) (Augier and Teece 2008: 1190).

The common assumption is that such possibility of charging prices above the marginal revenue (exercising market power) accrues if the intellectual property (IP) owner has a title that preserves her from being eroded by competitors. A firm that holds IPRs can use them to suppress competition, stopping potential competitors

I. De Leon, J. Fernandez Donoso, *Innovation, Startups and Intellectual Property Management*, DOI 10.1007/978-3-319-54906-4_2

from offering customers identical or similar products or services. The main goal of an IPR holder is to develop market power to emasculate competitors' activity from the market.

Positive law defines the extent to which local legislation allows businesses to exercise market power through IP, but this capacity varies depending on the country and depending on the IPR. The legal powers associated with the legal instrument itself vest right holders with differing degrees of protection. Each type of IPR gives its possessor a varying degree of market power to charge prices above competitive levels and thus increase its profits. Patents, utility models, copyrights, trademarks, industrial designs, and trade secrets grant different degrees of market power according to the legislation applicable. IPRs differ in their scope of protection; in the protection, they provide against encroachment from competitors, and in the protective efforts they require from entrepreneurs to use them effectively. For example, patent registration is considerably more demanding than utility model registration concerning information disclosure and registration complexity; they give varying term protection to their beneficiaries (typically, for patents, 20 years from the filing date of the application; 7–10 years for a utility model without the possibility of extension or renewal). Table 2.1 shows a comparison of these rights.

It is important to note that the market power afforded by law is not immutable. It has changed over time, and also is contingent to the nature of the intellectual asset protected. Its elusive nature makes it hard to value it and to incorporate it into an IP management strategy.

The degree of monopoly power legally afforded to patent and copyright holders has changed over the years. Before the Uruguay Round of trade negotiations (1986–1994), there was no explicit agreement on IPRs in the framework of the General Agreement on Tariffs and Trade (GATT) multilateral trading system. Instead, a myriad of treaties negotiated since the second half of the 19th century governed intellectual property in a fragmented way. Countries differed significantly in the extent of protection and enforcement they afforded to IPRs; developing countries typically afforded much lower standards for IPR protection than developed countries. In the words of Mercurio (2014: 4): "The TRIPS Agreement harmonized the scope and length of protection that patents provide. While tailoring the criteria of patentability and extending patent protection is [sic.] possible, the international system sets the perimeters for both the scope and length of a patent. The system does not attempt to differentiate between industries or sectors." The 1994 TRIPs Agreement is an effort to narrow the gaps in the legal protection accorded to IPRs around the world. Subsequent trade agreements have broadened the protection afforded by incorporating aspects not covered under the TRIPS agreement, implementing stricter IP obligations (referred to as TRIPS-plus). These include patent term extensions, patent linkage, data exclusivity, lower patentability criteria and additional enforcement measures. Examples of TRIPS-plus provisions appearing in trade agreements include the U.S. -DR/Central America Free Trade Agreement, the US-Jordan Free Trade Agreement and the currently under negotiation Trans-Pacific Partnership Agreement (TPP) between twelve Pacific-Rim countries, including several developing countries.

Table 2.1 Standard comparative protection of different types of IPRs (in the United States)

Type of protection	Utility patent	Design patent	Utility model (not in the U.S.)	Copyright	Trademark	Trade secret
Subject matter	Utilitarian features	Ornamental features	Utilitarian features	Forms of expression: authorial work, writing, music, photo, literary, musical, pictorial, architectural, sculptural, motion picture, and computer software	Identifying symbol: words, names, symbols, devices, sounds, smells, non-functional trade dress	Formulae, processes, products, software, plans, designs, pricing, devices, R&D information, business information
Protection standards	Novel, useful, and non-obvious	Ornamental, novel and non-obvious	Lower inventiveness	Originality, authorship, expression	Identify and distinguish goods or services	Economic value from maintaining the information secret
Source of rights	Registration at Patent Office; U.S. Patent and Trademark Office	Registration at Patent Office; U.S. Patent and Trademark Office	Registration at Patent Office (not in the U.S.)	No; however, notice and registration help monetary recovery; registration required to suit. Copyright Office of Library of Congress	Common law by use, federal or state registration based on use. U.S. Patent and Trademark Office	State common law under the Restatement, the Uniform Trade Secret Act and precedents
Acquisition procedure	Claims in filing tested by PTO examiner before patent is granted	Claims in filing tested by PTO examiner before patent is granted	Examination after issuance	Automatic upon creation in physical medium	Federal registration and regulatory compliance	Maintain secrecy

(continued)

Table 2.1 (continued)

Type of protection	Utility patent	Design patent	Utility model (not in the U.S.)	Copyright	Trademark	Trade secret
Term	20 years from effective filing date	10–15 years from grant (changes based on the jurisdiction)	8–15 years from filing date (it changes based on the jurisdiction)	Works after 1/1/78: Life of author plus 70 years	As long as properly used; registration lasts 10 years (if formalities are met); renewable for 10-year periods	Duration of secret
What infringes	Making, using, selling, offering for sale, or importing devices embodying the claimed invention or using claimed process	Designs that appear alike to the eye of an ordinary observer and use 'point of novelty'	Making, using or selling embodiment	Copying, distribution of copies, unauthorized performance or display	Likelihood of confusion, mistake or deception	Misappropriation, improper disclosure
Cost	High	Low	Moderate	Low	Low to moderate	Cost of maintaining secret
Continuing duties	Maintenance fee	None	Maintenance fee	None	Proper use; policing; renewals of registration	Maintain secret
Date protection commences	Upon issuance; 2–5 years from filing	Upon issuance; 2–5 years from filing	Usually 3–10 months from filing	When fixed in physical medium	First use; filing of U.S. intent to use application followed by registration	Creation of valuable secret

Moreover, the market power that IP owners can exercise is confined to the boundaries of a particular jurisdiction, because the enforcement of the IP legislation is usually territorial. There are no such titles as "international patents", though there is an international patent application under the Patent Cooperation Treaty, even in this case, the protection is only intended to grant a temporary protection (one year), subject to the final registry before the national authority. The IP system is country-specific, in the sense that follows their particular circumstances of political economy. There is no convenient reference or international entity that centralizes enforcement or law making. Finally, some countries enjoy exceptions granted by the international treaties, thereby applying different protection standard in various areas of patentability.

More importantly, the legal distinction does not say much about how much market power a firm can wield to overcome systemic uncertainty and protect their knowledge effectively. Market power ultimately rests on the capacity of IP holders to protect their underlying knowledge from reverse engineering or other forms of imitation.

Ultimately, protection from encroachment rests on the nature of the knowledge embed in the intellectual asset. In particular, the market power that arises out of these capabilities stems from them being unique and not imitable. This condition applies to what Hayek (1936 [1948]) and Polanyi (1958) defined as "tacit knowledge," that is, knowledge which is personal, subjective, contextual and therefore, hard to convey to third parties. The IP literature usually refers to this as "know-how." Trade secrecy is intended to protect this type of knowledge. By contrast, knowledge which is easy to classify, dissect, objectively interpreted and subject to aggregation is harder to protect from imitation.

Tacit knowledge or know-how is harder to convey, therefore, to be traded; but also, it will be harder to imitate. Therefore, it requires no additional protection from the law other than verifying the owner's diligence in preventing its unauthorized dissemination; in other words, the legal standard only requires the owner's effective control over its disclosure. As a means of developing a competitive advantage, know-how makes it harder for competitors to dislodge the owner's control of a key intellectual asset (Teece 1998). Yet, by the same token, the very problems of conveying tacit knowledge to third parties also makes these assets harder to trade in the market, thereby reducing their effective price. On the other hand, explicit knowledge embed in certain intellectual assets is easier to trade, but also to be imitated. Effective control of these assets requires additional protection from the law, usually in the form of exclusivity granted through patent or copyright protection.

In Teece's (1998) words:

> "The competitive advantage of firms in today's economy stems not from a market position, but from difficult to replicate knowledge assets and the manner in which they are deployed."

This form of intellectual capital is a differentiator in many types of new markets and therefore becomes a significant source of the competitive advantage of firms, because competitors can hardly replicate it. Know-how is the most important competitive factor influencing the firm's competitive behavior, more so than codifying or structuring such knowledge under a patent. This phenomenon happens because dynamic capabilities are idiosyncratic, discrete and inherent to the particular experience of the firm. In the words of Augier and Teece (2008: 1202):

> "This view represents the firm as an incubator and repository for difficult-to-replicate technological and organizational assets. Distinctive processes support the creation, protection, and augmentation of firm-specific assets and competences – all vital elements in the strategic renewal process. These assets and competences reflect individual skills and experiences as well as distinctive ways of doing things inside firms. To the extent that such assets and competences are difficult to imitate and are effectively deployed and redeployed in the marketplace (reflecting dynamic capabilities), they can provide the foundations for competitive advantage.

In short, know-how is more effective when coupled with IP protection. IP legal enforcement raises the bar against imitators, so that "while intellectual property can be traded, and can sometimes be invented around, it can no longer be infringed with impunity and without penalty" (Teece 2008: 10). In fact, building dynamic capabilities based solely on the possession of know-how is risky because it ultimately rests on the strategy of competitors' not to replicate it because of the relative costs involved. The fact that market power stems from non-replicable knowledge does not mean that products or processes are fully shielded from imitation. Current technology often allows decodification of encrypted knowledge, thus threatening owners unless the law provides them additional protection.

At the other end of the spectrum, codified or explicit knowledge is easier to be replicated. Here the law sets forth mechanisms providing for exclusivity, as long as the knowledge is articulated clearly under a set of claims that the authorities can distinguish from those of competitors. Take the case of molecular compounds developed in the pharmaceutical industry. The nature of these chemicals is usually found in their quantitative formula, which is easy to decode once it is chemically developed. As Bansal and Koradia (2005) note "reverse engineering of the innovator product's formulation is a scientifically sound and cost-effective strategy for accelerating generic product development." Clearly, the best way to protect such an easily decodable asset is to offer exclusive protection to its developer, on the condition that the information is disclosed, so that unauthorized copying can be easily established, i.e., to patent it. By contrast, a receipt on how to make a secret sauce for a hamburger such as MacDonald's Big Mac may depend on information that cannot be easily conveyed. Hence it becomes difficult to protect it.

Thus, the underlying knowledge embed in an intellectual asset drives the choice of IP strategy, whether leaning towards a patent-oriented one or a trade secrecy one. Empirical evidence supports this conclusion. Huang (2016) found in a study reviewing 362 firms and organizations in the knowledge-intensive genomics industry that under uncertain IPR conditions, firms reveal and accumulate more knowledge through open science (follow-on publishing) but shift to knowledge appropriation through commercial science (follow-on patenting) when IPRs are certain. This effect is most salient when firms develop their knowledge assets or operate under a strong IPR institutional regime. For highly science-based knowledge assets, firms continue tapping into open science for access and reciprocity in knowledge acquisition from the scientific community. Patenting is valuable because it levers businesses' capacity to monetize their intellectual assets. However, patenting is considered a viable strategy under a predictable institutional setting.

In this kaleidoscopic milieu, enforceability and protection scope depends on the underlying technology subject to analysis. Even about patents alone, there is no such a thing as a "standard" of protection applicable to all industries. As Mercurio (2014: 4) indicates "while 20 years of patent protection may be necessary for R&D in the pharmaceutical industry, it may not be appropriate in the software sector, where, in the words of Posner, 'after five years, these patents are mainly traps for the unwary.' Likewise, is 20 years of patent protection for the pharmaceuticals adequate given that a large proportion of the patent period is over before the product can be marketed?" As Cho et al. (2015) indicate, there appears to be empirical evidence justifying such differentiation.

In short, the nature of the underlying intellectual asset influences the degree of market power that one can expect to obtain from the law. The problem here is that some intellectual assets' knowledge are easier to protect by the law, as they are codified in a way that third parties can easily interpret. For this type of knowledge, legal disclosure, followed by exclusivity of use, seems to be the best fit. This situation induces entrepreneurs to choose a special blend of patents, copyrights, trademarks, and trade secrets protection that best matches their competitive strategies to build IP dynamic capabilities. These IP portfolios also strategize elements of IP protection with other means of developing competitive advantage in the market, such as lead start.

In short, IP managers overcome the problems arising from a fractionalized IP system by imposing their legal control over their intellectual assets. Faced with an array of legal instruments to help them ensure control, IP managers will likely seek the optimal combination of IPRs that will give them their best competitive advantage in positioning themselves in a given actual or prospective market. Each of these rights has different advantages and drawbacks, depending on the possibilities. However, the legal monopoly power vested upon patent and copyright holders is ultimately qualified by the nature of the knowledge involved.

Put it differently, IP protection relies not so much on meeting the legal formalities that businesses need to obtain a legal title but in their capacity to integrate such title into their competitive strategy, which should consider how likely it is for competitors to replicate the invention's underlying technology. This approach involves identifying their "core technological" endogenous capabilities, on the one hand, as well as complementary ones (i.e., manufacturing, and finance), which they can obtain from competitors through contractual means (i.e., licensing and sale contracts), or through litigation. Thus, even if SMIEs became skill users of the IP system, they would still have to be capable of exerting legal control over assets that other firms control. In short, they must learn how to commercialize their intellectual assets.

2.2 Choosing Between Patents and Trade Secrets

The ultimate goal of IP management is to reinforce a competitive advantage at the firm level, by strategically deploying tradable and non-tradable assets under alternative legal instruments.

Companies build their IPR portfolios looking to enhance their market power. Managers perceive their IP portfolio as a "basket" of instruments that they can tailor to the specific technologies they intend to sell or license, the presence of other competitors, and the varying degree of protection that the legal system affords to each instrument, to increase their capacity to maintain or reinforce the market power achieved through their pioneering exploitation of the new technology.

As said above, the patent filing could prove counterproductive if the underlying technology is easily replicable, as this would provide the blueprints of the invention to copycats. There is always the danger that the competitors reverse engineer or re-adapt the invention, and possibly, in a worst case scenario, obtain a patent on the invention, in which case the original inventor risks patent infringement in such circumstances. High litigation costs and the uncertainty of effective enforcement could make patent registration unattractive for innovators as a means of protecting intellectual assets.

There are cheaper and more effective means for SMIEs to protect their knowledge, provided the technology is suitable to that end. For example, trade secrecy offers businesses an opportunity to protect their intellectual assets by not communicating them publicly. This is convenient when such knowledge largely rests on know-how, as opposed to coded, patentable knowledge.

Trade secrecy is a very effective defensive intellectual property strategy for products or processes whose embodied knowledge cannot be easily replicated by potential business imitators. Trade secrecy is frequently the most natural and immediate form of protecting the know-how emerging out of the innovation process and could be the company's most valuable IP portfolio asset, even compared to patents (Hall et al. 2014). No matter how detailed manuals incorporating such knowledge are, know-how is inherently tacit and personal, hence difficult to relay onto third parties. Consider the complexity of the innovative design. A company may rely on the complex nature of its products when their composition and structure is such that it renders copying by competitors unattractive. Here, the protection results from the disincentive placed upon potential competitors, to do reverse engineering or to readapt the invention, or even obtaining a patent on the same.

In the context of IP protection, secrecy involves information that exhibits three traits: first, it is not known to a relevant portion of the public; second, it has commercial value; and last, reasonable action is taken to maintain its secrecy.

Coca-Cola holds one of the most famous trade secrets regarding the recipe of its original soft drink. Although the law does not protect trade secrets in the same way as patents or trademarks, they may still enjoy some level of legal protection (though the extent to which this is granted varies from one jurisdiction to another). One should distinguish between lawful means to obtain a trade secret (such as, by process of reverse engineering), and improper means (such as by industrial espionage) – which entails legal liability for the party acquiring it.

Also, trade secrecy is to be distinguished from abstaining from using IP, which displays the strategy of many SMIEs. This is usually a source of great confusion and is important to clarify it. Innovators may abstain from using the IP registry system because they do not appreciate its value, or simply they are unaware of its existence.

This is to be distinguished from the legal protection sought under a trade secret, where the entrepreneurs take concrete steps have to be conducted to ensure that know-how is protected, i.e. negotiating a non-disclosure agreement, notwithstanding the abstention from registering the IP.

As said above, the know-how protected through trade secrets has a disadvantage of being less liquid as compared to patents, for commercialization purposes. How can parties establish value upon tacit knowledge embodied in a trade secret? The economic value of trade secrets, like other forms of IP, lies in the proprietary competitive advantage it gives to its owner from use, together with the exclusion of third parties. However, unlike the right of exclusion that a patent gives to its owner, which stems from disclosing the information in exchange for a legal monopoly, trade secrets give a competitive advantage as long as they are undisclosed and owners make reasonable efforts to maintain them secret.

Under the legislation of some countries, statutory provisions protect this competitive advantage. For example, section 3(a) of the U.S. Uniform Trade Secrets Act (UTSA), as amended in 1985 states that competitive advantage unfairly gained through misappropriation becomes a basis for extending the period of protection.[1]

Like the case of patents, copyrights vest property holders with a legal monopoly. However, they afford differing degrees of protection in terms of time and the subject matter they protect (See Table 2.1). Also, there are significant differences in terms of the toil and costs of registering a patent as opposed to a copyright. Finally, unlike the patent system, copyrights protection is not administered through a system of 'claims,' because it does not use 'prior art' as a benchmark of novelty that entrepreneurs need to comply with in order to register their patents.

2.3 Building Large IP Portfolios

Companies build their market power by tailoring IP portfolios which combines the protection afforded by IP law with the capacity to obtain such power through technological means. Yet, companies may increase it even further by increasing the size of their IP portfolios, adding patents that protect adjacent technologies to their "core." Building large patent portfolios protects innovators because of their higher scale effects, and lower transaction costs. Parchomovsky and Wagner (2005: 32–42) argue that a collection of closely related patents defining a patent portfolio operates like a 'super-patent,' as it will exclude others from the collective scope of the individual claims. They ease in-house innovation as they ensure that a wider range of technological possibilities will be covered which reduces the concerns over infringement of others' patents. Also, a bigger scale enhances the ability to consolidate

[1] Such provision states: "Like injunctive relief, a monetary recovery for trade secret misappropriation is appropriate only for the period in which information is entitled to protection as a trade secret, plus the additional period, if any, in which a misappropriation retains an advantage over good faith competitors because of misappropriation" (Section 3a).

technological developments by giving the firm an unassailable market position in a particular field. A larger patent portfolio helps to avoid litigation because a broader scope of protection will make proof of infringement by others more evident; also, it improves the patentee's bargaining position and enhances the diversity of the technology supplied.

From an IP risk management perspective, large portfolios reduce IP risk, thereby attracting investors' interest. Hsu and Ziedonis (2008) examine the degree to which patents enable entrepreneurs to acquire financial capital across the new venture life cycle. The authors conclude that having larger portfolios of patent applications increases the likelihood that entrepreneurs will attract initial financing from a venture capitalist. Specifically, they found that a doubling in the patent application portfolio of a new venture is associated with a 24% increase in valuation, representing an upward funding-round adjustment of approximately $12 million for the average startup in their sample.

Finally, building larger portfolios reduces the transaction costs that otherwise would accrue if companies had to negotiate licensing contracts with third parties in order to outsource technologies they do not control.

Large companies often patent non-core innovations developed in the research of an activity production line to strategically build a larger patent portfolio, thereby becoming more attractive partners in cross-licensing negotiations or to defensively block other firms from accessing strategic assets in adjacent markets. According to the European Commission (2006) on average, 37.7% of the patents are not used. Of these, 47.6% are sleeping, and 52.4% are blocking patents. The same report indicates that large firms have higher shares of both unused patents and unused blocking patents on small and medium businesses. Small firms use about 80% of their patents, against about 59% for large ones. Patents may protect innovations that arise as by-products of a core research line or production activity. Firms might not use these patents because they do not master the downstream complementary assets for producing and commercializing the underlying products, or because they are uninterested in developing a position in these markets, or because the by-products could cannibalize other products of the firm (Gilbert and Newbery 1982).

In this setting, the system is tilted in favor of the big players, such as multinationals. Large companies, with sizable R&D budgets, are more likely to hold unused patents. Compared to startups, they are better positioned to manage the rights arising out of their patent titles. Hold-ups resulting from being blocked by others and of being sued for infringement is higher. The power of startups such as startups or single inventors to enforce their patents is weak, and thus the multinationals are acting similar to monopolies on IP markets (Bader et al. 2012).

The size of the IP portfolio is thus critical to ensure the innovator's competitive position, but at the same time, it raises a barrier to competitors with smaller portfolios. IP portfolio size effects create asymmetries between large operating firms on one side and individual inventors and small companies on the other hand (Jaffe and Lerner 2004). The patents that startups own or create are less likely to be monetized because they typically belong to smaller portfolios and because their owners usually have limited financial resources and legal expertise, which severely undermines their bargaining leverage (Hagiu and Yoffie 2013).

2.4 Pioneering as IP Strategy

Lead-time is a defensive strategy that prevents competitors from amassing market power through their IP portfolios by becoming the first mover in a market. Pioneering firms establish their market presence through branding (trademarks), supported on their control of know-how (trade secrets), or standards, and through developing relationships with major distributors.

This strategy leverages this position through IP forms difficult for competitors to replicate, such as developing a reliable trademark embodying sound commercial reputation. It is no surprise that firms that consistently introduce pioneering products in the market prefer lead-time advantage as a strategy. Relative to other means of control over IP, lead-time scores high in the preference of users. In the United States, Cohen et al. (2000) indicate that for process innovations, only 23% of respondents consider patents as an effective control mechanism as compared to secrecy (50%) and lead-time (38%). For product innovations, respondents consider patents slightly more effective (41%), but still less effective than either secrecy (51%) or lead-time (50%). In Europe, the results are no different, as seen in the following figure, indicating the SMIEs' preferred strategy of IP protection (Fig. 2.1).

These are companies constantly in the lead concerning its innovative activities. By applying such an approach, the inventing company always has an enhanced

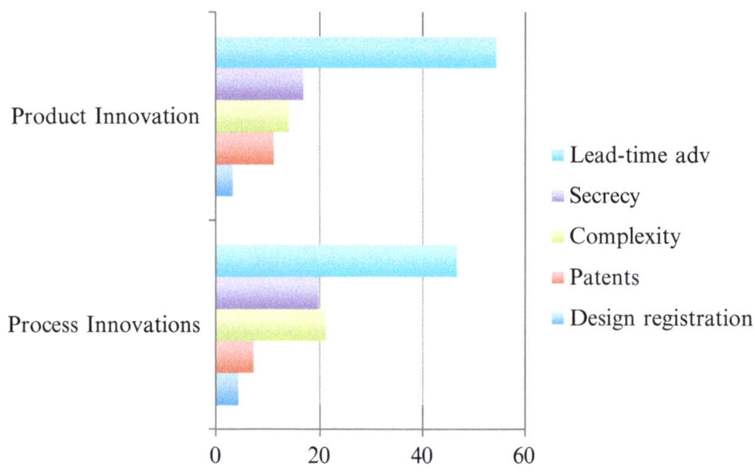

Fig. 2.1 SMIEs IP protection strategy in Europe (Source: Arundel 2001)

version of its products ready for release before a competitor has the time to successfully copy the product that is currently available on the market. A lead-time strategy complemented by the strategic use of trademarks and branding is a popular form of IP protection in the services industries, where know-how is also difficult to replicate.

Businesses engaged in becoming first movers usually position themselves through branding strategies. Trademarks protect against consumer confusion as to the source of the goods and can last indefinitely in the right hands. A strong branding strategy efficiently utilizes trademark protection to build goodwill during the early days of a product or service, such as during the early life of a patent and enforces the brand beyond the patent protection law provides. Eventually, patents expire, or a competitor will succeed in invalidating or designing around the patents. By that time, the product will have established market share and can continue to compete through branding even after patent exclusivity has ended. A branded drug, for example, will usually have a made-up name like Viagra®, Abilify®, or Lunesta®, which the generic newcomer generally cannot use without permission. The trademark and overall brand identity provide the opportunity for offensive licensing of an authorized generic to capitalize on the goodwill and brand recognition built by the 'non-generic' drug manufacturer (Rodriguez and Dunwoody 2014).[2]

Trademarks may be helpful to protect intellectual assets—reputation in this case—in the absence of other forms of protection. Adidas® is famous for its apparel and sportswear; it invested heavily in the marketing of its '*Three Stripes*' design mark to ensure that consumers identified that mark with Adidas in the sports equipment and apparel markets. Since fashion design typically is not eligible for patent protection or copyright protection, Adidas has utilized its multiple trademarks to protect and enhance its market position and earn additional revenue. For example, in 2008, a court ordered Payless ShoeSource to pay $304.6 million to Adidas, when the latter successfully claimed that the former sold shoes and sportswear that were confusingly similar to the Adidas 'Three-Stripe Mark' and 'Superstar' trade dress. A subsequent review reduced the penalty to $64.4 million (Rodriguez and Dunwoody 2014).

2.5 Defensive Publishing

Among IP strategies, defensive publishing is the one that highlights best why exercising IP market power may not always be a desirable option for businesses.

[2] Sometimes this strategy may be pushed too hard into an anticompetitive territory. A case in point is AstraZeneca's appeal of a patent settlement, which was dismissed by the European Court of Justice, in early December 2012. The Court imposed on the company for two cases of abuse of a dominant position relating to blocking or delaying generic copies of the anti-ulcerant drug Losec (omeprazole). The Court found that AztraZeneca misused regulatory procedures to delay generic competitors in the market, as it intended to extend the life of its patents on Losec. Therefore, it ordered AstraZeneca to pay €52.5 million for abusing a dominant market position in the market for ulcer medicines. A similar case was decided in Ecuador in 2011, against Pfizer.

Defensive publication, or defensive disclosure, is used to prevent another party from obtaining a patent on a product, apparatus or method, for instance. The strategy consists of disclosing an enabling description and/or drawing of the product, apparatus or method so that it enters the public domain and becomes prior art. This powerful preemptive disclosure prevents other parties from obtaining a patent on the product, device or method. It enables the original inventor to ensure that they have access to their invention by preventing others from later making patent claims on it. Therefore, the defensive publication of perhaps otherwise patentable information may work to defeat the novelty of a subsequent patent application.

Companies considering developing a technology that may affect other businesses' IPRs may choose to disregard the potential claims of rivals by making public the potentially infringing technology. This option may be more affordable for SMIEs than filing a patent application, which not only requires payment of the filing fees (often in several jurisdictions, but also maintenance fees of the patent). Moreover, defensive publishing may be useful if the competitive advantage rests not only on the coded technology subject to publication, but rather on the know-how needed to operate it: the SMIE may thus preempt the threat of a competitor undermining their use of the technology, while controlling its practical use through know-how, which is much more difficult to internalize and replicate.

This strategy seeks to render useless any future litigation by a competitor claiming ownership of the technology, because there is a chance that judges will regard the technology 'prior art', thus part of the public domain. If the SMIE disseminates the competing technology as wide as possible before litigation is initiated, there is a great chance that judges will regard the standard technology public, thus unprotected. Knowing this possibility, a wide dissemination of a closely similar technology will put pressure upon the competitor claiming IP ownership to grant a license on the company carrying this strategy before the judicial ruling is made.

Defensive publishing makes important information public, for example, by disclosing the knowledge embedded in a technology in a specialist journal. In principle this strategy seems to be counterintuitive, as publishing allows access to anyone, who would be free to use the invention; however, in closer inspection, making knowledge public also means that nobody would be able to patent the invention as it becomes part of the state of the art. Thereby, all novelty claims—one of the fundamental prerequisites for patentability—will be defeated. Large companies such as IBM and Siemens operate their journals for the purpose of defensive publishing.

Milstein reported (2002) the case of Plantronics, a U.S. telephone headset manufacturer that developed a technology for reducing microphone noise. The invention was not something the company could use right away, but Plantronics executives did not want to risk letting a competitor patent the idea first. The company sought to prevent competitors from patenting the design of the headset by posting a description of it on IP.com, a website that enables inventors to establish an idea's legal existence, transforming the novelty into prior art, and part of the public domain.

This is a highly risky strategy, because it ultimately rests on the decision of judges, not to construe the technology as similar or part of the public domain. As Fisher and Oberholzer (2013), there is a great chance that such judgments can run either way. Milstein (2002) justifies this strategy, because although "publishing an innovation means that competitors have access to it (…) the competitive risk is outweighed by the benefit of making it difficult for someone else to win a patent—a patent that could give the holder the right to demand licensing fees from all other users of the technology or technique." Moreover, as Henkel and Pangerl (2008) indicate, this strategy presents itself as an alternative to patenting and secrecy, because the increased number of patents today (particularly of low-quality patents) raises the risks of the innovative firm to be blocked by judicial means, and trade secrets tend to leak out.

2.6 Patent Donation

Very often, corporations develop technologies that fall outside their 'core' capabilities. At DuPont, researchers found a way to make a valuable chemical that leaves water as the byproduct instead of tons of acid. At Eastman Chemical, they devised a plastic packaging that could more than double the shelf life of beer and soda. At Procter & Gamble, there were discoveries that could help doctors reduce skin discoloration from burns, wounds and grafts. All these cases have a commonality in that none of the technology mentioned represented their 'core' knowledge, yet they prevent competitors from developing market power through closely related or similar technologies.

Through patent donations, companies put inactive but potentially useful intellectual property in the hands of other organizations, mostly academic research centers that will develop and apply it. That helps patentees to transfer their unusable patents to universities, hospitals and other non-profit or governmental institutions and that these organizations would then put them to work within their own research programs. This could help donating firms to have leverage on the new technologies developed on top of the donated one, or prevent competitors from holding-up by patenting competing technologies.

Yet, the reason that induced firms to use patent donation was not strategic but financial. Corporations use their patent stock much less than expected. As Feder (2002) indicates, "Good companies use only 20% of their patents," said Sam Khoury, the president of Inavisis International, a consulting firm that appraises patents, trademarks and related corporate assets. "Badly run companies use only 10%." The question arises, what to do with these idle patent stocks? Unused technologies entail a legal cost of protection, which in the case of corporations with large patent portfolios, can take a considerable financial stake of their balance sheets.

First, patent donation allows businesses to improve the overall financial return of their intellectual assets. Tax regulations in the U.S. allow enterprises to take a tax deduction for the value of a patent. Large corporations with large patent portfolios would review their holdings to identify ways to increase the financial return on their intellectual assets by doing away the expenses associated with patent maintenance expenses of patents that are not part of the corporation's 'core' or that are not used as a 'defensive shield' against potential patents of competitors.

Corporations have taken significant advantage of this opportunity to offer patents to a variety of non-profit institutions, sometimes to the point of raising the concerns of the IRS, due to excessive use or misuse of the deduction scheme.[3]

Dow Chemical Company introduced the concept when it discovered that 25% of their patents had no business value, they were able to save more than $40 million in 5 years by downsizing their portfolio by over 10,000 patents. According to calculations by M-Cam, who specializes in valuing and auditing patents, corporations received $3.8 billion in tax deductions for donating patents that may have had no commercial value at all.

Aside from the tax credit reasons, Fisher and Oberholzer (2013: 168) also see capital market concerns as a reason for donating patent stocks. By disclosing part of its non-strategic knowledge, corporations can signal its value to capital markets for their strategic technology stock, thus making it easier for them to obtain financing.

More recently, large international companies throughout the 2000s have increasingly adopted an 'open innovation' business model based on the premise that technology commercialization can be greatly simplified, expedited and accelerated by incorporating external IP, expertise and multiple partnership relationships into technology commercialization activities, instead of relying solely on internal IP and expertise.

Open innovation has thus enabled the financial sustainability of innovative startups, who have become suppliers of large corporations willing to reduce their inhouse R&D costs, and find alternative forms of producing innovation through outsourcing. Yet, in order to successfully trade their intellectual assets, startups need support from specialized partners who can provide them with business expertise, and IP strategic know-how.

As Polonenko and Chatterjee (2011) note:

> Patent protection is a key element in open innovation business models. However, unlike the closed innovation approach that regards patents as monopolistic 'fences' and 'barriers' to keep competitors away, the open innovation approach considers patents as 'currency' that can be used to acquire access to third-party IP to expedite technology development through non-exclusive licensing and/or cross-licensing. Moreover, the open innovation approach is comfortable with the selling or bartering of non-essential IP to secure at least some return on the investment for IP protection, instead of simply abandoning patents that have little or no direct value to the IP holder.

Open innovation represents a paradigmatic shift in the development of IP strategies. Whereas in the past businesses focused around how to create and protect patents, open innovation laid down an alternative road, focused on finding the scope of

[3] The popularity of patent donation is such that in a 2003 Treasury Issue Notice, it was declared that the IRS is aware of purported charitable contributions of intellectual property involving: (1) transfers of nondeductible partial interests in intellectual property; (2) the expectation or receipt of benefits in exchange for transfers; (3) inadequate substantiation of contributions; or (4) overvaluation of intellectual property transferred.

the public domain, and developing supporting strategies around it (Boyle 2008). Moreover, IP strategies designed around open innovation provide unique opportunities for institutional technology transfer offices and businesses to engage each other far beyond their traditional focus on securing exclusive license deals. The organic way this new approach has evolved elicits the adoption of fully-fledged incubation strategies that take into consideration not only IP but also other areas of business strategy.

2.7 Non-competition Clauses

Companies that deal with qualified employees who control delicate trade or industrial secrets use non-compete clauses in their labor or services contract to protect their secrets from being disclosed publicly. According to these contracts one party agrees not to compete with the other for a set period of time. These contracts are negotiated either upon contract signing or at the end of a business relationship to protect them. From the viewpoint of the IP holder, these contracts seek to extend their market power through contractual means.

Non-competition clauses are particularly relevant in certain industries where other forms of IP protection are unavailable, due to the nature of the secrets involved. Such is the case of the fashion industry, where creative and executive positions at the industry's most celebrated brands often swap seats. Such clauses could serve as more than merely a way for brands to ensure that their top talent does not switch to a competitor; non-competes, in a way, serve to protect brands' valuable designs from being copied, particularly given how easily it is for garments and accessories to be replicated. Fashion, after all, does not require the millions of dollars and lengthy timelines associated with innovation in the technology space, for instance. In this industry, a design may be taken to a new brand and replicated in a matter of days.

A case that exemplifies the relevance of IP management strategy based on non-competition clauses is the lawsuit for breach of contract that Carolina Herrera, the Venezuelan fashion designer based in New York brought against Oscar de la Renta, over Monse Founder, Laura Kim. The suit, filed in December 2016, was intended to enforce a 6-month long provision in the contract of the house's former senior designer, Laura Kim. The New York state court that is currently hearing the case, had issued a temporary restraint order that upheld the non-compete agreement, but on December 23rd lifted the preliminary injunction that barred Kim from working at Oscar de la Renta.[4]

In sum, this chapter highlighted how IP strategies rest around the pursuit of market power arising out of the non-replicable nature of the intangible asset protected, and of the legal monopoly power granted by patents and copyrights under the IP law.

[4] News available at: http://www.thefashionlaw.com/home/carolina-herrera-sues-oscar-de-la-renta-over-monse-founder-laura-kim.

The selection of alternative IP strategies may be directed towards increasing the control of such assets, either by reinforcing their legal protective shield; by enlarging their patent portfolios, so to shield entire sectors from likely challengers or simply by pioneering the new technology. Also, companies deploy defensive strategies against competitors that could threaten their competitive advantage by means of controlling adjacent technologies, or by preventing others from enjoying exclusivity of their own research. The array of options extends well beyond patent or copyright registry, and include patent donation; defensive publishing; and introducing non-competition clauses, where necessary.

Chapter 3
Sharing IP Strategy: Commercialization

The previous chapter explored how IP legislation affords patent and copyright holders with a legal monopoly over their intellectual asset; with a view to reducing the amount of uncertainty they have over them. Other IPRs also are intended to grant exclusive control over valuable features of those assets. However, the market power allowed by such legal title is far from giving absolute certainty and control to titleholders. Market conditions limit their real capacity to impose full control to their asset use, due to the qualifying circumstances the market presents to them. In principle, that situation leads IP holders to deploy strategies aimed at enhancing their power over the market, to impose economic limitations upon their rivals on their capacity to seize strategic competitive capabilities.

Alternatively, companies may prefer to trade strategic assets in order to develop their own competitive capabilities. This option allows them to obtain useful inputs that may allow them to develop competitive advantages needed to penetrate new markets. IP managers define what skills they may develop in cooperation with other businesses; and how their patent titles give them intangible assets they can trade with other firms as currency to obtain missing capabilities, either by trading them or by licensing them in exchange for other licenses (patent pooling). This chapter will explore in detail how these trades take place.

3.1 Drawbacks of Imposing IP's Market Power

Patent selling and licensing are the most popular instruments for commercializing IP. The IP licensing market has grown dramatically in the last 20 years worldwide. According to WIPO, from 2000 to 2015, IP licensing grew from 100 billion to approximately 500 billion. Patent licensing is by far the most popular IP traded, but also trademarks and copyrights enjoy an important share of the market. This situation is not surprising. IP licensing is perceived as an expedient way for IP holders to develop a competitive advantage, by cooperating with competitors, trading their

I. De Leon, J. Fernandez Donoso, *Innovation, Startups and Intellectual Property Management*, DOI 10.1007/978-3-319-54906-4_3

knowledge, as opposed to imposing their market power. Yet, IP licensing or sale has a tactical advantage that makes it very appealing, as we will see in this chapter.

Innovators may find it convenient to leave the hazards and uncertainties of commercializing IP in the hands of patent brokers and focus on the innovation activity. The way to do this is by selling or licensing the patent to a firm in need of such knowledge to develop a productive capability or to trade their IP portfolio (other than patents), either through a patent broker or directly to the buying or licensee company.

Alternatively, the innovator may prefer to retain a relationship with the business party, in the interest of fulfilling some other strategic corporate goal. For example, the innovator may be a researcher interested in using the business' facilities or teams to develop future research or may find it useful to obtain financial resources to carry out alternative scientific research, or may be interested in getting access to the network of contacts and financial resources available to the business party. An innovator may discover that he either needs to license technology from his company to augment his product development efforts or needs to create a new revenue stream by licensing technology that he has developed for other people. In cases such as these, a licensing agreement would enable the mechanism to do this, through a contractual arrangement between the innovator (licensor) and the business partner (licensee) in exchange for an agreed payment (fee or royalty).

According to Fisher and Oberholzer-Gee (2013), three factors may increase the costs of imposing market power for IP owners, thereby driving them to trade with potential competitors, instead. These are reasons why they may find it more convenient to share their IP with rival companies either through licensing, selling or even giving away their assets.

First, IP owners obtain market power from their legal entitlements, but their capacity to extract "rent" greatly depends on the strategic behavior of competitors. Competitors' actions may diminish the overall value of the market where IP owners expect to obtain their IP revenues. Faced with this contingency, IP owners may find it convenient to negotiate an understanding with their competitors to share the income resulting from their IPRs. The cutthroat competition between Procter and Gamble Company (P&G) and Colgate-Palmolive Company in the home teeth-whitening industry highlights this point. P&G introduced Crest Whitestrips in 2000, offering consumers a less expensive method to whiten their teeth. This approach had patent protection that made it very hard for Colgate to invent around. To Colgate's dismay, Crest began to rapidly gain market share, not only on the whitening strips but also across its portfolio of dental products traded under the Crest brand. To halt Crest's growth, Colgate introduced a less useful product at a lower price, thereby triggering a price war that dissipated much of the gains the market offered to both P&G and Colgate. Arguably, Crest could have retained a much larger chunk of the profits by adopting less aggressive marketing tactics and developing an entente with Colgate.

A second factor that justifies a sharing strategy is to prevent competitors from "inventing around." Again, here is a case where the exercise of market power through IP undermines the long-term profitability of the right's owner. This is particularly visible where the owner would want to transform its technology as the dominant "standard" of the industry at the early stage of the sector's development. One of the most well-known cases in point is Apple's self-defeating commercialization strategy in the 1980s, and the lessons drawn for their strategy in the 2000s over the iPhone.

In the early 1980s, Apple and Microsoft were partners in the development of the Macintosh. Apple required innovative software to develop its upcoming operating system iOS; Steve Jobs was to focus Apple on the computer business, thus leaving software development to Microsoft. By owning the patents that helped her to control the OS, Apple expected to impose her market power upon consumers and make customers pay accordingly, as well as managing software developers like Microsoft. However, Microsoft had other thoughts.

Apparently, Bill Gates did not want Microsoft to follow Apple's plan, as this would have made it dependent from her ordering. It realized that the Graphical User Interface was the future of computing, so he did not want Microsoft to be a small software developing company. Devising a strategy to avoid technological oblivion, Microsoft put their efforts into developing its own Graphical OS (Windows), capable of competing with Apple in the upstream market. However, to do that, they had to make this OS as widely available as possible. They allied with IBM, who was desperate to break into the personal computing market; so Microsoft reached an agreement with IBM to outsource their Windows OS on IBMs computers. Since IBM had wider brand recognition and reach among distributors, Microsoft immediately gained a competitive advantage over Apple. Also, Microsoft started selling its OS to any PC maker that would buy it. By contrast, Apple was foreclosing her possibilities, by imposing a market power strategy upon her distributors, who thereby increasingly started switching to IBM/Windows, and subjecting consumers to pricey offerings and technological idleness (it took Apple 7 years to produce Apple III, the sequel to Apple II). Customers and developers were familiar with the IBM brand and bought IBM computers. As Microsoft grabbed market share, developers started working on applications for its OS instead of Apple's Macintosh system. Microsoft became the dominant firm from then on. At the end of the 80s, Apple was primarily a minor player in the computer industry. The lesson is that they should have licensed in more favorable terms, until becoming the industry standard (which they never were, contrary to the general opinion).

Many people thought history would repeat itself with Apple's iPhone in the wake of Google's cheaper Android arrival. However, this time things were different for Apple. Apple's IP strategy was much more robust, as it had spent years building brand recognition through the iPod and the Mac and its constant innovation and development of product portfolio with the iPad.

As Yarow (2012) explains:

> Each year Apple has released a phone that is better than the phone it sold the year before. There was no seven-year opportunity for a rival to release a phone that was better than the iPhone.

Also, unlike its previous experience, Apple had no real challenger, comparable to IBM who could quickly switch into the personal computer market by just finding the right OS provider. When Google got into the smartphone industry, it was starting from scratch with Android. In 2007 Google was still widely unknown to most people. It was not a trusted brand like IBM. In short, this time Apple had to learn how to deploy a successful IP management strategy that could sustain its costlier licensing program, and that prevented competitors from inventing around.

The third factor is the development of network effects that lead to smaller markets for complementary goods. A product or services value increases with the number of users, as it happens with social networks: the value of the standard or network increases as more individuals use it ("direct network effects"). However, the value of the platform also increases as the number of users grows because a greater number of complementary products and services become available. Complements are products that increase the demand for another product.

For example, some readers may remember back in 2007 when Apple first told developers that to develop for the iPhone, they would need to build WebApps for Safari. Walter Isaacson (2011) recalls how Steve Jobs stubbornly opposed the idea of third party apps and wanted to create web apps that iPhone clients could only use through the iPhone's mobile Safari web browser. Art Levinson, an Apple board member, recalls that Jobs was against third party apps partly because he felt they could not handle all the complexities that would be involved in policing third-party app developers. This is a usual case of a top-down approach towards innovation that prioritizes policing the process as opposed to leaving it unleashed.

So, here we have the man reckoned to be the personification of innovation in the personal computer industry, the man regarded as *the* guru of business trends in the digital industry, who failed to see the trend of the market. This trend was driving the market towards making the iPhone a carrier for the development of apps, whether WebApps for Safari or not. He lacked a proper IP management strategy to capture profits arising from his IP over the iPhone's iOS mobile operating system, in a way that could not only guarantee Apple's market power exploitation as a mobile telecom carrier but also as an operating platform for the development of thousands of apps.

3.2 Contractual Flexibility in Licensing and Selling Patents

Depending on the specifics of the transaction desired, a variety of licensing agreements are available. These include Technology License Agreements, Trademark Licensing and Franchising Agreements, and Copyright License Agreements. In practice, these agreements may involve different types of IP, so it is usual for the parties to negotiate them concurrently.

Licensing is very flexible to adapt to whatever degree of business integration both the licensor and licensee desire. Usually, provisions enabling adaptation of capabilities between both parties include the following:

(a) *Subject matter*. What is the asset that the parties agree to license? Is it a patent, copyright, an image, a computer program, a song or a recipe?
(b) *Rights to be granted or conveyed*. License agreements allow the right to use, to sell, to make, or to have made by a third party the licensed IP. The parties will want to be certain to get the rights they need.

(c) *Exclusivity*. Is the license exclusive, i.e. is the licensee the only one authorized to use the intellectual asset? Is it non-exclusive or is it partially exclusive? The licensee may find it valuable to hold an exclusive license in markets where there are no competing technologies; also exclusivity may be needed if the technology still requires considerable development from the licensee.
(d) *Geographical scope*. Are there any geographic limitations such as regional, national or local?
(e) *Field-of-use restrictions*. A licensor may find it relevant to license the technology for use in one industry but not another. A nanotechnology developed for rapidly detecting changes in the composition of proteins may be used selectively in several markets where the technology may be applied, such as vector diagnostics and water or food contamination. Thus, it may be licensed to different licensees depending on their particular capabilities and roles in complementing the value offered by the licensed intellectual asset.
(f) *Sublicense*. Does the licensee have rights to license the technology again? These rights may be necessary if the licensee plans to incorporate it into her products.
(g) *Assignment rights*. If the licensee company gets bought, does the license get canceled or does it get assigned to her acquirer?
(h) *Payment*. Payment could adopt the form of an upfront fee, or through running royalties based, typically, on the sales of the product. One could negotiate a combination of these payment modalities. Choosing what payment system is tricky if the intellectual asset to be licensed gets embedded into a larger product that is sold by the licensee. How are royalties calculated then? What if the licensee does not charge for her product? Usually, startups will pay the upfront fee with equity, because they typically don't have much cash.
(i) *Diligence*. The licensor may impose on the licensee company duties to commercialize the technology within a certain timeframe or by showing some milestones.
(j) *Patent litigation*. Sometimes licensors require licensees to protect the technology by paying litigation expenses in case of infringement by third parties.
(k) *Confidentiality*. Clauses requiring confidentiality are standard to protect know-how implicit in the intellectual asset.
(l) *Improvements*. Does the licensor yield to the licensee rights on any improvements developed by the latter?

The flexibility allowed by the contractual mechanisms offered by the licensing and sale of intellectual property is the most obvious way of dealing with cognitive problems arising from the IP system. The parties' cognitive expectations about potential business outcomes resulting from their relationship drive their actions towards specific business goals.

As WIPO (2015) indicates:

> All of these mechanisms either on their own or in combination will provide a startup, as a licensor or licensee, a wide variety of possibilities in conducting business in your own country or elsewhere. As an intellectual property owner and a licensor, your startup can

expand its business to the frontiers of your partners' business and ensure a steady stream of additional income. As a licensee, your startup can manufacture, sell, import, export, distribute and market various goods or services which it may be prevented from doing otherwise.

The complexity of the IP system creates new challenges that cannot be solved only by contractually resorting to patent licensing or selling. Indeed, IP commercialization strategies do not need to involve patent registration. In fact, of their total investment on innovation, firms seldom appeal to patent registration due to its high costs and convoluted process. Disclosure requirements put innovators in a difficult position: trusting the effectiveness of an expensive enforcement mechanism to redress any infringements against their entitlement by third parties.

More often, firms resort to a combination of strategies, and a portfolio of IP protection that extends well beyond the scope of patent registration.

The threat of patent litigation arising from the lack of clarity in the assignment of patent claims increases with the level of complexity featuring the industry concerned. That could discourage businesses from making their inventions public through the patent registry, and they therefore may prefer to rely on commercial or industrial secrets or to develop preventive strategies such as the reciprocal licensing of patents to avoid traffic jams ("patent thickets"), which may restrict competition.

3.3 Forms of Patent Trading: Brokerage and Pooling

Trading parties in the IP market have developed a myriad of ways in their attempt to furnish such transactions with information needed for the exchanges to take place. We will examine in this section only two primary forms of IP trading: patent brokerage and patent pools. For simplicity's sake, and given their higher liquidity in the market, we will assimilate patent trading to IP trading, which covers a broad range of IPRs different from patents, such as copyrights, trade secrets, trademarks and utility models.[1]

First, patent brokerage plays an important role in reducing transaction costs between producers and consumers of IP by supplying specialized information to the market in the form of specialized valuation services. Given the difficulties of attaining a patent market value, broker's experience is critical to determine the most accurate value achievable under these exceptional circumstances. They also are helpful to bring useful third party information (information about the industry, the technology involved, the competitors, and so on) to the negotiation table. This aid could be critical to reducing information asymmetries between a seasoned firm on the one hand, and a smaller first-time seller, on the other.

In the past, brokers were lawyers and patent agents who matched inventors looking to sell new technologies to investors or buyers seeking to commercialize them. However, the booming development of the patent registration has made this work

[1] Millien and Laurie (2009) find 17 highly particular types of intermediaries, including distinctions between Patent Licensing and Enforcement Companies, and IP/Technology Development Companies.

more difficult. Today, technologies overlap and are valuable depending on the size of the portfolio where they belong. Wang (2010: 164) acknowledges: "the new focus on patent assets has not corresponded to a rise in sophistication among parties to intellectual property transactions."

Perhaps this explains why patent brokers' presence in the market is limited; they are small in scale and tend to focus on facilitating high-end licensing transactions bearing hefty price tags (10% of the value of the deal and sometimes 20–30%).

Although some authors (Wang 2010) seem to suggest the recent emergence of the market for IP, and hence the novelty of these patent intermediaries, the truth is that brokers have existed since the very inception of the patent system. Lamoreaux and Sokoloff (2003) account for the positive effect of agents on the US market for patented technology between 1870 and 1920. Today it includes players such as Inflexion Point Strategy,[2] iPotential (Epicenter Group),[3] Ocean Tomo,[4] IP Value[5], Pluritas[6] and Thinkfire[7] (Wang 2010: 171; Hagiu and Yoffie 2013).

The second form of patent commercialization, patent pooling, may be best grasped by looking at the experience of Oracle Corporation, one of the most innovative firms in the software industry. This company refused to patent its inventions to avoid the costs of potentially infringing a myriad of existing competing patents related to the technologies Oracle applies while producing complex software products. In fact, Oracle did not obtain its first patent until 1995 and acquired only 161 patents during the 1990s, although patents have been issued on database techniques at least since the early 1970s, and especially since 1990.

In the course of the USPTO Hearings in 1994, Jerry Baker, Senior Vice President of Oracle Corporation, the software firm specialized in innovative database management systems explained why, despite all their innovative capabilities, he had consciously decided not to give priority to patent applications to protect their technologies.

Of course, not all technology firms have Oracle's advantage of an established brand name in the market, so they have to rely on patents, rather than other intangible rights. Their options are limited to finding some way of avoiding the potential clash of patent claims whose technology boundaries may collide or overlap. In the wake of patenting proliferation since the 1980s, this is a very real problem. "Patent thickets" resulting from this phenomenon have created "a dense web of overlapping intellectual property rights that a company must hack its way through to commercialize new technology"[8] (Shapiro 2001). Alternatively, in other words, "an overlap-

[2] http://www.ip-strategy.com/

[3] http://www.IPotential.com

[4] http://www.oceantomo.com/

[5] http://www.ipvalue.com/

[6] http://www.pluritas.com/

[7] http://www.thinkfire.com/

[8] Patent thickets may have ambiguous effects on patent transactions. On the one hand, they may discourage patent deals because patent ownership is not centralized but scattered among many patent holders. As the number of patent owners with whom buyers and licensees have to strike deals increases, transaction costs rise. However, they may also encourage licensing deals because

ping set of patent rights."[9] In the absence of patent pools, patent thickets require firms seeking to commercialize new technologies to negotiate individual patent licenses with multiple patentees. That gives rise to as many conflicting claims of intellectual property ownership as there are patent owners.

Thus, patent thickets create a problem of royalty stacking. In this situation multiple parties that hold market power in a chain of production are collectively forced to increase their prices above the level they would have in the absence of the other firms with overlapping technologies. In other words, stacking reduces their joint profits (Hagiu and Yoffie 2013: 50). Harper (2015) notes that patent thickets reveal an "anticommons problem" that induces innovative firms to underuse the patented invention because they are faced with their competitors' veto since no firm has an existing right to use the IP. In his view, this situation arises because IP owners apportion IPRs into too many small fragments, so it creates prohibitive asymmetric transaction costs that make it harder to regroup them into alternative bundles, according to the needs of entrepreneurs and end-users.

The solution is agreeing to cross-license each other's technology; hence the rationale of "patent pools." A patent pool is an agreement between two or more companies to cross-license their patents relating to a particular technology. The consortium that runs patent pools sets forth the rules whereby participants submit their IP to a joint venture. This joint venture helps firms developing highly sophisticated technologies protected with different layers of patent claims to share and transfer intellectual property and, ultimately, facilitate innovation with a minimum of disturbance from IP-related legal issues.

Sometimes SMEs create unique forms of patent pooling around standard-setting institutions to raise their chances of finding third party clients interested in their technology. Standard-setting organizations endorse a particular technological standard: to execute this arrangement, SMEs members agree to cross-license or to pay royalties to the single standard owner (Hagiu and Yoffie 2013). In other words, several pooled patents set down a standard that increases the potential value of individual patents by raising probabilities of trading them under the norm umbrella. By reducing transaction (negotiation) costs between small companies, the standard enables more transactions to occur between the pool and potentially interested third party clients (licensees). This way of conducting patent pooling has limitations, however, as the number of industries and technologies involved is relatively small. Therefore, their significance in terms of total patent market share is relatively lower.

---

the presence of overlapping patent rights may reduce the value at stake in each patent licensing negotiation. Furthermore, incumbent firms (especially in mature industries) may use patent thickets as a strategy to raise the entry costs of potential competitors, if patent standards are low, and the technologies are complex (Bessen 2002). Patent thickets are thus used to defend against competitors designing around a single patent. When they assert these patents through the threat of litigation, innovators are forced to share rents under cross-licenses, making R&D incentives sub-optimal. On the other hand, when lead-time advantages are significant, and patent standards are high, firms pursue strategies of "mutual non-aggression."

[9] The expression "thicket" comes from the SCM Corp. v. Xerox Corp. patent litigation case (SCM Corp. v. Xerox Corp., 645 F.2d 1195, 1203 (2d Cir. 1981), wherein SCM argued that that Xerox assembled a "patent thicket" to prevent competition.

Closson (2009) explains the historical development of the patent pools, associated with the technological development of competing technologies used in sewing machines. In 1856, four companies[10] held the patents related to the sewing machine; however, they employed much of their endeavors suing each other for patent infringement. Accordingly, they resolved to enter their patent portfolios into a technology pool (held in a trust) that would allow each company to freely cross-license the technology from the pool. In this way, they saved resources from litigation to use instead for manufacturing and marketing sewing machines.

Patent pools are difficult to form because they require the participation of all key patentees. If they are not in, it is likely that the pool will not be sustainable. For this reason, sometimes the government has stepped in and forced the creation of a pool, to preserve resources from being squandered in wasteful lawsuits. As an example, in 1917 the US Secretaries of War and Navy 'recommended' (i.e., forced) the Wright Company and the Curtiss Company, two principal owners of essential airplane patents, to set up a patent pool. At the time, the United States was about to join the First World War. Until the brink of the war, multiple patent suits had prevented new airplane construction. On this 'recommendation' coming from the US Federal Government, Wright, Curtiss and other essential patentees formed the Manufacturers' Aircraft Association. Of course, in the arms industry the government usually has a high leverage to stir things following the dictates of "national security."

Other historical examples of patent pools include several industries. For example, in the film industry, in 1908, Armat, Biograph, Edison and Vitagraph agreed to assign "all the patents in the early-day motion picture industry." The agreement also stated how much royalties movie exhibitors would pay to the pool as licensees (Wanamakert 2003; Aberdeen 2005). In 1916, in the consumer goods industry, the owners of various folding beds patents agreed to provide the Seng Company an exclusive license to manufacture and sell under the pool patents. Under the terms of the contract, 33% of the total royalties was allotted to the Pullman Couch Company. Two companies and two independent inventors signed the licensing agreement: the Davoplane Bed Company (7 patents), the Pullman Couch Company (13 patents) and two inventors. In return, the Seng Company paid a fixed percentage to the pool, and then, pool members split the royalty according to a contractual formula. A few years later, in 1924, in the radio industry, an organization first-named the Associated Radio Manufacturers (renamed Radio Corporation of America) pooled the resources and technology of American Marconi, Westinghouse, General Electric, Telegraph (AT&T) and American Telephone. This pool would lead to the establishment of standardization of radio parts, airway's frequency locations and television transmission standards.

The development of patent pools in the high-tech industry is emblematic in recent years. In 1997, several patentees of key technology created a patent pool in the video industry[11] and Philips Electronics N.V. to pool some essential patents related to the MPEG_2 compression technology standard.

[10] Grover & Baker, I.M. Singer & Co., Wheeler, and Wilson & Co.

[11] The parties were the Trustees of Columbia University, Lucent Technologies Inc., General Instrument Corp., Fujitsu Limited, Matsushita Electric Industrial Co., Ltd., Mitsubishi Electric

Similarly, in 1998, Sony, Philips, and Pioneer formed a patent pool for technologies necessary to comply with some DVD-Video and DVD-ROM standard specifications. Finally, in 1999, Toshiba Corporation, Mitsubishi Electric Corporation, Hitachi, Ltd., Time Warner Inc., Matsushita Electric Industrial Co., Ltd., and Victor Company of Japan, Ltd. set up a patent pool to administer technologies manufactured in compliance with the DVD-ROM and DVD-Video formats.

Finally, sometimes cross-licensing may result out of a strategy initiated after a litigation settlement has taken place, so it becomes a preventive strategy for future claims. A case in point is the dispute between Nokia and Apple, analyzed above, whereby Apple agreed to pay Nokia an undisclosed amount for smartphone technology allegedly stolen. The agreement provided a one-off sum payable to Nokia followed by ongoing royalty payments. Apple noted this payment was the result of a cross-licensing agreement because it also considered its patent claims against Nokia and contended it did not include "the majority of the innovations that make the iPhone unique."

Notwithstanding the clear advantages that patent pools bring about to firms that find it very expensive to commercialize their closely related patents separately, they do not eliminate financial risk in full, only temper it. Nevertheless, the pool does help to assure a common interest will emerge should one member be accused of infringement by a third party.

3.4 Patent Exchange Online Platforms

A clear problem arising out of the difficulty to measure IP value objectively became apparent in the failed attempts to develop broader IP market trade with the help of digital technologies.

Given the steady rise in the number of patent registries in the U.S. (and elsewhere) following the new perception of patents as a "core asset class" (Palfrey 2012), the conditions were seemingly ripe – or so it was thought – to institutionalize a comprehensive patent market exchange mechanism. Throughout the 2000s several companies built online platforms in an attempt to create more efficient ways to bring buyers and sellers of patents closer. These digital infrastructures were intended to facilitate transactions without taking ownership of the patents involved. Two types of platforms emerged: online marketplaces and live auctions.

Online marketplaces attempted to replicate the Alibaba or eBay model, by enabling better information about patent owners and technology sellers and potential buyers and licensees. Web sites such as Yet2 or Tynax list information of the patents that are for trading together wish special conditions for the sale or licensing. Special tools give buyers an easy search of the valid patents both by patent classes and by keywords, as well as descriptions of specific intellectual assets of particular interest.

These platforms allow applicants to search without disclosing the buyers' identity, coupled with curation carried out by the platform over the parties offering bids;

Corp., Scientific_Atlanta, Inc., Sony Corp.

screening is critical to ensure the presence of active investors and to filter weak patents from accessing the platform. Confidentiality ensures that the parties will withhold their strategic competitive research advantage vis-à-vis other potential offering parties present in the platform. Moreover, trading partners hold no transactions online; rather, the platform connects buyers and sellers once the potential traders commit in a posting. Intermediaries appointed by the platforms then perform person-to-person deals. The platform charges commission fees for these services. In a nutshell, these platforms act as brokers for highly specialized patent deals.

However, high hopes were placed upon the capacity of technology to support patent trading through auction mechanisms administered by online platforms. Hagiu and Yoffie (2013) explain this mechanism:

> These auctions functioned like other live auctions, for example, like art at Sotheby's and Christie's – with an auctioneer taking bids for each lot, which could be a single patent, copyright, trademark, or domain name right, or a bundle of such assets. The lots were sold to the highest bidder on condition that the highest bid exceeded the seller's reserve price.

Possibly IPXI was the most visible online auction mechanism for patent licenses, so it deserves closer inspection to understand the hurdles imposed by the patent system in allowing the emergence of efficient trading mechanisms.

This platform was launched in 2008 amidst high expectations that it would capitalize the richness of intellectual property scattered throughout the vast U.S. innovation ecosystem. IPXI expected to build an open and extended mechanism to help patent owners (particularly favoring SMEs) monetize their intellectual assets more efficiently and give them access to risk management tools to hedge their exposure. Its founders expected to develop a transparent marketplace for patent license exchanges that would lure investors to speculate on emerging technologies as opposed to investing in the equity of the companies that operate those technologies, with the ability to trade those rights as the value increased. In this way, IPXI expected to reduce investors' risk exposure.

IPXI's online auction trading platform could fulfill its harmonizing role as long as different trading parties could easily compare the information traded. To harmonize the information arising from specific technologies, IPXI created a new standard, the Unit Licence Right (ULR). This commodity or exchange-traded product offered purchasers a title to a license on a non-discriminatory basis, at a market-based price and could be sold on a standardized technology-unit basis that IPXI determined according to the underlying technology or IP of the ULR contract. Presumably, each ULR Contract offered its buyer a sound right to manufacture and sell a particular number of products or services employing the patented technology without the threat of an infringement suit. Thus, for example, a patent owner, i.e. licensor, could list on the IPXI a ULR contract that covered a patented nanotechnology for rapid detection of pathogens in organic liquids. The buyer of a ULR Contract could then manufacture diagnostic devices, use and sell the technology, or, a pre-defined number of devices with the patented nanotechnology. So, if the purchaser or licensee wanted to make and sell 500 devices and each ULR contract represented a single use of the IP, then the purchaser had to buy 500 ULR contracts. Each ULR contract expired when one device was manufactured. A secondary market for unused ULR contracts was also expected to emerge.

IPXI divided available patent licenses into a defined number of ULRs; by slicing the implicit IP entitlements, potential investors could buy just the optimal number of ULRs they wanted to invest in; thus, the mechanism allowed them to hedge their risk more efficiently, as the system would minimize financial risk associated with idle ULR contracts. The IPXI published market-based pricing of the vetted technologies and presented potential investors with a URL standard-terms contract similar to that of public equity offerings of corporations. Moreover, buyers could sell ULRs if the licensee found it had too many; or it could buy more if necessary. IPXI offered a large market of ULRs to invest in, and that presented (at least in theory) a more efficient way of investing in emerging technologies than entering into murky, tortuous, and expensive bilateral deals.[12] Commentators at the time highlighted this point:

> One of the biggest advantages of the ULR Contract for both IP licensees and licensors is the removal of the lawyer-intensive traditional bilateral licensing process (…) One of the IPXI's initial objectives was to build an exchange that operates under two core principles that do not exist in the traditional bilateral product/technology licensing scenario: transparency and efficiency. Regarding transparency, the IPXI starts the ULR Contract process by performing in-house a legal analysis designed to give the marketplace confidence in the quality of all patent rights listed as available ULR Contracts.

IPXI's business model was simple: both ULR contract sponsors, i.e. licensors, and investors, i.e. licensees, had to pay an annual membership fee of $5000 each, and sponsors had to pay a $100,000 listing fee per patents or patent portfolio. Also, IPXI's processing commission fee was set at 20% of the ULR Contract price.

Moreover, IPXI's founders put great effort into signing up members to the platform, to trigger initial use of the platform that could be followed by newcomers. Its membership included 70 leading innovative companies among the world's top owners of IP assets including several U.S. universities like Rutgers, Northwestern and the University of Utah. At some point, these institutions committed to issuing ULR Contracts with a market value of at least $50 million (Boger and Ziegler 2012). Other sponsors included names such as Ford Global Technologies, MetaPower Inc., the University of Notre Dame, the Regents of the University of California, JP Morgan Chase and electronics giants Sony USA and Philips. Even the U.S. Department of Energy and various national laboratories committed to the IPXI as sponsors.

In short, all the odds seemed for IPXI's business model. The platform the auction mechanism provided was transparency to the licensing and created an open database of royalty rate data. Also, it standardized contracts used to do the patent licensing, thereby reducing transaction negotiation costs, and allowed parties to obtain licenses at comparable rates. Finally, it established a royalty database that could have allowed

[12] Critics had complained that IP licensing was an inefficient and costly way to do business. Most of these complaints centered on the fact that negotiations raised many transaction costs that outweighed the value of the license. These included value determination of the IP and the market potential of the technology; identifying possible licensees; once the licensee candidate was chosen, it was necessary to do a due diligence; and only then, negotiations over the license agreement conditions. In the most optimistic scenario, this process usually took several months to complete (Boger and Ziegler 2012).

third parties to increase their predictability about future potential licensing transactions or set damages in case of litigation. Moreover, it also provided access to technology users of all types: small companies, research organizations, and universities would have similar access to ULR contracts, as Fortune 100 companies. Finally, IPXI provided a rules-based approach to directed enforcement. What went wrong?

IPXI's model would prove more fragile than it looked on the surface. In his farewell memo, CEO Pannekoek told staff and members that the exchange was forced to close because the "time was just not right, and the obstacles – including potential licensees who challenged us to litigate instead of work with them – simply too insurmountable."

Given the lack of particular IP value, licensee candidates prefer to chase an expected "litigation price" that potentially yields them higher returns, as opposed to the "auction" price they are offered through standardized terms, such as the ULRs. IPXI was held up by the potential patent licensees' unwillingness to obtain required licenses unless threatened with litigation.[13] It seemed obvious that licensees found it more lucrative to free ride on the technical innovation of the patentees, members of the IPXI's platform, than to pay royalties, no matter the curation services provided by the platform.[14] Rent seeking presented them with a lower "litigation price," that yielded higher returns for the use of technology, than the amount of royalties calculated by IPXI's technicians. Even if ULR valuation included a significant price discount for litigation contingencies, and that legal due diligence was duly executed by supporting law firms, licensees were driven by the price potentially attainable in out-of-court settlements. Reality sank in, as everyone realized that given the murkiness of the IP system, betting on the judicial enforcement would be more lucrative than the hardships of negotiating IP prices.[15]

---

[13] Pannekoek explained: We were astonished by some of the initial responses to our marketing efforts. We decided to go directly to the business operations of our potential licensees and approached CEOs and others in the executive suite to make a business case. When we sat down with those who got back to us, in most cases, the initial discussions went very well – people understood what we were saying about it being an efficient, transparent process which allowed the licensee to get fair terms based on a market price. But then, the process would stall. At some point, the door was shut and eventually the response was "we don't need to do anything until you file in court."

[14] IPXI put together a package for a collection of nearly 200 IEEE standard 802.11n compliant patents. But as IPXI's CEO explained, "we provided in-depth due diligence on essentiality history, determination, claims charts and more, plus a 75 percent discount on payments relating to alleged past infringements, as well as the ability to be on a level playing field with market-based pricing," he explained. "But still they were not willing to transact or negotiate."

[15] Contreras and Reichman (2015) argues that IPXI's demise was due to a complexity of factors. First, the patents whose licenses would align under ULRs were not essential to manufacturers, so IPXI would not serve as a one-stop solution for alleviating the burden of negotiating bilateral license agreements about the standard. Second, IPXI's sponsors were not necessarily perceived as key players in the licensees' market, nor did they have a tradition of license enforcers; hence, these manufacturers may not have seen these sponsors as a threat that could be forestalled through preventive licensing. Finally, and one could say, paradoxically, URL standardization of contractual terms between licensors and licensees, which was intended to enhance market trading and pricing, was inflexible, hence unfit to accommodate specific transaction needs. Thus, ULRs were a less convenient option, compared to cross-licensing and patent pools which enable the licensee to use its patents as a currency in obtaining a desired license from the patent holder, thus offsetting part of their license cost.

IPXI's management failed to note that litigation is also another form of IP strategy that emerges out of the convoluted nature of the patent system. IP patent litigation is an inherent element of the IP system as much as a patent award because it is tough to value IP, so parties have incentives to leverage their market power if they have one. Far from the idealized Platonic assumption that people would eagerly submit their IP for an exchange forum like IPXI, he should have better started by questioning whether it would be more attractive for licensors to exploit their technology voluntarily, or to avoid exposure simply by not patenting their technology at all.

3.5 Patent Trading as IP Management Strategy

Patent trading remains the most important IP management strategy today, although its shape and goals are becoming more versatile as the popularity of competitively designed IP increases.

Given the pace of technological change, many companies are turning to new paradigms and models of innovation such as open and collaborative innovation. These models challenge the protection mindset and could give rise to new thinking and practices on IP ownership, sharing and licensing. An example is the 10-year-long broad patent cross-licensing deal recently signed between Google and Samsung. Patents may continue to increase, but the manner in which they are utilized and deployed are likely to evolve to accommodate the dynamism of the marketplace.

First, IP management today devises patent filing as a strategy to sense the market. A program of monitoring and reviewing filings that have the potential to influence one's space empowers companies to anticipate emerging threats and identify trends. This can support effective blocking strategies, such as defense patenting, whereby companies pursue IP in the unoccupied ground or white spaces where substitutes may emerge or where the competition may be going. Using analysis of patent filing activity can reveal where tomorrow's most important innovations will be gauged. This could help IP management strategists to anticipate where their competitors may be headed. For example, in terms of geography, since 2010 there have been five countries with the highest volume of filings: China, the U.S., Japan, Germany, and the Republic of Korea. Also, this data shows the relative specialization of countries in certain technologies: Japan in optics, the U.S. and China in digital communications.

Second, filing patents preemptively could be used to drive M&A activities, to block out current or potential competition, to create new business structures and partnerships or to establish a culture of innovation. For example, research on patent filing may clarify what technologies are "in" and what technologies are "out", thereby allowing businesses to plan their innovation strategies. For example, the recent increase of solar energy filings among patent applications in energy-related technologies in the U.S. shows that this technology is likely to be the prime technology dominating this market, above fuel cells, wind energy and geothermal.

Third, the convergence of technology acceleration and patent reform has created an urgent need for business leaders to reassess their IP strategies, to become much more assertive than in the past. By assertiveness we do not mean to be always on the offensive; defensive strategies are also part of the portfolio of IP management strategies. The point is, rather, that corporate leaders must acknowledge the nature of the battleground waged for the control of competitive capabilities. More and more, corporations fight in this war using a mix of technology and intellectual property. Players that do not understand this reality not only run the risk of becoming technologically obsolete from competitors they did not anticipate but also face the prospect of not being able to meet their challenge because patents have completely blocked them out of the game.

Of course, like any other market, IP trading needs information to function. However, it is evident that IP markets suffer from various forms of information asymmetry that undermine their transparency and place SMIEs in a delicate position, as they can hardly obtain information because of their comparative weaker financial resources to obtain such missing information about clients, interested investors, complementary technologies, cost-effective jurisdictions, where to avoid being sued by a stronger party, and so on. If the potential licensor and licensee knew how much the technology involved in the deal was worth, they could quickly reach an efficient agreement that would be mutually beneficial in the absence of transaction costs (Coase 1960). This is far from the case. IP market murkiness is geared against SMIEs because they lack resources to obtain such information. Their weak position enhances the impact of transaction costs arising out of the lack of transparency featuring IP markets.

Institutions emerge to fill this gap by allowing IP trading parties to communicate information effectively. This conclusion sounds simpler than what it is. As IPXI's failure shows, the inherent murkiness of the IP patenting system tends to prevail upon the efforts across the board aimed at creating stable IP market prices. Participants in the IP market preferred to litigate than coalescing into the information mechanisms provided for by the IPXI market. Clearly, this is a case where the Coasean transaction costs inherent in the underlying discretion within which patents are afforded it impossible to reach the optimal solution that an alternative institutional arrangement would have brought about.

In general, these platforms failed to allow trading to occur, and its promoters quickly migrated to consulting services or brokerage.[16] Online marketplaces, as well as auction platforms, proved unviable due to the complexities and information asymmetries of the IP market. These asymmetries forced platform managers and hosts to become advisors and brokers supplying the market with information, as the working of these infrastructures alone failed to encourage transacting parties to disclose such information by themselves. Naturally, that undermined the business model implicit in the very concept of platforms, namely, to promote exponential growth by minimizing entry thereby easing curation mechanisms.

[16] These include platforms such as Yet2 (http://www.yet2.com/) and Tynax (http://www.tynax.com/).

In the IP markets, particularly patent trading would prove too complicated for the trading partners to assume this activity by themselves. Searching for the "right" technology, assessing the legal title of those claiming to be owners of that technology, and the hurdles implicit in facilitating the legal exchange[17] could prove enormous.

Very often, IP players apply business tactics intended to leverage the system in their favor to tap the information gaps created by the IP system. Thus, it seems that the development of IP strategies in the U.S. does also include that of making a tradeoff between the amounts of information that the innovator will be interested in disclosing in a patent application, versus staying quietly on the sidelines, trying not to be noticed. The excess of litigation indicates a very responsive system that highlights the gaps of information accruing from its failure to assign IP claims in a non-contested manner. Let us turn our attention to that problem in the next chapter.

In the case of Latin America, we associate the cognitive problem arising from the use of intellectual assets with a failure to understand the system, but in a different way; rather than availing from the legislation to exert rents through abusive litigation, in Latin America innovators seem to adopt the opposite direction.

[17] These difficulties include coordination costs between potential co-owners, coordinating costs with the sellers assessment of potential market success for the technology and IP valuation.

Chapter 4
Offensive IP Strategy: Litigation

On June 21, 2016, *Wall Street Journal* reporter Juro Osawa (2016) described the lawsuit that the Chinese smartphone maker Huawei Technologies Co. filed against South Korea's Samsung Electronics, Co., claiming that this company violated 11 of its mobile patents. Huawei's strategy of becoming one of the world's top smartphone manufacturers was the first significant legal challenge by a Chinese smartphone maker in U.S. courts.

In addition to strategic patenting and licensing technologies from other industry players, litigation is also part of a broader intellectual property (IP) strategy that Chinese smartphone giant manufacturers increasingly apply in their quest to become international players in the lucrative smartphone market. Entrepreneurs have come to view litigation as a complementary instrument of the patent award system, due to its propensity to create conflict between potential patentees.

Designing an IP litigation strategy is far from simple. IP managers cannot design litigation strategies in a structured or serial way, focusing on positioning one patent at a time. A single product may involve a growing IP network of multiple patents—perhaps hundreds. The complexity that such a structure involves may create a situation where the patentee needs to seek a solution through cross-licensing to preempt an infringement action, or may not be in a position to assert his title because the threat of a countersuit could be high. Potential claimants may involve parties representing different positions and views, for example, Non-Practicing Entities (NPEs) or shareholders asserting a lack of process and control of an intellectual asset. Such complexity forces patentees to address patent risk holistically for each product or service introduction, in an attempt to bring down probability costs arising from litigation charges. That requires a sense of strategy that underlies the IP management agenda.

What factors are involved in designing an optimal litigation strategy?

I. De Leon, J. Fernandez Donoso, *Innovation, Startups and Intellectual Property Management*, DOI 10.1007/978-3-319-54906-4_4

4.1 Patent Litigation as an Investment Asset

Clausewitz said that war is the continuation of politics by different means. One can say the same about litigation being an extension of IP commercialization by alternative means. Firms develop IP litigation strategies to seize opportunities opened by the litigants' asymmetric savvy over their knowledge of differences in IP protection in various jurisdictions across the world.

Litigation over intellectual assets has become an attractive business for investors in the U.S., and this perception is quickly spreading into other jurisdictions. Trends in global patent litigation show an increase in the number of cases brought for dispute in the most popular jurisdictions for litigation: China and the U.S.(Fig 4.1).

Litigation in the U.S. has risen astonishingly. The highest number of patent lawsuits occurred in 2015 if one adds the number of district court cases to patent disputes that are resolved through the process of "inter partes review." If only district court cases are measured, 2013 was the year with the most filings.

Jaffe and Lerner (2004: 9–18) explained the popularity of IP litigation in the U.S., as a by-product of the improved prosecution mechanisms introduced in the 1982 patent system reforms. These legal changes centralized decision-making around the Court of Appeals for the Federal Circuit and vested specialized judges with adequate powers to reach decisions, thus overcoming the previous scenario of concurring appeal courts, which promoted forum shopping among litigants. The kaleidoscopic layout of the IP judicial system led to contradictory case law and created an enormous uncertainty in the expectations of patentees about the extent of

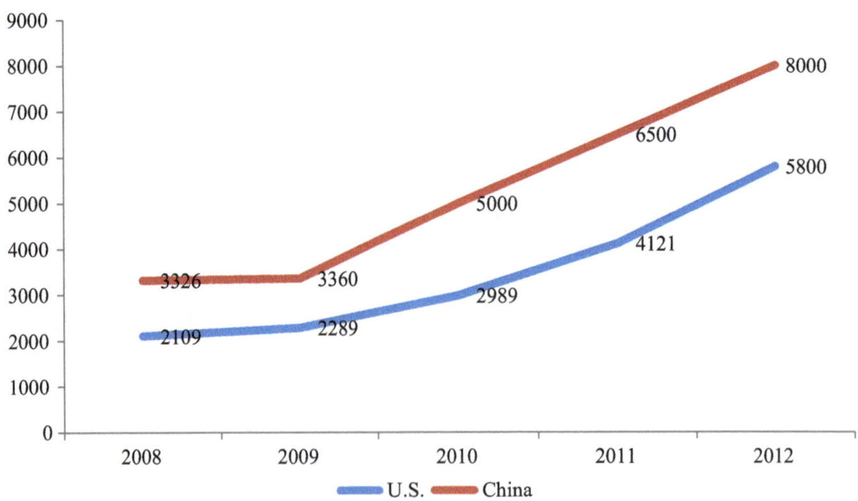

Fig. 4.1 Trends in Global Patent Litigation, China vs. U.S. (Source: Global IP Project 2015)

their rights. Paradoxically, the very efficiency displayed by these reforms would lead the system into another turmoil, as patent claimants would see litigation as an opportunity to obtain conditions that voluntary agreements (i.e. licensing or sale) could not attain.

In our view, by contrast, it is precisely the perception of asymmetric opportunities for litigation that has created the setting inducing corporations to launch more aggressive litigation strategies at a global level. Uncertainty about the scope of IP raises the likelihood of abusive litigation because it allows the emergence of concurrent claims over a given technology. This situation raises the cognitive hazards that can derail the creation of markets for patents and other IP.

Litigation offers IP managers a powerful tool that induces firms to rearrange the patent scope because it allows them to qualify ex post facto the extent of patent awards, which, as mentioned in Chap. 1, above, are forcefully imprecise and open. Litigation either whittles it down against the patentee or expands it against potential competitors. In either case, due to the incomplete nature of the patent system, both sides will be potentially placed into opposing camps the very moment the authority grants the patents. For this reason, a successful global patent litigation campaign requires careful selection of the targeted IP and sophisticated strategic planning that takes into account the differences between the major jurisdictions in timing, procedure, and substantive patent law.

Traditionally, firms sued potential competitors who attempted to develop alternative technologies threatening to erode the incumbent's market power. However, businesses have realized that litigation is not only attractive as a defensive strategy against a possible violator of one's IPRs. The lack of transparency in the IP market, particularly in regards to patents, has encouraged businesses to use it as an offensive strategy.

Litigation is more likely in countries where the system provides the means to grant legal monopolies over patents and copyrights relatively easy, and establish litigation mechanisms to protect them. For example, Jaffe and Lerner (2004: 19) note the following:

> Patents have become so easy to get, and are enforced so ruthlessly by the courts, that the winners of the technological competition in crucial industries are sometimes those with the best attorneys, or those simply lucky enough to have been awarded a key patent they did not really deserve, rather than those that have created the best product or services. Some firms have embarked on explicit strategies to make their money by collecting patent royalties on existing technologies rather than by developing new technologies …

The proliferation of litigation, far from ensuring the transparency of the patent system through effective allocation of patent entitlements, has reinforced its convoluted functioning. The failed experience of Chicago-based Intellectual Property Exchange International, Inc. (IPXI) examined earlier clearly proves the point.

Perhaps a good approach to understand the "litigation business" over IP (particularly, patents) is to highlight how potential litigants perceive it as an "investment." From this perspective, we can construe patent litigation as an investment asset (i.e., the legal claim) whose risks they can hedge against probabilistic trial outcomes.

The fact that no patent title can decisively give assurance of who will be in control of the underlying asset (i.e. technology) makes litigation an attractive vehicle in the absence of voluntary contractual agreements.

Let us examine the case of Priceline.com. Still being a growing startup, in 1998 this company introduced a revolutionary e-commerce business model: it reversed the traditional auction mechanism by which sellers auction their price; instead, it offered buyers a name-your-own-price scheme, giving them the option to accept the seller's offered price. In this model, sellers do not quote a selling price, but buyers make a suggestion for a product's price; the transaction occurs if a vendor accepts this quoted price. This innovation helped the Priceline Group become the global leader in online travel services, thanks to this competitive advantage.

In an attempt to replicate this competitive advantage, Expedia (and its then parent Microsoft) developed a similar Expedia® Price Matcher™, which allowed customers to place bids on unsold airline tickets and hotel rooms. Priceline sued for patent infringement at the end of 1999; 18 months later, both companies reached an out-of-court settlement by which Expedia agreed to pay royalties to Priceline for using the reverse auction model. Priceline's stock rose 16% in the aftermath. Clearly, for Priceline.com litigation was an investment that paid off.

The degree of risk involved in these "investments" is high, though. A strong 50% of patent litigation suits fail to obtain results (Hagiu and Yoffie 2013). Also, litigation assets are less liquid than alternative forms of investments, because those who invest on litigation rights cannot transfer as easily as other investment assets such as bonds, or stock or treasury bonds.

How do investors determine whether there are incentives for them to invest in patent litigation? Dent and Victor (2004) propose a decision tree methodology based on the following algebraic formula:

$I = (A - C) \times L,$
where:
I = *Expected income ($)*
A = *Trial award value, or expected damages ($)*
C = *Trial costs ($)*
L = *Litigation risk (percent)*

Award value is contingent to the damages calculated by the court. This amount should subtract the costs that the parties anticipate at their trial. Sometime these costs decrease, or are negative, if the law of the jurisdiction penalizes the losing party to redeem them (e.g., the winning party attorney's fees). Several factors influence this variable, including resolution period and the complexity of the technology under dispute, both of which influence the attorney's fees.

Litigation risk is one of several factors that include the presence of parties with capacity and interest to challenge the patentee's title, the nature of the technology or underlying intellectual asset involved, and the changes in the legal system and centralized judicial mechanisms.

Costs and benefits drive the decision of the parties involved; they change depending on the particular procedural and substantive rules applied in the jurisdiction where the litigation takes place, and that also changes the odds of obtaining a favorable decision. Given the territorial nature of IP legislation, each jurisdiction has a different appraisal of the substantive and procedural legal approach towards patents and other IPRs. This situation creates relative costs that vary according to the jurisdiction, thereby driving the parties' choice to seek redress of their IP entitlements.

Finally, we need to add a "cognitive discounted factor," to this cost and benefit calculation, to assess the cognitive awareness of the parties doing such risk calculation. IP litigation strategy.

Let us examine in detail each of these factors, in the following sections.

4.2 Award Value and Litigation Costs

Compared to large corporations, SMIEs face strong incentives not to litigate in support of their patents, due to the procedural rules in place, because they of the high risk surrounding such trials. According to the 2009 AIPLA survey, discovery roughly represents 60% of costs litigants incur in these proceedings. During a pretrial stage in a lawsuit, discovery procedures allow each party to obtain evidence from the other party through interrogatories, depositions, requests for production of documents, and requests for admissions. Discovery makes litigation expensive, particularly to SMIEs, which cannot afford such expenses in IP cases. Speaking about the state of patent litigation, Federal Circuit Chief Judge Randall Rader (2011) commented the following:

> Patent cases, in particular, produce disproportionally high discovery expenses. In one 2010 report, the Federal Judicial Center determined that Intellectual Property cases had cost almost 62 percent higher, all else equal .... We all understand as well that those expenses multiply exponentially when attorneys use discovery as a tactical weapon. The production burden of expansive e-requests outweighs their benefits. I saw one analysis that concluded that .0074 percent of the documents produced actually made their way onto the trial exhibit list – less than one document in ten thousand. And for all the thousands of appeals I've evaluated, email appears even more rarely as relevant evidence.

The exorbitant costs arising from IP litigation build the setting for an imbalanced position between litigants of diverging financial strength, which naturally strains SMIEs' position. Regardless of whoever has to pay for the litigation costs under the procedural rules of the litigation forum, whether each party or just the losing party, both systems are prone to abuse by the party that has deep pockets.

Because of this problem, the law sometimes takes steps aimed at offsetting these costs, as happens, for example, in Germany, the most attractive jurisdiction chosen to litigate patents in Europe. In this jurisdiction the value of the dispute determines legal costs; the judge fixes the costs according to the plaintiff's request, and the loser party must reimburse them. However, judges could use a split value to even the financial risk of economically unbalanced parties.

However, the position faced by a potential litigant in financial distress hardly changesafter the litigation has been launched because the stronger party can always raise the stakes of the weaker one, knowing that discovery costs for her would have a comparatively lesser impact in preparing litigation. Moreover, no matter the split judicial value, the enormous cost involved in a patent litigation usually will exceed what is tolerable for an SMIE in financial distress. The SMIE cannot afford to lose such declaratory judgment or to file a plea and to refund the resulting costs (in the case of losing the case) (Table 4.1).

The following table summarizes a compared view of litigation costs in several jurisdictions.

Table 4.1 Patent litigation costs under selected jurisdictions

Country	Characteristics of the legal system	Average duration	Average cost
France	Civil law Unified litigation No specialized courts	First instance: 18–24 months Appeal: 15–18 months	€80,000–150,000 (1st instance)
Germany	Civil law Bifurcated litigation Specialized court for invalidity	First instance: 12 months Appeal: 15–18 months	€50,000 (1st instance) €70,000 (Appeal)
Italy	Civil law Unified litigation Specialized courts	First instance: up to 24 months	€50,000–150,000 (1st instance) €30,000–70,000 (Appeal)
Spain	Civil law Unified litigation Commercial courts	First instance: 12 months Appeal: 12–18 months	€100,000 (1st instance) €50,000 (2nd instance)
U.K.	Common law Unified litigation Specialized courts Mediation promoted	First instance: 12 months Court of appeal: 12 months House of lords: 24 months	€750,000–1,500,000 (1st inst.) €150,000–1,500,000 (appeal) €150,000–1,500,000 (H.L.)
China	Civil law Bifurcated litigation Specialized courts	First instance: 6 months Appeal: 3 months, no limit with foreigners	US$150,000 (1st instance) US$50,000 (appeal)
Japan	Civil law Bifurcated litigation Specialized courts	First instance: 14 months Appeal 9 months	US$300,000 (1st instance) US$100,000 (appeal)
U.S.	Common law Unified litigation Specialized Court of Appeals (CAFC) Jury trial available Mediation promoted	First instance: up to 24 months Appeal: 12 + months	Up to US$4,000,000 (1st inst.) US$150,000–250,000 (appeal)
Mexico	Civil law Unified litigation Specialized court	First instance: 24–48 months Appeal: 15–18 months	€50,000–100,000 (1st instance)

Source: WIPO (2010)

The resolution period of the patent litigation is also relevant for establishing litigation costs. "Patent litigation carries a high price tag and is time-consuming" (Schutz 1999). The trial and settlement speed and the patentee success rate are usually correlated. A quick litigation victory can leverage the patentee's position in an overall global battle. In 2011 the Finnish mobile phone maker Nokia filed patent infringement actions in Mannheim, Germany against Apple, to take advantage of this jurisdiction's swift timeline for deciding infringement claims. According to Ben-Aaron and Pohjanpalo (2011) the rationale behind Nokia's strategy is to preempt Apple's chances to launch a successful counterclaim in U.S. district court and the ITC. Her strategy worked. As a result, Nokia won an almost 2-year patent dispute with Apple Inc., in a settlement that awarded a one-time payment and royalties to the Finnish handset maker. Although the parties never disclosed the specific financial terms of the settlement, pundits estimate the amount could be around €500 million, or about $720 million (Lawton and Chopping 2011).

On December 21, 2016, Nokia tried its successful strategy again by filing patent infringement against Apple in 11 jurisdictions, the first two of which were the U.S. District Court for the Eastern District of Texas and three regional courts in Germany (Dusseldorf, Mannheim, and Munich). The other jurisdictions are Helsinki, Finland; London, United Kingdom; Turin, Italy; Stockholm, Sweden; Barcelona, Spain; The Hague, Netherlands; Paris, France; Hong Kong; and Tokyo, Japan, as well as with the International Trade Commission in the United States.

Given the hourly rate of the billable hour of IP attorney costs, which is not very different from what precise IPR is subject to litigation, the costs indicated above are very much similar (Table 4.2).

In the United States, possibly the most popular patent litigation forum, the litigation costs are even more astounding. The American Intellectual Property Law Association (AIPLA) commissioned a survey in 2009 that assessed total litigation costs, which increase up to $3 million in patent infringement cases with disputed amounts ranging between $1 million and $25 million; and can multiply twofold if the amount in dispute is higher than $25 million. In litigations where the amount disputed is less than $1 million, the total expenses

Table 4.2 Intellectual property litigation costs by type of IPR

Patent litigation		Trademark litigation		Copyright litigation	
Litigation amount (US$)	Cost (US$)	Litigation amount (US$)	Cost (US$)	Litigation amount (US$)	Cost (US$)
Less than 1 M	873 K	Less than 1 M	354 K	Less than 1 M	325 K
1 M–10 M	2.2 M	1 M–10 M	670 K	1 M–10 M	663 K
10 M–25 M	3.5 M	10 M–25 M	1.1 M	10 M–25 M	1.1 M

Source: 2015 AIPLA Report of the Economic Survey

Table 4.3 Top 10 largest initial adjudicated damages awards: 1996–2015

Year	Plaintiff	Defendant	Technology	Award ($M)
2009	Centocor Ortho Biotech Inc.	Abbott Laboratories	Arthritis drugs	$1673
2007	Lucent Technologies Inc.	Microsoft Corp.	MP3 technology	$1538
2012	Carnegie Mellon University	Marvell Technology Group	Noise reduction on circuits for disk drives	$1169
2012	Apple Inc.	Samsung Electronics	Smartphone software	$1049
2012	Monsanto Company	E.I. du Pont de Nemours and Co.	Genetically modified soybean seeds	$1000
2005	Cordis Corp.	Medtronic Vascular, Inc.	Vascular stents	$595
2015	Smartflash LLC	Apple Inc.	Media storage	$533
2004	Eolas Technologies Inc.	Microsoft Corp.	Internet browser	$521
2011	Bruce N. Saffran, M.D.	Johnson & Johnson	Drug-eluting stents	$482
2014	Masimo Corporation	Philips Electronics N. America Corp.	Device measuring blood oxygen levels	$467

Source: PWC (2016)

normally exceed the disputed amount, with discovery costs raising up to 60% of the total litigation costs.

In the European Union, the situation is more or less similar. According to a European Commission report (2015: 72), once the forthcoming Unitary Patent Court is launched, the losing party to a legal dispute will be required to pay the winner's court fees. This report calculates the winner's legal expenses up to €3 million. Also, the losing party would be required to pay damages.

The average cost of patent infringement litigation is $2.8 million, and the average length of business disruption due to an IP lawsuit is between 1½ and 3 years. These are numbers that hardly can be sustained financially by a standard SMIE.

Clearly, given the substantial expenses involved, corporations will be inclined to litigate only if the potential benefits are also rewarding; and they are indeed. The rewards accruing from a favorable patent award are potentially abysmal. Table 4.3 illustrates the amount of damages awarded between 1996 and 2015 in landmark IP trials.

Not all the big awards are from patent disputes, but that does not mean the amounts are less impressive. Witness Trovan, Ltd. was awarded $143 million in a trademark case against Pfizer, Inc. The point is made: IP litigation is not for the faint-of-heart or the light-of-pocket.

4.3 Patent Litigation Risk

In order to establish the likelihood of success in a patent litigation case, companies take into account three factors: first, the chances of being sued; second, the nature of the intellectual asset under dispute; and third, the changes on the law and structure of the IP system.

Being a possible patent trial target is, of course, contingent on the existence of credible competitors likely to challenge a patentee. Patentees should take into consideration the presence of potential claimants that may put forward concurrent claims over a similar technology. Also, the likelihood of patent trial has increased over the years due to the proliferation of numerous idle patents that are never exploited by their developers. These potential claimants are often parties that do not develop technologies themselves but merely arbitrage the opportunities opened by the uncertainty of the IP system, also known as Non-Practicing Entities (NPEs), which we will examine later on in this chapter.[1] In the meanwhile, we should note their relevance as part of the tactical considerations that IP holders should have in connection with potential sources of patent litigation affecting their "investment."

In the presence of potential claimants, patentees must balance whether they have enough resources to defend themselves against potential countersuits. They should evaluate their counterparty's capacity to launch a retaliatory attack by looking at her patent portfolio and previous litigation experience on IP affairs. Given the global scope of IP strategies, any counterparty with resources at hand may look around IP offices in the world for prior art, in an attempt to have the plaintiff's patent invalidated. On the other hand, it is also important to evaluate a potential defendant's ability to satisfy the judgment that the plaintiff hopes to achieve.

Recent cases have demonstrated how active firms engage in countersuits as a strategy to offset any tactical advantage gained by a potential plaintiff. A successful countersuit could put pressure on the original plaintiff for a quick settlement. After being sued in September 2015 by Fitbit for patent infringement over the technology of wearable fitness trackers, Jawbone, a company in the wearable technology market, countersued. Jawbone claimed that Fitbit misused its patents as part of its efforts to protect its market power and that Fitbit stole trade secrets after she hired some of Jawbone's employees. The case is still pending resolution, but the media is reporting the effect that it already is creating on the price of Fitbit's stock (Neiger 2016).

In another case, in May 2016, Groupon, the online deals company, brought a countersuit against IBM claiming that the latter had violated Groupon's patent related to a technology that allows businesses find customers based on their loca-

[1] See Sect. 4.4, below.

tion at a given moment. This action came as a response to IBM's suit against Groupon claiming it had infringed her 1993 and 1996 patents related to the "Prodigy service," technology that allows signing into an app with Facebook. This technology, said IBM, developed new methods for presenting applications and advertisements that allowed efficient communication of Internet content. Interestingly, Groupon spokesman released a public press note indicating that "IBM is trying to shed its status as a dial-up-era dinosaur," thus highlighting a public relations strategy that is intended to tame IBM's strategy in the courts, influencing the perception of juries.

A second factor influencing the risk of litigation is the nature of the intellectual assets involved. Some technologies are easier to bring to trial than others, because they are easier to understand by the public. These technologies, usually found in consumer goods, could wield higher influence over courts.

Some technologies are more likely to create an impression on the public in case of conflict because the public at large will likely be familiarized with them. In these cases, public relations also have an impact on the strategy to follow. Patents with highly visible features are likely to have the greatest impact on the alleged infringer. In April 2016, Bridal designer Jenny Yoo filed two lawsuits, including one claiming design patent infringement of her protected bridesmaid dresses, against David Bridal (Grimes 2016). Also, the legal dispute in the U.S. between Apple and Samsung in the U.S. over iPhone highlights the issue. The court was familiar with the technology involved in this litigation, namely utility patents protecting design features such as the graphical user interface used on the iPhone, as well as patents on the design of the electronic device. That understanding of the technology under dispute played an instrumental role in Apple's favorable outcome.

For this reason, technologies that are widely known by the public, or that are more accessible to them, are easier to protect than obscure technologies. Finally, a third factor is the implicit price that the effective legal enforcement assigns to the intellectual asset under legal protection. The scope of protection may change according to the structure of the legal system or because of legal change. According to a PWC report (2016), the decline in the number of patent cases filed and patents granted since 2015 in the U.S. is likely been driven by the 2014 decision in Alice Corp. v. CLS Bank, which significantly impacted the ability to obtain and assert software patents.[2] Interestingly, in China too, the legal changes are unfolding but in a different direction, which is changing the relative price that businesses perceive in connection with the protection that the law grants in that country to software patents, as Brachmann (2016) reports:

> In late October, China's patent office unveiled new patent examination guidelines which make it clear that software and business method inventions are patentable. Given a very high winning percentage for plaintiffs in Beijing's IP court, more foreign entities are deciding to duke out patent infringement cases in Chinese courts rather than American ones.

[2] See Sect. 1.5, above.

The factors mentioned above influence the odds of getting a favorable decision in a patent case. Here, the statistics show that only 1% of any randomly selected patent will be subject to litigation. Naturally, some patents have a higher chance of being caught in litigation throughout their life span. Pharmaceutical patents, for example, have a greater than 25% chance, while patents covering other key technologies have higher than 10% chance. The reason for this differentiation lies in the fact that some patents embody technological breakthroughs that introduce pioneering advances over the current state of the art. These original findings represent valuable knowledge that the parties will dispute through litigation, to win legal battles over that technology.

Similarly, patentees hold a special interest in asserting their patents over essential industry standards, because they allow them to leverage their position vis-a-vis potential patent infringements more easily compared to remaining outside of the industry standard. These standards are widely adopted in technology industries and include the following: MPEG movies, DDR memory, JPEG images and WiFi wireless Ethernet, and 3G/4G mobile phone communication. Patentees can prove infringement by mapping the claims against the industry standard, as opposed to focusing on the specific product. In the second case, they would be forced to engage in expensive reverse engineering to prove the infraction; in the first one, they would only need to check the industry standard to prove the infraction. The Federal Circuit noted inFujitsu Ltd. v. Netgear Inc. noted the point as follows: "if an accused product operates in accordance with a standard, then comparing the claims to that standard is the same as comparing the claims to the accused product" (620 F.3d 1321 [Fed. Cir. 2010]). However, the court also noted limits to this approach, where "an industry standard does not provide the level of specificity required to establish that practicing that standard would always result in infringement" (Casino et al. 2015).

Countries vary widely in their degree of patent protection, but on the whole, they tend to favor patent challengers. According to the Global IP Project, patentees only win 35% of cases (based on 2006–2008 data from 16 countries). In a similar way, a PWC Report (2015) records a slightly lower success rate (33%). The same study also adds that patentees achieve slightly higher rates of success in the following industries: consumer products, biotech/pharma, medical devices and computer hardware/electronics.

The parties anticipate the profit that they can obtain under a litigation strategy; yet, this assessment is increasingly undermined as IP litigation has become global, because that has made any attempt to predict litigation outcomes almost impossible. Although IP enforcement is legally national in scope, business considerations have turned litigation part of the global IP strategy executed by IP management corporate teams. This perception is particularly strong because dispute settlement usually confronts the same competitors in multiple countries. Therefore, the result of one lawsuit in one jurisdiction may affect litigation in the settlement negotiations conducted in other jurisdictions.

What then, drives IP managers' decision to launch a litigation or multiple litigations under alternative jurisdictions?

4.4 Choosing the Litigation Forum

The selection of the litigation forum is a key element of IP management. This step involves critical assessment of the odds of successfully litigating under alternative jurisdictions.

The winning rates of patentees asserting their entitlement changes according to the jurisdiction, as seen in Table 4.4.

In multi-jurisdictional litigation cases, these differences may lead to patently absurd results, as in the litigation between Novartis and Johnson and Johnson, on patents for extended wear contact lenses, reported by Elmer (2010). In this case, different jurisdictions produced different outcomes, in the evaluation of the same facts: the European Patent Office upheld the patent; the Netherlands upheld Novartis's European patent and granted an injunction against Johnson and Johnson; the U.K. declared the patent void; France declared valid and infringed; and Germany declared invalid. In the same vein, a PWC report (2015) indicates that 52% of appealed cases in the U.S. are modified in some regard, and if they involve the Federal Circuit addressing damages issues in an appellate opinion, the chances of such decisions being modified increases to 80%. However, it is precisely on those absurdities that patent lawyers leverage their knowledge of such probability asymmetries to calculate their chances of implementing a successful global IP management strategy.

Perhaps no other case shows the nature of global IP litigation as the turf of war between Nokia and Apple for the control of the mobile phone technology in the late 2000s.

In October 2009, Nokia first launched a patent lawsuit against Apple over wireless patents. Nokia sued Apple for alleged patent infringements of touch interfaces, caller ID, display illumination, and 3G and Wi-Fi technology. Nokia's corporate management was aware of Apple's iPhone success in the high end of smartphones, the most lucrative segment of this market. By suing Apple, Nokia's strategy was intended to position its own Symbian and Maemo platforms. As a defensive measure, Apple countersued Nokia. Ultimately, the two companies settled out of court almost 2 years later; under the terms of the settlement Apple agreed to pay negotiated royalties and signed a limited cross license of patents.

Then it was Apple's turn to bring a suit against Samsung, as part of its strategy to obtain a competitive position regarding the design of smartphones and tablet computers. Lawsuits and countersuits proliferated across Europe and the U.S. but neither Apple nor Samsung obtained a decisive win until 2012, when the former won a crucial ruling in the U.S. (California) that awarded $1 billion in damages. However, the award, which had been withheld down to $548 million, was appealed to the

Table 4.4 Patentee winning rate by selected jurisdiction

Dusseldorf	London	Brazil	Russia	India	Texas	Guangdong
63%	14%	30%	29%	37%	80%	100%

Source: The Global IP Project (Elmer 2010)

U.S. Supreme Court. In turn, the U.S. Court of Appeals for the Federal Circuit ruled for Samsung, indicating that it had not violated Apple patents on the iPhone's slide-to-unlock feature as well as technology turning alphanumeric characters, such as phone numbers, into links (Reisinger 2016).

To weigh the magnitude of this strategy, one has only to look at the number of countries involved in the litigation war between these two giants: 19 ongoing cases in nine countries by August 2011, and 3 months later the legal disputes expanded to 10 countries (Albanesius 2011). By July 2012 the two companies were battling more than 50 lawsuits around the world (Mueller 2012). Evidently, patent litigation as an IP management strategy has gone global.

Why suing simultaneously in different jurisdictions for patent infringement may pay off to companies that can afford it? This plan may give the patentee significant strategic advantages. Choosing the best first-strike forum is, therefore, critical in establishing a "first-strike strategy" as a means of obtaining a good first result that the winning party can leverage to settle disputes in other jurisdictions favorably. This phenomenon is not a trivial issue. Early wins largely determine the shape of patent trial strategies; this is more so in today's globalized economy, which forces patentees to file for protection in several jurisdictions, each weighing a different risk of patent protection. The broad variety of expected trial outcomes induces patentees to do forum shopping to cherry-pick specific authorities and forum or forums according to their expected winning odds.

The question, then, is what factors govern the decision of litigants, i.e., patentee and patent challengers, to file a lawsuit in a particular jurisdiction?

First, litigation goals influence the litigation filing process. Patentees weight the goals they expect to achieve through litigation; these goals may include maximizing licensing fees in one jurisdiction; forcing the exit of a competitor from the market; or preventing his entry into the market. For example, Texas Instruments' strategy relied on successfully licensing its vast patent portfolios. Once the largest semiconductor maker in the world, TI lost market share to rivals in the 1980s. In response, TI began supplementing its declining operating revenues by aggressively asserting its patent portfolio and licensing key technologies to competitors. In this way, TI was able to capture billions of dollars in licensing revenues while transitioning its research and development toward new technologies.

In devising an offensive patent strategy, patentees usually choose a jurisdiction where the alleged infringer has sales or permanent manufacturing or distribution sites, and the patent seekers are likely to obtain an injunction in their favor that will put pressure upon the alleged infringer. If several jurisdictions are involved, a quick order in one of them may force the alleged offender to seek a global settlement. Given that patent protection does not extend beyond national jurisdictions, the patentee may be compelled to obtain injunctions in multiple jurisdictions if he is seeking to force a competitor to exit the market or design around key patents. Global litigation can force a financially less robust litigant to decide to redesign its product or exit the market, due to the expense and risk involved. The alleged infringer's jurisdictional and global activities concerning the allegedly infringing products also shape the patentee's litigation goals.

Second, a key decision in any patent infringement case involves selecting the defendant. There may be scores, hundreds or more potential target defendants. However, once the patentee identifies these potential defendants, his strategic mapping only begins. For example, he has to decide whether to sue them in sequence or simultaneously; then, he has to consider the relative jurisdiction costs he will face along the way, and so on. Various forums contemplate different rules regarding payment of legal fees, but usually, each party is in charge of its expenses. Hence, the burden on the alleged infringer of paying legal fees in multiple jurisdictions may foster settlement. Also, a publicly held company may be an easier target to obtain a quick settlement, because it is accountable to its shareholders.

Third, the centralized or decentralized structure of IP jurisdictions in some countries may influence the level of protection. Litigation may also be contingent to whether the jurisdiction where it takes place sets forth a single court that hears IP cases – either statutorily or de facto – or whether there are several competing courts. Courts act haphazardly in countries with centralized IP jurisdictions; even more so in countries where concurrent jurisdictions exist. Such varying litigation options range from jurisdictions that tend to favor a low patentee rate (e.g., the Patents Court in London), to countries with a reputation for being patentee-friendly (e.g., Dusseldorf, Germany).

Overall, the trend is increasingly pushing towards a single IP specialty court. For example, Taiwan moved to one specialty court (2008); France followed soon (2010); then Switzerland followed (2011). Other countries like Germany, Spain, and Italy remain sided with the multi-court system, along with the U.S., Japan, China and South Korea (Elmer 2010). Obviously, forum shopping in countries where several first instance IP courts coexist triggers incentives to deploy first-strike strategies.

Obviously, in the forum shopping calculation, the plaintiffs usually consider their home-court advantage. Plaintiffs often favor suing in their home court, which may give them an emotional strategic advantage. Sometimes the results are perplexing. In August 2012, a California federal jury awarded Apple Inc. over $1 billion in its smartphone patent infringement suit against Samsung Electronics Co. Ltd.—the largest patent verdict ever. The same day, a Korean court issued a split decision widely seen as more favorable to Samsung, and, recently, a Japanese court ruled against Apple outright, ordering the U.S. company to pay Seoul-based Samsung's legal costs. Moreover, suing an opponent on its home court can provide substantial leverage where the alleged infringer's exposure is high in its home court. As said above, much of the IP strategy rests on intelligently using the media coverage, to get the attention of the opponent's management. Samsung employed this strategy in its dispute with Sharp, in which it countersued Sharp in Japan Sharp's home country (Seah 2012).

The foregoing shows why patentees must weight comparative law before deciding to sue. Due to different legal standards, available defenses and protective scope, the outcome of litigation could differ significantly. Patentees could lose validity or infringement claims in one jurisdiction but not another. The notion of what constitutes "prior art" differs between Europe and the United States, with the likelihood of obtaining different results. This contrast is particularly evident in the area of software protection, for example. Due to this phenomenon, global patent litigation strategies requires costly planning and coordination among several law firms operating in different jurisdictions. Although consistency is ideal, it is unlikely that a loss in one case will cause a loss in another case in a different jurisdiction.

4.5 Non-practicing Entities: The Two Sides of Offensive Patent Aggregation

One recent example of litigation is the offensive use of patents by shell companies with no real assets but patents that threaten litigation with other firms supported on their patent portfolios. Ambivalent as the Yin and Yang of the Chinese philosophy,[3] these companies, referred to as NPEs, are seen by some as an eminently predatory patent ("patent trolls"), and by others as useful "Patent Monetizing Entities." These entities NPEs come in all types and sizes from the lone inventor in his garage to multi-billion dollar patent aggregators and consortiums. Examples include Intellectual Ventures, an investment company and one of the top five holders of U.S. patents. This NPE has acquired over 70,000 patents, mostly through purchases, and makes its money by licensing the technology to operate companies in virtually every technology sector. Another example is Acacia Research, a publicly traded patent licensing company with 160 different patent portfolios across all industries. Acacia licenses and enforces through various subsidiaries.

NPEs do not make any products but license their patent portfolios to operate businesses. They seek no other objective but to profit from the information gaps that the complexity of the patent system creates. Uncertainty about IP ownership in times of disruptive innovation can multiply the number of disputes between firms that seek to occupy disputed niches through a strategic accumulation of patents. Litigation then becomes an alternative to the priority registration mechanism.

Innovations that their developers cannot commercialize boost the emergence of specialized companies that sell technologies in "hibernation." In these cases, the NPEs acquire portfolios of technologies that then allegedly used to intimidate and get financial compensation from companies with a little financial capacity to maintain extensive litigation. In this view, the defendants obtained the reason in 92% of cases initiated by NPE plaintiffs. However, patent traders seek out of court settlement in 86% of cases due to the inability of small firms to keep the costs of such litigation innovative companies.

Let us measure the size of the problem. In 2015, NPEs filed around two-thirds (66.9%) of all patent lawsuits. According to Unified Patents (2015), "that is up from 61% last year. About two-thirds of patent lawsuits are filed in the high-tech sector.

[3] In Chinese philosophy, Yin and Yang ("dark—bright") describe how opposite or contrary forces are complementary, interconnected, and interdependent in the natural world, and how they interrelate to one another. People often think tangible dualities (such as light and dark, fire and water, expanding and contracting) are physical manifestations of the duality that Yin and Yang show.

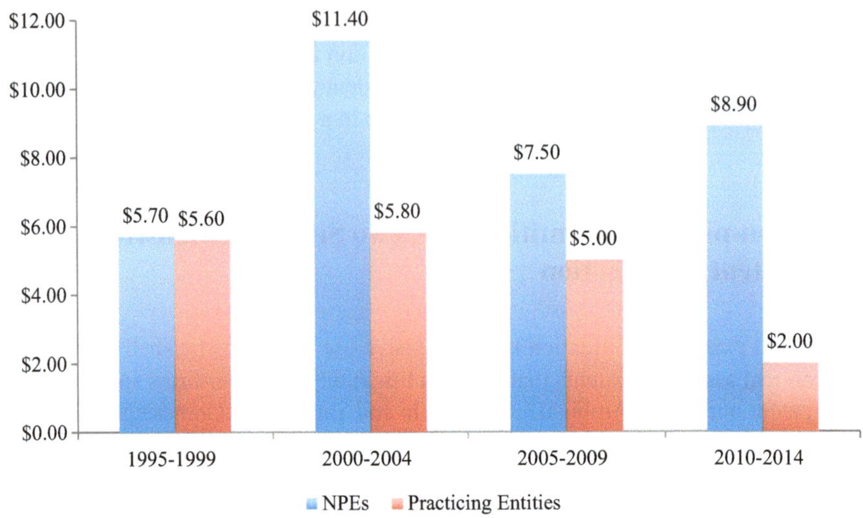

Fig. 4.2 Median damages awards in the U.S.: NPEs vs. practicing entities (X US$1000) (Source: PWC 2015)

Of the high-tech cases, more than 88 percent involved NPEs." To put this in perspective, 1998 had fewer than 250 companies engaged in litigation against NPEs; by 2010, the number had risen to 2600 (Ghafele and Gibert 2009: 23). The White House published a report in 2013 indicating that the cost of these (allegedly) predatory tactics reached only the sum of $29 billion in 2011 (money that could have been invested in innovation but had to be used to pay litigation), and $300 billion in the preceding 4 years.

Why are NPEs so influential in IP markets? The answer is their high litigation success rate. NPEs take advantage of the uneven legal treatment afforded by different courts to the same substantive issues involved in patent litigation.[4] As a result, their success rate is very high. Even though at the summary judgment stage NPEs only win in 4% of identified decisions, as opposed to 10% for practicing entities, their scores at the trial success rates are comparable, at roughly two-thirds. Over the last 20 years, the overall success rate for practicing entities is almost 10% higher than that for NPEs, which speaks of the latter's success in wielding their clout over practicing entities (PWC 2015).

The market for NPEs remains highly attractive. NPEs perceive much higher damages awards about practicing entities. Since the early 2000s, NPEs awards increased to almost 4.5 times the median for practicing entities (Fig 4.2).

Closson (2009) traces one of the earliest cases of patent trolling back to the sewing machine patent pooling case referred to above. In this case, one of the five participants of the pool was Mr. Elias Howe, who did not manufacture; nevertheless, he held key patents needed for the pool to be sustainable. Leveraging his strategic

[4] See Sect. 5.2 below.

position, Mr. Howe obtained a higher royalty on each license made using his technology from the patent pool entered by all sewing machine manufacturers, compared to the rest of the patent pool members.

On the one hand, those who object to NPEs activities argue that their business model is inherently predatory. Such predation stems from the opportunity NPEs perceive in high litigation costs. Out-of-court settlement typically is lower than patent litigation costs because of the way litigation rules are structured. Many jurisdictions do not impose liability against frivolous prosecution; indeed, it would be hard to prove malicious intent from a plaintiff in patent trials because judges usually have competing allegations about patent claims that often constitute reasonable probable cause. Even if the victim party could seek compensation, it is unlikely that it could bear the high litigation costs until the trial ends. NPEs take advantage of this institutional flaw, so they can aggressively put pressure on SMIEs to yield their patent holdings at a discount, or face bankruptcy, as there is little the company can do to offset its exposure to the "troll."

On the other hand, others, like Khan (2013) perceive the NPEs as relevant entities in a world where disruptive technologies multiply the number of innovative companies, but at the same time, they cannot place their technologies on the market for financial reasons. The NPE supplement this deficiency, acquiring portfolios then sold on the market. Now thousands of single patent owners and small high-tech start-ups are able, for the first time, to monetize the enormous investments in time, money and ingenuity that they have made in their inventions. If NPEs were not able to sue for the patent portfolios they acquire, these technologies, acquired from start-ups, would lack value; it follows that the original owners of these patents would not be able to liquidate their investments either. As Benjamin (2010) indicates:

> "What should (small start-ups) do? Not sell out (to NPEs) so large multinational high-tech firms will not be harmed when the patent trolls try to extort money from them with "frivolous lawsuits" and "jeopardize the future development of key technologies"?
>
> Forcing the multinationals to spend money to take 'troublesome patents' off the market has created a new investment market for owners of intellectual property to be able to liquidate them and monetize all their hard work and investment."

In this perspective, the NPE agents are not only necessary but also essential, to arbitrate technology markets, given to involving significant information asymmetries. They identify valuable, yet idle technologies, and enforce them, thereby facilitating their release. From this perspective, far from encroaching technology markets, NPEs act as arbitrageurs of profit opportunities, enabling newer transactions to take place, hence they enlarge the size of the market, which in turn allows further possibilities for innovation and labor specialization to take place (Smith 1776; Young 1928). This reality is far from the outcry that the NPEs "stifle the future development of technology." Benjamin (2010) notes that such a claim has no bearing on a court case; it is only profits that suing companies care about, not future technological trends. A new study by the Federal Trade Commission (2016) acknowledged that the term "patent troll," does not help to differentiate those abusing the patent litigation system, and those patent owners that are not. In the Commission's words:

> "... a label like 'patent troll' is unhelpful because it invites pre-judgment about the societal impact of patent assertion activity without an understanding of the underlying business model that fuels such activity," the report reads. So the FTC officially took a stand against the use of the term "patent troll" despite how loudly that phrase has echoed on Capitol Hill in recent years."

Clearly, the level of increased litigation during periods of the introduction of disruptive technologies marks no evidence of any intention per se of preying technologies financially among weaker companies. This phenomenon simply shows that in times of rapid innovation institutional uncertainty grows because conflict ensues over entitlements affecting the new technologies and the realm that belongs to the "prior art."

Beyond the allegations in favor or against NPEs, the factual question remains: will NPEs activity increase in future years? The answer is negative, because of the legislative efforts in the U.S. aimed at offsetting them. The U.S. has introduced a sweeping overhaul of its legal framework on patents, in an attempt to curb the activity of NPEs. That effort includes important legal changes in the Leahy-Smith America Invents Act, which was passed on March 16, 2013. This law changed the basic U.S. "first-to-invent" patenting standard for the "first-inventor-to-file," which the rest of the world applies. That change modified the U.S. standard applied since 1952. In the new system, as long as the inventor is the first to file, she is the rightful owner of that invention. By contrast, in the previous first-to-invent system, the patent would be awarded to whoever could prove to be the first to develop the technology.

- Other changes introduced by the AIA include: NPEs cannot file infringement suits against dozens of defendants in a single action.
- A third party can take control of a transferred patent (for example, inventor sells his/her patent to third party) as it goes through the application process.
- Proceedings in the USPTO make it more efficient to challenge issued patents.
- The "micro entities" filing fee is substantially lower than fees for larger entities.

Moreover, by 2016 thirty-two states had introduced legislation to create or amend state laws that punish bad faith patent assertions. At the federal level, two current bills address "litigation abuse by patent trolls." The Innovation Bill aims to curb abusive practices through provisions such as heightened pleadings requirements, limitations on discovery, shifting attorney fees for SMIEs, the disclosure of real-party-in-interest information and stays of customer suits. The Protecting American Talent and Entrepreneurship Act ("The Patent Bill") covers heightened pleading standards, early infringement contention disclosure, stays of suits against customers, limits on discovery and provisions allowing for attorney fee awards (Pelletier 2016). One can expect the U.S. Congress will pass Federal legislation (the Innovation Act and the Patent Act) soon regarding this problem.

The legislative trend follows previous recent case law. In 2014, the U.S. Supreme Court created conditions for a more favorable litigation environment towards SMIEs victims of NPEs. In Nautilus Inc. and Biosig Instruments Inc.,[5] the Court narrowed

---

[5] https://www.supremecourt.gov/opinions/13pdf/13-369_1idf.pdf

the scope of frivolous claims over software patents, which in this particular case the judges perceived linked to an "abstract idea." In other words, they interpreted the patent claim to be so vague that it should be dismissed. Moreover, in Octane Fitness LLC v. Icon Health & Fitness Inc.,[6] and in Highmark Inc. v. Allcare Health Management Systems, Inc.[7] the Court expressly shifted attorneys' fees against plaintiffs who bring weak patent claims. However, even though Mullin (2016) indicates that "the price of beating a bad patent is, potentially, 80 to 90 percent less than it was a few years ago" there may still be space for patent trolls asking for $25,000 or $50,000 to score settlements. The reason is simple: In the event of final success at the end of the trial the SMIE knows that it will have to spend a few hundred thousand dollars in litigation – a hefty sum.

Far from discouraging them, these costs have induced corporations to increasingly include litigation into the portfolio of tactical options to execute their IP management strategy at a global level. This is by no means confined to corporations in developed countries; emerging markets are also adopting this strategy very quickly.

4.6 Avoiding Litigation Through Defensive Patent Aggregation

To reduce their exposure to NPEs some corporations have adopted so-called "Defensive Patent Aggregation" (DPA) tactics. They purchase patents or patent rights to prevent SMEs from acquiring such patents.[8] Acquiring patents from potential competitors expands the purchaser's patent portfolios, with all the benefits associated with it.[9] DPAs identify patents that might threaten subscribers of their services, acquire those patents (or the right to grant sublicenses) in the open market, and provide all of its subscribers with licenses to those patents.

Given their preemptive litigation origins, DPAs do not manufacture nor do they conduct much research. Rather, they pursue other goals of interest to their founders and investors. They purchase patents and patent rights pre-litigation and also acquire assets as early as possible out of active litigation. Members of DPAs have access through their membership and syndicated acquisitions to obtain a license to every patent and right the DPA owns. Patents and rights to which they are licensed can never be used defensively against them. DPAs often include significant high-tech names such as Apple, eBay, Google, Intel, Microsoft, Nokia, and Sony, as well as the universities of Pennsylvania and Notre Dame. Nations such as China, France, South Korea, and Taiwan even have their mass aggregators to varying degrees.

---

[6] https://www.supremecourt.gov/opinions/13pdf/12-1184_gdhl.pdf

[7] https://www.supremecourt.gov/opinions/13pdf/12-1163_8o6g.pdf

[8] The threat of potential litigation has induced this particular form of patent trading. See Sect. 3.3 below.

[9] See Sect. 1.4 above.

Defensive patent pools entities are not intended to generate revenues per se. Rather, these objects render a service analogous to an insurance policy. Membership fees are set up to provide a pool of resources that supports IP acquisitions and the administrative costs to operate the pool. However, unlike traditional insurance costs, where the payment becomes available only if accidents happen, patent pools are designed to reduce the likelihood of accidents (i.e., being sued for patent infringement) from happening at all.

Therefore, the goal of these entities is patent aggregation alone, not to exploit the technology underlying the patents they acquire for the portfolio. As noted above, businesses enjoying large patent portfolios stand a higher chance of succeeding in the market, due to the difficulties of patent brokers to evaluate the scope and validity of any given patent claim. Orr (2013: 526) explains this rationale:

> "Practicing entities thus enter a virtual "arms race" under which they seek to build portfolios that will deter potential infringement claims by signaling their ability to bring substantial infringement counterclaims, thus encouraging would-be complainants to cross-license or settle disputes rather than resorting to costly and potentially disruptive litigation." Accordingly, an aggregated patent portfolio provides a stronger patent position than the sum of its patent parts – a kind of "super-patent."

Patent aggregation strategies are not limited to SMIEs. In July 2011, several high-tech big players (including Apple, Microsoft, Sony, and Research in Motion) outbid Google's attempt to acquire 6000 patents auctioned in the Nortel Networks' liquidation process for $4.5 billion. Shortly afterward, on another deal, Google acquired Motorola Mobility for $12.5 billion, including the latter's patent portfolio that included 17,000 existing patents and 7500 pending patent applications.

Sometimes, membership or association with a patent defensive aggregation consortium could backfire. In a 2012 case, SoftView LLC v. Apple Inc. and others, the District Court of Delaware found that membership to a Defensive Patent Aggregation (DPA) service showed that the parties had pre-suit knowledge of an allegedly infringed patent. Thus, they had willful intent to infringe the patent; therefore the Court imposed treble damages. In such a case, membership to a DPA consortium would not be a sound IP strategy.

In May 2009, SoftView entered in negotiations with RPX, a patent aggregation service, to explore the possibility of licensing some of its patents associated with the scalable display of Internet content on mobile devices. To this effect, SoftView disclosed its patents to RPX. SoftView alleged that the defendants acquired pre-suit knowledge of SoftView's first patent as a result of their corporate membership in RPX Corporation and that these defendants acquired pre-suit knowledge of the newly issued patent through their relationship with RPX.

The court supported the plaintiff's charge that the accused had pre-suit knowledge of both its patents. Specifically, it found that the very business model of this corporation induced her to communicate with its clients, i.e., the defendants about patents that would be of their interest. In fact, RPX would not have pursued the purchase of the SoftView patents if its members were not interested, and that RPX presumably determines what is of interest to its members by communicating with them (Brunsvold et al. 2012).

Thus, while patent aggregation provides a valuable service for firms preempting litigation, it can also work to their disadvantage. It depends very much on the side the relevant parties take. This finding provides an interesting insight into how the outcome of IP management is contingent to the position of the parties in a potential or actual litigation, and therefore, may not be a suitable IP strategy to follow.

Let us move one step further. Litigation costs, albeit difficult to predict and measure, in the end are knowable. However, there is another source of costs that the usual metrics do not compute. We refer here to the expenses of "not knowing" the institutional mechanism through which ideas can be turned into income. From a quantitative point of view, these are fees that probably exceed significantly the perceived legal costs arising out of the complexity of the legal system. We claim that legal expenses arising from not knowing the value of IP management are far higher than litigation costs. This chapter attempts to bring these costs to the attention of the reader.

Chapter 5
Hiding IP Strategy: Trading Secrets

So far we have seen the inherent uncertainty that the IP system creates as a result of its structural complexity. The way patent claims are conceived generates a multi-layer, intertwined system of broad and narrow mixed claims that is very hard to fathom, and that adds to the lack of resources by patent offices, thus leading to imprecise decisions granting patents, which are a constant source of conflict. In other words, the supply of patent services is cumbersome, and therefore expensive; its price is usually defined through less-than-optimal preemptive strategies or simply by expensive court settlements or litigation.

SMIEs often adopt secrecy as their IP strategy because of the high costs imposed by the patent system on them, as we learned in the previous chapter. However, often these costs do not present themselves in clear fashion, but underlie the system regarding transaction costs, as do the costs of finding the right licensees to contract with and the costs of searching for the best jurisdiction to choose in order to protect intellectual assets.

However, other costs are related to the SMEs' position in the production chain, which renders their technology too complex to disclose publicly under patent rules, or simply their lack of awareness about the potential lost by not protecting their assets.

In this chapter, we explore a third strategy used by businesses protecting their intellectual assets. It highlights how this strategy operates in the context of the SMEs, particularly concerning the Latin American experience, and develops some hypotheses about the possible cognitive causes explaining this phenomenon.

5.1 Secrecy as an Optimal IP Strategy

What do Facebook and Google share in common with Ford Motor Company in 1913? Surprisingly, a lot. As Hunshell (1984) described in his chapter about Ford and the rise of mass production:

I. De Leon, J. Fernandez Donoso, *Innovation, Startups and Intellectual Property Management*, DOI 10.1007/978-3-319-54906-4_5

Henry Ford allowed an extensive amount of experimentation to be carried out in the factory [...]. Ford had attracted to his factory a core of perhaps a dozen or a dozen and half young, gifted mechanics, none of whom had developed set ways of doing things. Encouraged by Ford, this group carried out production experiments and worked out fresh ideas [...]. Until about two years before the introduction of the Model T the factory of the Ford Motor Company resembled more closely a poorly equipped job shop than a well-planned manufacturing establishment.

Hounshell's description seems very similar to the story of any Silicon Valley startup. Just a hundred years earlier.

Indeed, one of the most remarkable innovations of the twentieth century is Ford's moving assembly line. Ford's innovation marked the culmination of the second industrial revolution, transforming industrialization and mass production before World War II.

However, was this innovation the result of a single genius invention? Historian Siegfried Giedion (1948) would write 35 years after the launch of the first Fort T:

Ford did not have to spend his life, like Oliver Evans, furthering ideas ungrasped by his contemporaries. He may have had the same indomitable energy; but he also had the advantage of coming not at the start but at the end of the mechanic phase. Success does not depend on genius or energy alone, but on the extent to which one's contemporaries have been prepared by what has gone before.

The idea lies in the hypothesis that Ford's success was a culmination of a stock of available knowledge at the time of mechanization (Giedion 1948). Moreover, the moving assembly line may have been inspired in continuous flow production methods used in industrial bakeries, mills, along with the 'disassembly' process in Chicago's meatpacking plant. According to this historical interpretation, Ford's innovation was, in part, a natural process of successfully incorporating available technology to his automobile's assembly line.

Nevertheless, this historical interpretation of Ford's innovation fails to explain a critical fact. If Ford's innovation was the result of available knowledge, and widely disclosed (Anton and Yao 2004), then why was the Model T Ford not perfectly imitated by competitors? By 1921, the Model T's market share was 60% of new cars.

Henry Ford's company never applied for a patent to protect the moving assembly line of the Model T. In fact, Ford had to fight a patent from 1879, claiming intellectual ownership of all vehicles powered by a gasoline engine. Moreover, Henry Ford disclosed all the principles of the moving assembly line. He even disclosed how much his employees were earning per day.

Indeed, Henry Ford disclosed general principles of the moving assembly line of the Model T Ford, but the public information was insufficient for a competitor to replicate the manufacture of the car (Hunshell 1984). An important part of the innovation remained secret. We have no further information of what type of contracts' provisions and disclosure agreements Ford's mechanics signed with the company. In other words, we do not know if Ford protected these secrets using NDAs to avoid strategic leaks to competitors. We do know, however, that Ford workers were paid higher wages than any other worker in any industry.

> *Henry Ford possessed a rare gift –or was unusually lucky- in attracting to his company well-educated mechanics who believed that "work was play."* (Hunshell 1984)

In the fourth industrial revolution, we would only need to change the word 'mechanic' in Hounshell's sentence for 'software engineer.' As with 1913's Ford Motor Company, today most innovative companies do not use formal intellectual property to protect their intangible assets. According to the U.S. Census and the National Science Foundation's Business Research and Development and Innovation Survey (Wolfe 2016), only 24.3% of surveyed firms consider design patents critical, 27.2% consider copyrights crucial, but 57.2% consider trade secrets paramount. In the U.K., the Intellectual Property Awareness Survey of 2015 found that confidentiality agreements were the preferred method of protection.

Why do businesses prefer secrecy to intellectual property rights that involve disclosure? So far, we have seen the inherent uncertainty that the IP system creates due to its structural complexity. The way the patent claims is conceived generates a multilayer, intertwined system of broad and narrow mixed claims that is very hard to fathom, and that adds to the lack of resources by patent offices, thus leading to imprecise decisions granting patents, which are a constant source of conflict. In other words, the supply of patent services is cumbersome, therefore expensive; its price is usually defined through less-than-optimal preemptive strategies or simply by expensive court settlements or litigation.

If we consider the decision to use formal intellectual property rights, we should evaluate factors such as disclosure, the simplicity to delimit and describe the invention, the costs of potential reverse engineering, the timing of protection, or the costs of obtaining and enforcing the intellectual property right.[1] As with all economic trade-offs, the decision weights the costs of keeping an innovation secret, versus the cost of disclosing and owning a legal right to the disclosure. Hence, an optimal strategy should consider whether the disclosure is sufficient to transfer tacit knowledge, or if the invention itself has a low cost of reverse engineering.

Therefore, several factors affect the optimal IP strategy, and in particular, the action of disclosing the invention using formal IP. Some factors are related to the specificity of the innovation, while others depend on external conditions (e.g. institutions, the rule of law, absorptive capacity, etc.). As an example, it would not make much sense to apply for the 20 years protection granted by an invention patent for products soon to become obsolete (Bilir 2014), or if the technology is extremely complex for any competitor to imitate it without the disclosure of a codified knowledge (Fernandez Donoso 2014). A well-designed strategy would take into account all internal and external factors, design the optimal codifiable knowledge to be disclosed in the patent, and use alternative strategies to protect secrecy (e.g. non-disclosure agreements, non-compete clauses, etc.).

[1] For a detailed literature review, see Hall et al. (2014).

5.2 Secrecy as a Sub-optimal Strategy

SMEs often adopt secrecy as their IP strategy due to the high costs imposed by the patent system on them, as we have seen in the previous chapter. Often these costs do not present themselves in clear fashion, but underlie in the system regarding transaction costs, as are the costs of finding the right licensees to contract with or the costs of searching the best jurisdiction to protect their intellectual assets.

However, other costs are related to the SMEs' position in the production chain, which renders their technology too complex to disclose publicly under patent rules, or simply the lack of awareness about the potential foregone of not protecting their assets.

5.3 Knowing and Not Knowing the Unknown

We have seen in the previous chapter how potential information gaps created by the convoluted patent system foster transaction costs, and how the system deals with them through insurance. In this chapter, we focus on a different kind of costs: those arising from not being aware of foregone opportunities that could have arisen otherwise.

The distinction is subtle yet important. Kirzner (1997) describes two kinds of ignorance: ignorance of specific knowledge, but having the knowledge of how specific knowledge may be obtained, and sheer ignorance – not knowing how to access specific knowledge because we do not know what we do not know. Kirzner says that sheer ignorance requires an entrepreneurial role to overcome it, which allows entrepreneurs to discover demand for products and services that consumers did not even know they needed or wanted.

This distinction perhaps explains where the missing entrepreneurial skills among SMEs may be. It is not so much on their talent to develop technical knowledge, but rather in their failure to be aware of the social setting (specifically, the set of IP rules) they need to wield to monetize their intellectual assets. The problem is relevant for us to gauge entrepreneurs' behavior towards IP management rules.

The current IP literature does not usually emphasize the distinction between 'known-unknowns' and 'unknown-unknowns.' In this literature, there is only one kind of 'costs': those that IP agents are aware of. The most extended opinion about why SMIEs do not use the IP system has to do with their fear that the system is tilted against them, in the sense that it favors businesses with deep pockets. Financially powerful firms may blackmail SMIEs, because procedural trial rules do not compensate the risk of the latter, and always create incentives for the former to impose their conditions. Either through forced licensing under disadvantageous conditions for SMIEs or through extended and costly litigation.

However, this is not in the calculation of entrepreneurs like Marie Sharp, who simply ignore the relevance of the use of IP rules altogether. Hers is a cognitive problem that brings us into a different discussion about subjective costs, and the source of SMIEs' poor IP management.[2] Ignorance, rather than fear of imitation, is what drives many innovative SMEs to fail to align to IP management rules and strategies, thereby keeping their intellectual property away from the IP markets, in secret.

Notice the very specific meaning of the word 'secrecy,' which we associate with 'hidden costs' of the IP system because of not being perceived by her users. Usually, the assumption of the literature is that secrecy conveys an express intention not to disclose information considered commercially important or strategic. Secrecy is understood as a rational reaction towards a threat — in this case, the fear of being imitated or stolen. However, in this context, secrecy takes a different meaning: the cost in which the parties incur without a clear sense of their consequences.

Many SMEs are simply unaware of the relevance of the IP rules, and the potential value that they embody. By not using them, the practical effect is that of concealing information that otherwise the system would process, turning potentially valuable knowledge enshrined in an innovation into a stream of revenue, i.e. monetization. Given these cognitive limitations, many SMEs will rather be inclined not to pursue patent registration but to remain in the dark, by keeping their trade secrets and know-how undisclosed for as long as possible.

5.4 The Cost for SMIE's of Using Formal IP: A Survey in Latin America

To understand the secrecy puzzle among small businesses, in De Leon and Fernandez Donoso (2016), we evaluated the perceptions of entrepreneurs towards the efficacy of the intellectual property system in six Latin American countries: Chile, Colombia, Costa Rica, Ecuador, Mexico, and Peru. The study assessed the perception of 352 businesses on four dimensions: (i) the time for obtaining intellectual property rights; (ii) the definition of what is likely to be protected; (iii) the uncertainty of imitation while obtaining the right is processed, and (iv) the ability of institutions to exercise protection of innovation after obtaining intellectual property (Table 5.1).

[2] Cost theory is traditionally related to utility theory. Under economic theory, costs are inextricably linked to the subject's projected want satisfaction. Therefore, the only way in which cost can influence choice is the perception at the very moment of choice of the satisfactions foregone (Wicksteed 1967: 391, quoted by O'Driscoll and Rizzo 1985: 48). Failure to spot an opportunity that the system offered through better IP management is clearly a 'social cost' that undermines wealth creation in society. For these reasons, we refer to these failures as 'costs' that could have been avoided.

Table 5.1 Number of firms interviewed by country

Country	Number of innovative firms interviewed
Chile	50
Colombia	50
Costa Rica	61
Ecuador	70
Mexico	50
Peru	71
Total	352

Source: De Leon and Fernandez Donoso (2016)

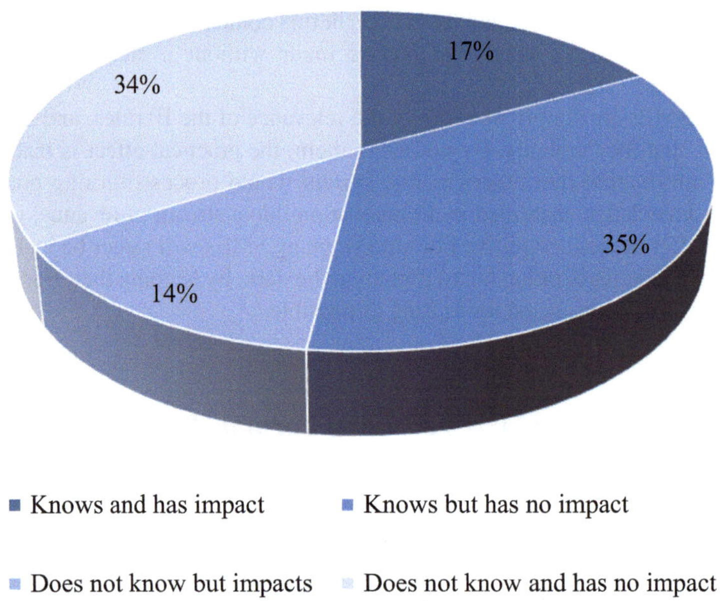

Fig. 5.1 Knowledge of IP system and perceived impact of IP strategies to innovative firms (Source: De Leon and Fernandez Donoso 2016)

Overall, 69% of interviewed firms considered that knowing how the IP system works has no impact on the performance of their business. Among those who believe that IP knowledge is relevant for business performance, only 54% think they know the system good enough to use it (Fig. 5.1).

On the costs side, firms do not seem to perceive unanimously that there are important costs of using the IP system, and in particular legal costs (i.e. hiring legal services). With a 40–60% distribution of firms considering that hiring legal services are not needed and needed respectively, the proportion of businesses considering that legal services are required is much lower than the share of firms that have never used the patenting system (Fig. 5.2).

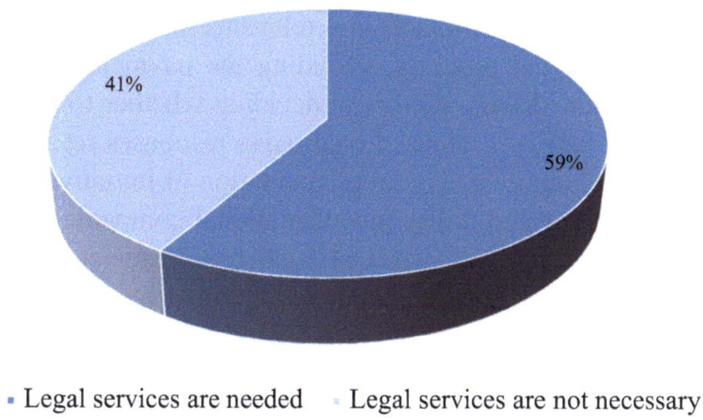

Fig. 5.2 Are legal services needed to successfully apply for an IPR? (Source: De Leon and Fernandez Donoso 2016)

Fig. 5.3 Innovative firms declaring if need for legal assistance and IPR enforcement (Park 2008) (Source: De Leon and Fernandez Donoso 2016)

In the study, there is a negative relation between the perception of needing legal services to use the formal IP system, and the IPR protection (Park 2008) of the country (Fig. 5.3). In other words, in countries with lower institutional IPR enforcement, a higher share of entrepreneurs perceive that legal aid is needed to apply for an intellectual property right.

The study noted that SMEs attach low relevance to the costs associated with registering their intellectual property, including the payment of fees to lawyers; therefore, these are their driving factors in deciding whether to use the IP system. Rather, the great contradiction accused qualitative responses regarding the need to hire legal services for patenting. The implementation of initiatives to reduce registration fees for inventions and utility models national companies, universities, and research centers ratifies the irrelevance of legal fees to register: despite reaching 75% of the amount of the original rate, they did not involve increases in the number of applications. Similarly, in Chile, the majority of respondents indicated that such costs were borne by the intellectual property office, INAPI. Neither firms perceived high risk to make public its invention by patent registration, fearing to become a victim of copying or imitation better positioned in the market competitor.

Most of the companies surveyed said they ignored the use of the registration system. Their responses reaffirmed this finding, which showed misconceptions and misperceptions about the costs of use and overall performance of intellectual property rights. The respondents' answers suggest that legal costs do not limit the utilization of the formal intellectual property rights system, but the beliefs of innovators. In other words, SMIEs do not realize that the system is conditioned on you; simply they do not know what it is.

Although the type of study did not allow to discern the precise innovators not to patent a case, it is possible to conclude that there is a link to the perception of the innovators who create an obstacle to greater use, either on patenting or other forms of intellectual property protection. In other words, innovative Latin American entrepreneurs perceive their creative and intellectual heritage unrelated to the legal system established for its defense, and thereby erode their chances of capitalizing on such intangible assets through ownership systems. There is a 'confirmatory bias' that limits their ability to return to a mismatch between the SMIE perceived utility of the IPR system, and what the IPR system can offer.

Confirmatory bias is a subset of cognitive bias that undermines inductive reasoning. People display this flaw when they selectively gather or process information because of their personal emotions or deeply entrenched beliefs. This bias leads them to interpret ambiguous evidence as supporting their existing position. Biased search, interpretation, and recollection of facts have been invoked to explain behavioral responses such as attitude polarization—when a disagreement becomes more extreme even though the different parties are exposed to the same evidence, belief perseverance—when beliefs persist after the evidence for them is shown to be false, the irrational primacy effect—a greater reliance on information encountered early in a series, and illusory correlation—when people falsely perceive an association between two events or situations.

In our case, the bias is reinforced as follows: given the perception of the system being useless, the entrepreneurs abstain from using it, which in turn renders the system useless. In the end, the negative perception is reinforced by a vicious circle.

To illustrate this result, we first must answer the question "How do entrepreneurs perceive the efficiency of the IP system"? Our claim of underutilization of the IP system may be partly explained simply because users (and potential users) perceive that the system is slow or unsafe. First, mover advantage is a key competitive variable when it comes to commercializing innovation. If the system fails to enable this benefit, either by slowing down with excessive bureaucracy or by not effectively keeping the secret of the invention while the IP is being reviewed, then using formal IP may no longer be the best tool to protect an innovation against imitators. However, the system may be well designed, efficient and functional, but if potential users perceive it as inefficient, the vicious cycle described above is reinforced.

Hence, we explore the perception of innovators about the effectiveness of the system and not just the official data of IP use. To do so, we asked firms to rate their perception of the IP system and then allowed them to expand their answers. Analyzing the text of their answers allowed us to confirm if the grading is consistent with their perception of the system. On the speed at which SMIEs perceive how quickly their IPR filings are processed and reviewed, we classified the answers according to the scale: 'very slow,' 'slow,' 'medium,' 'fast,' and 'very fast.'

Our interviews show that there is no unanimity in considering the institutions inefficient. Considering the extremely low use of the patenting system in these countries, we would have expected over 75% of interviewed innovators having a bad evaluation of the system. Except for Chile, no country has levels above 65% of interviewed innovators considering the system slow or very slow, or offering little or no protection while the IPR is being processed and reviewed (Figs. 5.4 and 5.5).

When we asked the surveyed SMIEs about their perception of the informal IP protection efficiency, in countries like Mexico and Ecuador, where innovators had a real perception of the effectiveness of the formal IP system, SMIEs also believe that NDAs and secrets are effective to protect their ideas. However, the evidence shows that most of them are using none.

Most innovating firms in these six countries do not patent their innovations, do not use NDAs, nor do they use confidentiality clauses in their contracts with partners and employees. If we contrast the percentage of respondents evaluating the system as slow or inefficient with Park's (2008) index of IPR enforcement, we do not find a clear negative (nor positive) relation either. We do not find that in countries where IPR enforcement is lower, more potential users evaluate the system with poor grades (Fig. 5.6).

Several causes might explain this confirmatory bias among Latin American SMIEs:

- Ignorance of the extent of their rights and the mechanisms to enforce them; that is, a lack of knowledge about the very existence of a functional system. This ignorance covers not only cases of absolute ignorance of the very existence of the IP system, but also ignorance about the quality of the claims ('claims') that can wield over his invention, because the system transmits no clear information on possibilities to enforce them in markets where the SMIE expects to place its product;

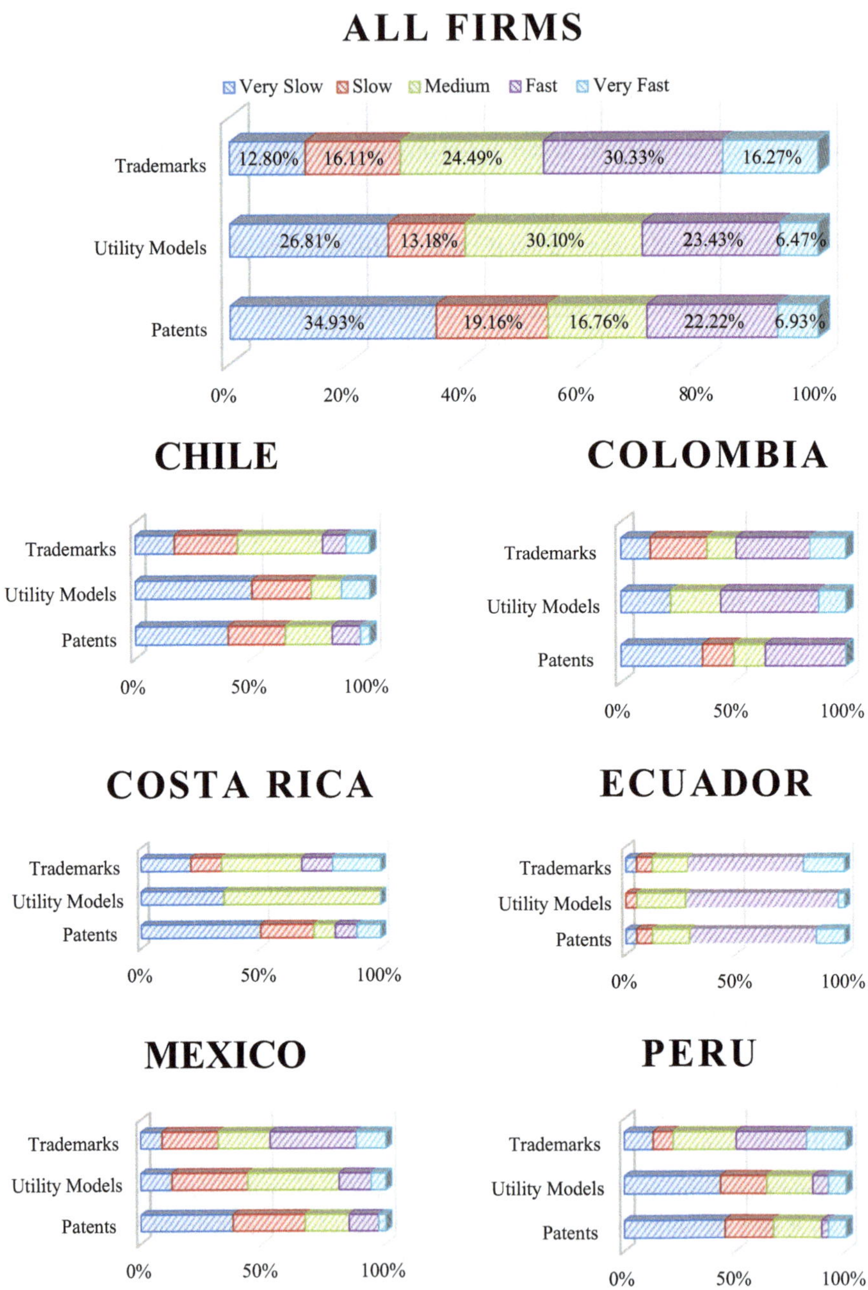

Fig. 5.4 Perception of process efficiency (time to process application) (Source: De Leon and Fernandez Donoso 2016)

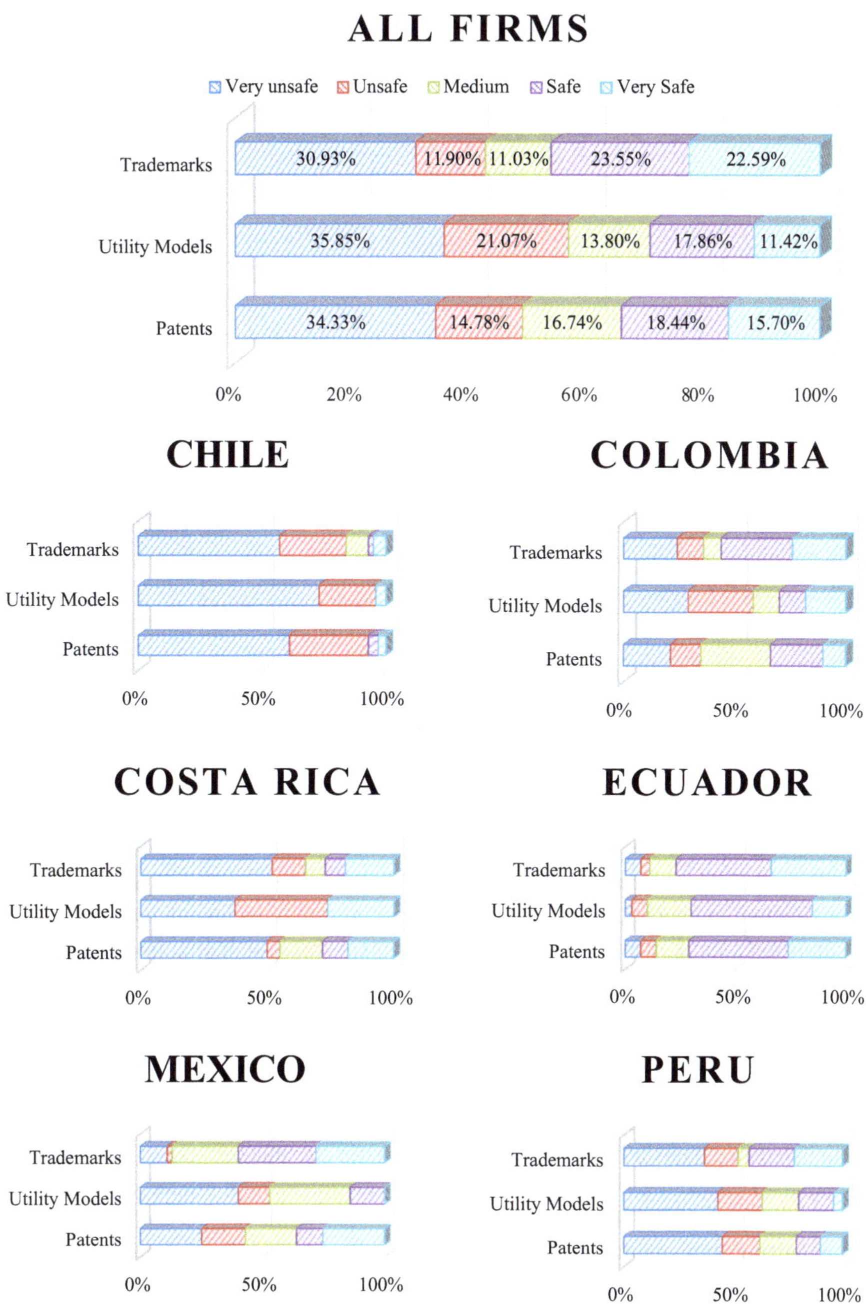

Fig. 5.5 Perception of system safety (likelihood of being imitated while processing) (Source: De Leon and Fernandez Donoso 2016)

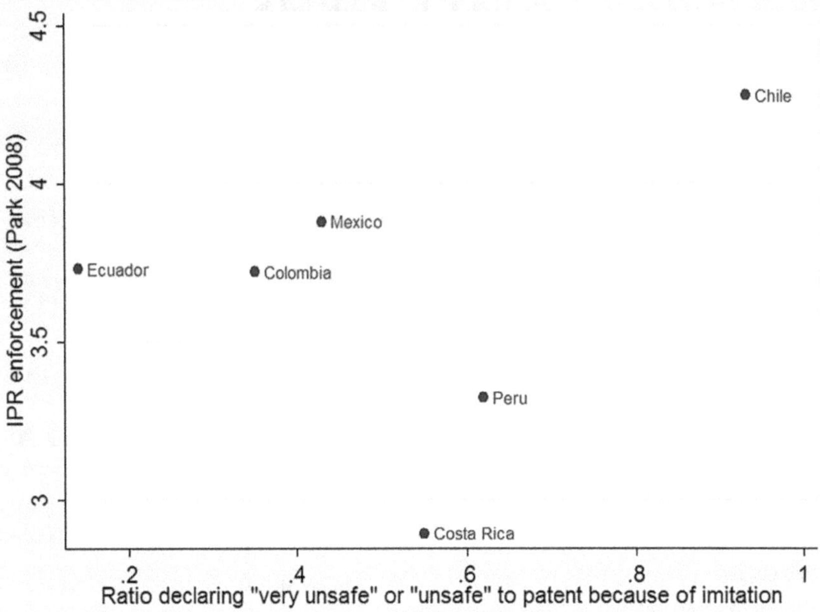

Fig. 5.6 Safety perception (imitation risk) and IPR protection (Park 2008) (Source: De Leon and Fernandez Donoso 2016)

- Their beliefs about the futility of using competitive strategies based on intellectual property and a tendency to act on these beliefs, despite knowing that there is a functional system;
- Their inability to structure based on intellectual property because they must use cognitive resources in many areas (management, technical knowledge to innovate, etc.), leaving little or no cognitive load to learn, internalize and implement competitive ownership strategies ('cognitive overload').

In other words, the entrepreneur does not fail to recognize the existence of the system or be convinced of its usefulness. He or she does not attribute the relative importance that it has, compared to other sources of his management attention. As a result, the Latin American entrepreneur has a problem of inability to size institutionalized mechanisms to capitalize their ideas in the market. These mechanisms begin their lack of knowledge about the use of the intellectual property system.

Another aspect of this cognitive bias is expressed in the perception between innovative entrepreneurs and potential venture capital investors about investment risk. Lerner et al. (2014) show evidence that proves how averse Latin American businesses are towards risk, which results in an obstacle to entrepreneurial activity. Possibly this hostility is linked not so much to the cultural malaise in Latin American entrepreneurial risk but systemic risk, due to the inability to 'internalize' the legal framework for the protection of intangible assets.

Naturally, lack of warning about the importance and use of the system indicates the unfamiliarity of Latin American entrepreneurs with international best business practices, and its remoteness from centers of venture capital. However, cognitive bias unfamiliarity evidenced in the use of the IP system, accused by a significant share of Latin American entrepreneurs could explain their inability to access capital to fund technological risk. Perhaps their reliance on family and friends for venture capital is then due to their limited knowledge about where they are and what the protocols are that one should follow to access venture capital funds.

In short, economic agents build their market expectations when they have a clear notion of goods or services exchanged for others; when there is no such certainty, because of cognitive bias that prevents them from recognizing the extent of their deliverables, markets simply do not occur. Empirical evidence shows that this is the case for Latin America.

Chapter 6
The Impact of IP Risk in the Development of IP Markets

In December 2006, Xiang Dong Yu, an engineer hired at the Chinese branch of Ford Motor Co., stole 4000 proprietary documents from the company before tendering his resignation and leaving to work for a competitor. The value of the secrets contained in those papers was calculated at $50 million. Yu was sentenced to 70 months in federal prison and ordered to pay a fine of $12,500 after pleading guilty to two counts of theft of trade secrets (U.S. v. Yu, U.S. District Court, Eastern District of Michigan, No. 09-cr-20304).

In another case from 2010, David Yen Lee, technical director in Valspar Corp.'s architectural coatings group since 2006, used his access to Valspar's secure internal computer network to infiltrate databases containing trade secrets and to download approximately 160 original secret formulas for paints and coatings. The employee was caught with the intent to hand them over to a competitor. An FBI study (2010) valued these formulas at $20 million.

These two cases highlight how IP risk can have disastrous consequences for firms that now handle their IP portfolio with particular care. Usually, people associate IP risk with the threat of becoming the victim of dispossession or theft by copyright pirates, patent flouters, trade secret thieves or brand impersonators. The concept of risk involving IP management extends way beyond the danger of exposure to open vaults or hacking.

We explored in the previous chapters how, in the event of uncertainty around the scope or enforceability of IP, traders confront three alternative strategies. The first is commercializing their IPRs over new technology; second, seeking rent through litigation; and third, refraining from trading (and litigating) by keeping their technology secret. Selecting among these three options is a matter of risk assessment, where parties evaluate the costs and benefits of resorting to any of these three strategies. However, IP traders not only confront uncertainty regarding the scope or enforceability of IPRs. In addition to the "systemic" uncertainty, they also face uncertainty on the value of the innovation itself.

In this chapter, we evaluate how businesses make efforts to control their stakes in the IP market through the valuation of their intellectual property, which may be

I. De Leon, J. Fernandez Donoso, *Innovation, Startups and Intellectual Property Management*, DOI 10.1007/978-3-319-54906-4_6

relevant to estimate the impact of IP theft, but also by missing an opportunity to seize a market spot. Such value is not confined to the technology developed but is contingent on the size of the portfolio of patents that businesses develop as a means to create particular zones or areas of influence in the technology input used in the production of a product or process. Next, we identify two emerging institutional mechanisms intended to hedge the risk of uncertainty over the value of IP. The first is insurance, which provides a mechanism that guarantees compensation in the case of damage occurring from IP enforcement, representations, warranties and IP value. The second mechanism is securitization of loans with IP used as collateral.

Next, we lay out the scope of our discussion exploring the notion of IP management risk.

6.1 What Is IP Risk and Why Does It Matter?

Companies face potentially devastating economic damages as a result of IP mismanagement. According to a PWC survey (2016), of 6000 respondents in the U.S. who have experienced economic crime, 15% have suffered IP infringement. The annual losses of international IP theft reach $300 million/year in the United States. Data theft, on average, costs $1.2 million per incident (2013).

Moreover, in the U.K., according to a study by the Office of Cyber Security and Information Assurance, in 2010, $11.6 billion was lost through IP theft, $9.6 billion from industrial espionage and $2.7 billion from extortion, with large companies being targeted. In total, U.K. businesses lost $26.5 billion, while the cost to individual Britons hit $3.9 billion and the government, $3.9 billion. Companies operating in the pharmaceutical, biotech, information technology and chemical sectors were the worst affected. A report developed by Create (2012) noted that 73% of companies surveyed had been hacked via their web applications within the past 24 months; 88% of them spent more money on coffee than on securing their web applications.

In principle, the theft of critical IP includes trade secrets, but it can also extend to product information, to negotiation strategies or client lists. For this reason, these are 'extinction level events' (PWC 2016: 14).

Assessing and mitigating IP risk is a central element of consideration for companies interested that undertake IP management. However, to understand IP risk management, one has to clarify first what is IP risk and what type of events lie under such definition.

In a strict sense, IP risk falls within the realm of phenomena that is foreseeable; therefore we can measure it (i.e. the probability of a judge deciding on the extent of exclusive rights on a contested patent).[1] Therefore, it is an insurable risk. The value loss resulting to a victim of intellectual property theft is also measurable.

[1]According to Knight (1921) risk applies to situations where we do not know the outcome of a given situation, but can accurately measure the odds. Uncertainty, on the other hand, applies to situations where we cannot know all the information we need to set accurate odds in the first place.

The possibility of measuring how some unknown event may put IPRs at risk implicitly means the possibility of such right being valued so that IP holders can transfer their risk to the insurance company by setting a price and underwriting a policy. Usually, such transfer involves four different situations of risk: infringement, enforcement, representations and warranties, and value insurance.

IP infringement claims reduce the value of the insured's IP. Litigation creates the potential for overturning the legal exclusivity granted for the underwriter. Insurance of this type of risk protects the underwriter against damages he is legally liable for towards third parties, such as customers and distributors because of a judicial decision or out-of-court settlement. Insurers have experienced traditionally substantial losses due to the adverse selection of the policy beneficiaries, who underwrite these since they are inclined to litigate their IP.

IP enforcement insurance protects the underwriter against the risk of not being able to enforce their IP. In this situation, the IP owner will be forced to pay legal expenses to protect his property. This type of insurance covers payment of professional fees and other costs resulting from the prosecution of infringers. Sometimes the liability is broadened to include contractual disputes against a third party for non-payment, and enforcement of an agreement to indemnify the underwriter.

Another form of risk has to do with the representations made by sellers or licensors, that the technology they trade belongs to them. This type of coverage defends against infringement/misappropriation liability and provides reimbursement for defense expenses and loss (awards or settlements).

Finally, IP value insurance protects the policy underwriter from risks involving legal claims against the IP that result in loss of revenue or value associated with the invalidity of findings. IP value can arise from future sources of income, licensing revenues, royalty receipts, valuation by IP experts of patent portfolios, research and development expenditures, and financial arrangements, in loan applications, securitization, monetization and investments in companies.

Some sources of IP risk are unavoidable in the short-run because their elimination requires institutional reforms that can only take place in the long run. Legal reforms addressing frivolous IP litigation clearly fall into this category. Legal reforms instituted to reduce the activity of NPEs, whether right or wrong, will take years before they take place. Moreover, due to the claim structure of the patent system, and the vagueness of other IPRs (both of which are unlikely to change) the probability of being sued without foundation exists, whether the legal system works well or not.

Other sources of risk are avoidable; these risks the company management can prevent or minimize if they are sufficiently aware of the need to act. Unfortunately, this is not always the case or easily anticipated. Sometimes, the harm deriving from faulty IP can go unnoticed, until it is very late. In an attempt to lower their production costs, Mattel began in the 2000s to produce inputs in China. However, it did not realize that for years the Chinese supplier had falsified quality inspection documents to sell illegal lead-based paints to Mattel's manufacturing contractors in that country. In 2009 the scandal erupted, and Mattel had to pay a $2.3 million fine and recalled more than two million toys after finding it was selling accessories and toys contaminated with lead. Besides the penalty, Mattel's brand heavily suffered in the process.

The patent insurance market is still incipient. Currently available patent infringement-related insurance products inadequately meet clients' needs in many respects. Policies tend to be limited, expensive, and maximum policy coverage is inadequate, placing restrictions on the owners' control over licensing and litigation decisions. Most insurance products only provide risk transfer and do not address the other important aspects of an IP risk management program. One way the market is addressing this problem is through patent litigation insurance, an extended industry in the U.S. In other regions, such as in the European Union, governments are increasingly subsidizing this service.[2]

The existence of IP litigation insurance shows that regardless of the unpredictable outcomes that litigation can produce, the parties know these costs in advance; therefore, they can provide insurance because they can quantify them through probabilistic analysis. Frank Knight's distinction between risk and uncertainty (1921) encapsulates the nature of these litigation costs as "risks." They include the risks of being liable to pay for litigation expenses, including fees for outside counsel and other service providers, such as witness experts; counterclaims, or declaratory judgment costs; and the risk of unfavorable settlement payments.

Valuation is a critical element of IP risk management. Assigning a monetary value to IP can be a strenuous exercise, but it is essential in understanding the damage that infringement can cause because it helps prioritize risk management activities. Additionally, the process of arriving at a monetary value can help IP managers identify how to integrate specific pieces of IP within an organization and may suggest ways that that IP can be better protected.

6.2 IP as Lottery Tickets

The way the patent claim system is layered makes it tough for the entrepreneur to establish a precise value on its patented assets. The scope arising from the statutory and treatise limitations as well as judicial interpretation of the patent claims open an array of objective probabilities allowing the issued patent to be challenged throughout its life. Once granted, a patent's validity hinges on the expectations of rivals that their legal attempts to challenge it will ultimately fail; their understanding of the interpretation of courts is, therefore, critical to encourage them to pursue this road or abstain from it. On this question, however, the terrain is uncertain: one court may reject patent invalidity in one suit, but another might reach opposite results.

For these reasons, it may be better to assimilate the IP system to a scheme that sets forth probabilistic outcomes that the parties involved interpret subjectively, by their particular position in the system as creators, IP brokers, research centers, litigants, and so on. Lemney and Shapiro (2005: 76) define patents as "lottery tickets" that confer their holder's certain probability the odds of keeping the integrity of the

[2] See Sect. 7.4 below.

legal monopoly and exclusive economic rights vested upon them. Such rights allow them to exclude third parties from commercially using the protected knowledge from the moment the Patent Office grants them to the time they expire, thereby such knowledge becomes part of the public domain. Other IPRs also convey probabilistic rights with respect to their scope of protection over their specific subject matter.

Of course, understanding patents as legal mandates adopts a formalistic approach to positive law that perceives their power arising from an act of government; it does not examine how likely it is for these legal mandates to produce their expected results. It is impossible not to consider the second issue, since the structure of the patent system, through overlapping, and often with conflictive claims, makes it tough to endorse the formal, even candid legal approach of patents as giving *unqualified* entitlements over their title holders.

Patents are in essence probabilistic rights. No one knows for sure at the time of the patent filing whether anyone will challenge her filing. Furthermore, even in the event of obtaining a patent, that does not ensure its integrity, since courts may well reverse them. A report by PWC (2016) explains that litigants in the U.S. appeal 80% of district court decisions; also, that the courts modify in some regard 53% of appealed decisions. Hence, only probabilistic calculations can establish how much one should expect traders in the market to value the technology embodied in a patent. Also, the fact that patents are perceived as opportunities to seize value, and not as unfettered rights to exclude others from commercializing an idea, explains why, despite being uncertain of how the market will value their ideas, inventors seek to patent many of them anyhow, knowing that most of the resulting patents will turn out to be worthless because they also hope that a few will pay off big time.

The probabilistic nature of these claims emerges from the fact that their scope and validity changes according to the intervention of reviewers as well as judges who analyze the extent to which these claims are legitimate. To be legitimate, these claims should be broad enough to encompass technological knowledge without conflicting with prior art, and narrow enough to differentiate them from other competing claims. Moreover, the interpretation by courts has changed over time; in fact, the scope of what is patentable and what belongs to the public domain has changed drastically in the last three decades, as the scope of patentability has broadened and the standards for granting patents have loosened (Mercurio 2014: 4). All this has added to the perception of patents being subject to probabilistic calculation.

How probabilistic are these titles? There are several layers of uncertainty that new technologies have to overcome before they can be traded in the market.

As Fig. 6.1 shows, the value of the patent increases incrementally depending on the certainty obtained at each level of progression, from the moment the patent is filed to the moment it is commercialized.

How much does value increase, as the technology gets closer to the market? Employing a dataset that combines information about cooperative licensing and the timing of patent allowances (the administrative event when patent rights are clarified), Gans et al. their (2008) find that pre-allowance licensing is quite common, occurring in about 27% of their sample. Furthermore, the administrative resolution of uncertainty over patent rights significantly increases the hazard rate for achieving a cooperative licensing agreement, and this effect is particularly salient in

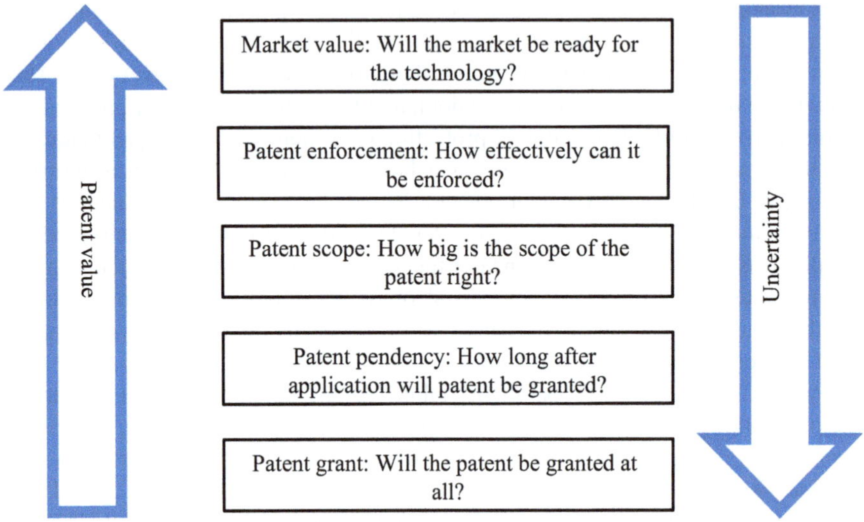

Fig. 6.1 Levels of certainty in patent grants (Source: Gans et al. 2008)

the period immediately following the patent allowance date. Empirically, the rate of licensing increases by 70–80% post patent grant.

Therefore, the likelihood of patent trading depends on how efficient the market for technology licenses is. If the information to obtain allowances is hard to get, the process may take longer. The need for disclosure of unprotected knowledge on the part of the inventor, asymmetric information between the licensor and potential licensees, or search costs may retard efficient technology transfer. In these cases, uncertainty surrounding the scope and extent of IP rights may make it harder to trade in the market for ideas. By contrast, if the market is efficient, the timing of licensing will be independent of whether the patent has already been granted, and productive efficiency considerations will determine license timing (which likely will be as early as possible after invention).

Finally, SMIEs face comparatively less favorable odds to commercialize their technologies. According to the European Commission, "The cost exposure for IP rights and particularly patent litigation is significant, hits SMIEs disproportionately hard and acts as a serious deterrent for SMIEs to engage in patenting in the first place." If we take patents titles as lottery tickets, it is undeniable that SMIEs are clearly at a disadvantage due to the number of "tickets" they can afford to buy.

6.3 The Challenge of Valuing IP

IP value assessment is the critical component of IP risk management.

The complexity of the IP system creates entitlements that are very hard to value; this phenomenon affects the alchemistic process of turning IP into valuable economic assets. In other words, perhaps the most visible sign of institutional uncertainty surrounding the market for patents and other IPRs – where risk failure is most apparent – is their value assessment. Even if one could figure the probability of these rights throughout their lifetime, this would not automatically ensure that market exchanges would occur. Parties to IP markets need to know the value of the underlying knowledge or technology protected by the IP.

Measuring value is the heart of IP management, and critical to calculate the risk threatening intellectual assets. Any trade, including both on tangible and intangible assets, needs a valuation. However, in the case of intangible assets, valuation is often overlooked because it is not easy to grasp. In the first place, IP valuations are needed to support transactions involving the sale of intellectual assets, licensing-in and licensing-out, joint ventures, mergers and acquisitions, and other negotiations where these assets are a critical component. Also, they are important to assess the value of collateral of secured lending transactions (Burton et al. 2014).

However, the list does not stop there. Valuation is also helpful to make strategic decisions involving tax or transfer pricing. IP asset valuation is critical to establish the quality of the intellectual assets to be traded. It signals to potential investors what startups have more sustainable competitive advantages because of their higher and more valuable IP portfolio.

Giving value to IP is way trickier than one would expect. Valuation of tangible assets is subject to less disputed rules. Accounting methods can give you a value of a company's inventory; they are usually internationally standardized and settled. Moreover, there is a good deal of market data that will give information about how much such tangible assets are worth.

By contrast, intangible assets like IP are much harder to assess due to the alternative methodologies available. These methods have different uses, depending on the specific features surrounding the technology or its state of development. In principle, we can classify all valuation methods into one of the three following classes: cost-based valuation, market-based valuation, and income-based valuation. Selecting any of these methods very much depends on the development stage of the company involved in the asset valuation process.

First, cost-based valuation takes into consideration how much it takes to create the asset historically and how much it would cost to replace it given current rates. This method is best suited to the initial stages of the company's development and before its technology commercialization because, at this juncture, there is no proper vantage point of value except for the costs of inputs. The cost approach is also better suited to the analysis of technologies that are easy to replicate because it takes into consideration the costs a company could avoid by purchasing the inputs in the market, as opposed to incurring in them internally. However, because of its reliance on past information, this method is unsuited to assess the degree of innovation inherent to the IP asset.

Next, market-based valuation examines comparable market transactions in comparable IP assets to establish a value. In this approach, valuation analysts typically research "the market" for both sales operations and license transactions that may be useful in estimating the value of the subject IP. Under this method, the analyst evaluates intellectual assets by comparing the subject asset to publicly available transactions involving similar assets with similar uses. This approach would be possible if there are other examples of new arm's length transactions with information about terms and conditions of such exchanges.

However, this is easier said than done. Hagiu and Yoffie (2013: 46–49) explain why valuing patents is tough, and no market reference exists. First, "comparables" for patents are hard to find because they are inherently unique, i.e. "novel." Second, even if the technology market had comparables, their value is contingent to the size of the portfolio they belong to, as well as the value they add to such a portfolio. Thus, if the portfolio they belong to is small, very likely there will be fewer buyers interested and their liquidity will diminish. In other words, entrepreneurs heavily discount the value of individual patents. Third, parties in the IP market face high search costs, as we noted above.[3] Finally, a patent value is highly skewed by patent litigation threat; therefore, many patent settlements reached out of court have more to do with the opportunity costs of avoiding litigation than with the fundamental economic value of their patents.

As with the cost-basis analysis, this method does not take into account the particular qualities of each IP asset but draws a comparison from other IP assets traded in a similar situation.

Third, income-based valuation measures the historical earnings and expected future earnings to establish the likely income stream of the intellectual asset under review. This methodology calculates the present value of future income streams that we can expect from selling the IP asset. It employs forecasted financial results based on factors such as historical financial performance, industry trends, and the competitive environment. Obviously, this method works best for technologies that have already been commercialized. For example, Dimech-DeBono (2016) thinks that the most accurate way of measuring IP value is the "Royalty Approach." In this class of income-based analysis one hypothetically assumes what a business would pay to license intellectual property assets as opposed to owning it; however, this method is sensitive to royalty rates and sales forecast used in the calculation.

Weingust (2016) takes a pragmatic approach that chooses a particular method depending on the case. In his words:

> [W]hen valuing IP, the analyst will typically consider the three basic valuation approaches – cost, market and income – and will further consider many different methodologies within these approaches. Ideally, the valuation analyst will try to implement multiple methods to 'zero in' on the appropriate value estimate but, on a case-by-case basis, the analyst will often find that a number of the methods may be precluded due to a lack of reliable data or because the facts and circumstances of a particular valuation do not support their use.[4]

[3] Section 1.4 above.

[4] These are the most conventional valuation methods; yet, valuing intellectual assets may be harder than it looks. Anson (2015) gives us a list of 25 alternative methods. Some commentators identify almost 30 different methods of value assessment – a fact that highlights the level of methodological imprecision surrounding this area. Let us highlight a few of these. For instance, the "Brand Contribution" measures the contribution of the brand, as opposed to other elements of the business profit. The "Replacement Cost" calculates how much money we need to develop a substitute for

The presence of so many methods highlights the difficulty of conducting IP valuation, and above all, the overall uncertainty that prevails today in this area. The multiplicity of alternative methodologies shows how difficult it is to measure the real value of an asset until market participants do gauge its qualities and use. As Barzel (1997: 4) notes, a full specification of the rights to an asset would require that both the existing and potential owners of an asset have complete knowledge of all its valued attributes. This endeavor is futile because of the novelty that features innovation. In the words of Harper (2015): "the emergence of new property rights to newly discovered attributes of assets is unpredictable in principle."

Apparently, certainty over intellectual assets ownership does not only rest on the novelty of the technology that innovators claim to have discovered. Rather, it depends on the conditions within which that technology will be effectively commercialized in the market, i.e. its capacity to be combined and recombined with complementary assets to deliver further value on other entrepreneurial plans. Novelty is just one criterion among many evaluated by an IP office. If innovators could not trade or license their patents, their capacity to complement other entrepreneurs' assets would vanish and their value would be nil.

In other words, the value of a patent does not only rest on the exclusive commercialization rights it confers to the patentee; but it ultimately rests on the ease and expediency to which entrepreneurs can trade it. One can easily understand why ceteris paribus patents are more valuable than trade secrets, because secrecy makes them harder to any value assessment.[5] The legal monopoly that allows exclusivity in the sale of IP would be of little value if they cannot market them.

As seen above with the cases of Kodak, Nortel and others, failure to do proper IP valuation can carry disastrous consequences to unaware firms. More broadly, too, assessing the value of innovations is essential to create innovation markets; if hypothetically the price of a good were entirely unknown; the transaction costs that emerge would render the exchange impossible (Coase 1937).

Here is precisely where the challenge lies, due to the nature of innovation. Patents' value is uncertain since their commercial exploitation is unknown at the time the Patent Office grant them. It is necessary for patentees to incorporate them into a business model that brings the innovation into the market. However, that alone is no guarantee that the technology will succeed in raising capital funds mak-

the IP with the same functionality. The "Reproduction Cost" measures the aggregate costs necessary to produce an exact duplicate. The "Technology Factor" measures a technology's contribution to a business' total revenue; it calculates a net present value and then is multiplied by an associated risk factor (the "technology factor"). The "Venture Capital Method" analyzes the value of future cash flows over an asset's life. It employs a fixed, non-market-based discount rate (generally, a rate of between 40 and 60%), and it makes no adjustments to account for the probability of success (e.g., a patent's success). Finally, the "Liquidation Value Method" measures the liquidation value for any piece of IP, which is the lowest price that the asset is virtually guaranteed to obtain in a distressed situation.

[5] Sometimes, though, there are still valuation methods that entrepreneurs can apply. In April 2015, Kolon Industries Inc. paid $275 million in restitution to Dupont Co. to settle the litigation involving the theft of their trade secrets relating to Kevlar bulletproof vests.

ing worthwhile the investment made to obtain the patent. Things are more complicated than a mere mechanical exercise; regardless of the efforts made, technologies need to be valuable to users or consumers to be tradable.

6.4 IP Monetization: The Alchemy of Transforming Risk into Cash

In 1997 the late rock star David Bowie revolutionized the world of copyrights by launching the very first sale of bonds on his music catalog. The securitization structuring involved Bowie's future royalties on copyrights he owned over his catalog. In exchange for financing, Bowie converted his future royalties from his record sales into securities and sold these in a private bond offering for $55 million. Thus the commercialization of IP receivables began. Later the popularity of this financial vehicle extended beyond the creative industries, such as patents and trademarks. IP securitization is becoming an attractive option for large enterprises; the question is whether it is so for SMIEs. To explore this possibility, we need to analyze this instrument closer.

In general, asset securitization involves a financial mechanism in which one party, the IP owner, called "originator," pools different financial assets and uses them as collateral to apply for loans or to raise capital from potential investors. The rationale behind securitization is simple. Assets are claims over "things," whether tangible or intangible; as long these assets generate predictable cash flows or even future receivables, they have a value that potential investors may be interested in negotiating for dividends.

Any future royalty generator asset may qualify for securitization, including intellectual assets such as patents, trademarks, trade secrets, or copyrights. All these assets generate royalties in the form of licenses; they represent the most valuable untapped resources for many SMIEs, which usually lack physical assets or credit score to back their loans. However, it is not an instrument only used by SMIEs. During its bankruptcy proceedings, Kodak used its patent portfolio as collateral to raise a $965 million line of credit that helped to keep its doors open.

How does securitization operate? The international financial practice has quickly developed alternative legal structures intended to adapt to the investors' needs and the extent to which the operator wants to hold her asset as collateral. These legal structures include IP collateralization, also known as IP-backed loans and IP royalty securitization.

IP collateralization is the standard IP monetization contract. It allows a company to borrow a percentage of the value of certain IP assets using them as collateral. It allows the originator to raise funds or loans by using a percentage of her IP asset's value as collateral. This contract does not involve the originator transferring her ownership over the asset to the lender.

SMIEs may be interested in looking for lenders, rather than investors. IP collateralization allows them a financial vehicle that helps them monetize their IP to use it as back-up for a loan operation. Collateralization also allows them to combine their IP as part of a package that involves other guarantees, as opposed to using IP in a stand-alone deal. Such IP collateral enhancement deals allow initiators to reduce credit risk, increase their leverage and to obtain lower interest rates. An example is a 2004 transaction involving a loan to BCBG Max Azria Group, a manufacturer of women's apparel, footwear, and accessories. Out of the $53 million deal, collateral comprising the company's portfolio of trademarks raised $12 million, through a guaranty issued by a third party specialized credit enhancement firm.

Collateralization allows the originators not to sell their property upfront, but to obtain up-front capital in exchange for a promise (usually, debt or equity certificates such as convertible bonds) of dividend payments at the end of the contract period. In return, the originator temporarily gives away the rights to her future royalties in exchange for the up-front capital.

By introducing a time delay in the repayment of the debt, the collateralization mechanism does a financial alchemy: it transforms the originator's potentially valuable assets into immediate cash without yielding their ownership of the asset. Not giving away ownership is intended to preserve the integrity of the originator's future capitalization, because, at the end of the contract, the originator can rearrange another securitization, on better financial conditions, if needed. To this extent, this option significantly improves the financial position of SMIEs throughout their critical initial development stages, without compromising their equity.

Before IP securitization emerged, companies usually exchanged future receivables into cash by giving away their exclusive rights entirely for a lump sum. For example, artists sold their receivables by giving away their royalties earned on copyrights protecting their artistic work. Following the same principle, patent holders, too, sold their rights over their patented technology. Of course, yielding their copyrights or patents would make these artists and innovators lose control over their intellectual assets; therefore, they could not celebrate new contracts under higher royalties as their artistic popularity increased or if the technology protected strengthened its value over time. Securitization, then, requires an asset that generates a cash flow. The more likely the generation of cash flow is, the higher the value of the asset-backed security will be.

A significant disadvantage of this mechanism is that it leaves the risk of the asset integrity entirely on the shoulders of the originator. Therefore, investors are unprotected from third party claims over the originator's assets in case of liquidation or bankruptcy, including their IP.

To tame this bankruptcy risk, IP royalty securitization allows the IP owner pooling and selling future IP-related income streams in exchange for a current lump sum upfront payment. In exchange for this service, the IP holder would transfer the IP assets to a bankruptcy special purpose vehicle (SPV) in return for a lump-sum payment. The SPV then repays the asset-backed security to the investors with the cash flows that the asset generates, usually by issuing securities. Thus, while the contract lasts, the IP holder is technically no longer owner of the stream of royalties produced by the asset, but the SPV's, who distribute them to the investors. In the case of bankruptcy, the SPV assumes all the liabilities arising from that operation, and the assets are shielded from creditors in the case of the original SMIE's bankruptcy.

The IP securitization program Sears promoted in 2007 around the brand names Kenmore, Craftsman, and DieHard shows how sophisticated these programs have grown. The company created a Special Purpose Vehicle called KCD IP, which acquired the ownership of the brands. At the same time, it issued $1.8 billion worth of bonds for investors. KCD charges Sears royalty fees to license those brands and uses the royalties to pay the principal and interest on the bonds.

From the viewpoint of the investor, IP securitization eliminates uncertainty because she will get a promise from the SMIE that she will obtain dividends and the nominal value of the bond at maturity. The bond the SMIE issues contains a promise of paying the bondholder the future stream of cash.

Of course, the reader will immediately see that the securitization does not eliminate the underlying risk of the asset-backed security. The whole premise supporting the operation rests on the assumption that the underlying asset will preserve its value. However, what happens if the artist whose image supports the future sale of the music portfolio (the asset) sickens? What about if a parallel technology catches the attention of the market and displaces the one embodied in the patent used as collateral? In the case of the Bowie's Bond, rating by Moody's fell considerably after illegal streaming of his music became freely available, through Napster. In the event of technology SMIEs, the risk is higher because it not only depends on the quality of the knowledge but on the capacity for the asset to be commercialized. This capability is contingent upon the successful execution of the IP strategies indicated throughout this book.

Given this risk, SMIEs require something else that adds up to the sense of trust potential investors see in this mechanism. Governments in some countries step in, as guarantors of the underlying value of the IP asset, by giving insurances or guarantees on the value of the IP for a defined duration. This backup reduces the risk of foreclosure and improves the overall credit profile of the SMIEs applying to a loan solely by their IP. We will examine these government programs more in detail in the next chapter.

No matter its weaknesses, IP securitization is increasingly becoming a favorite instrument for conducting IP transactions. Securitization is an attractive mechanism because it makes funds available that otherwise investors would not commit to purchasing or acquiring IP. Securitization has the following advantages: it gives the IP holder seeking funding immediate cash, at higher rating/cheaper finance, and a broader array of investors. Using intellectual assets as collateral for commercial loans is a growing practice, especially among Internet-based SMIEs, in the music industry, and in high technology sectors.

6.5 Uninsurable IP Risk

Some risks are not insurable. These are risks arising from unexpected events or future valuation that may be subject to entrepreneurial risk and technological evolution.

An old Chinese folk story tells us about arriving at rash conclusions for the apparent loss of value as a result of unexpected changes of fortune. The story is about a farmer who loses a horse, and goes like this: A farmer had only one horse. One day, his horse ran away. His neighbors said, "We're so sorry. This is such bad news. You must be so upset." The man just said, "We'll see." A few days later, his horse came back with 20 wild horses following. The man and his son corralled all 21 horses. His neighbors said, "Congratulations! This is such good news. You must be so happy!" The man just said, "We'll see." One of the wild horses kicked the man's only son, breaking both his legs. His neighbors said, "We're so sorry. This is such bad news. You must be so upset." The man just said, "We'll see." The country went to war, and every able-bodied young man was drafted to fight. The war was terrible and killed every young man, but the farmer's son was spared since his broken legs prevented him from being drafted. His neighbors said, "Congratulations! This is such good news. You must be so happy!" The man just said, "We'll see."[6]

Innovation is inherently uncertain because we do not know in advance its full implications. We do not know the value of things but in hindsight. Like the farmer of our folk story, we cannot know how new events will play out in the context of an uncertain future. IP is intended to narrow the array of possible changes of fortune by creating boundaries to the expectations that innovators build around the likely behavior of those with whom they trade their intellectual assets. However, we do not know in advance its value, and because we do not know it, we find ourselves lost in trying to establish whether trading IP under specific terms is convenient or not.

Take the case of Kodak. This company was the market leader of chemical photography during much of the twentieth century, yet their failure to gauge IP value doomed it. Kodak had paid attention to digital photography innovations developed in the early 1990s, such as the film-based Photo CD and computer printing docks for photos. However, chemical technology provided Kodak with the lion's share of its income. That led the management to maintain their old chemical technology despite the fast innovations happening around them in digital photography.

In fact, the company made a huge investment ($5.1 billion) in 1988 into the acquisition of Sterling Drug, a pharmaceutical company, with the hope of obtaining high profits by using its expertise in chemical engineering to develop drugs. Kodak, however, lacked the ability to transform this knowledge into a robust patent portfolio of pharmaceuticals. The diversion into the chemical industry proved fatal for Kodak, which was forced to sell Sterling for less than $3 billion only 6 years after its acquisition. However, the worse was yet to come.

By failing to migrate to the new era of digital photography wholeheartedly, Kodak sealed its fate, and that of its new digital competitors. In 2011, while Kodak was filing for Chapter 11, Instagram, the startup based on digital photography, hit the $1 billion mark.

[6] http://ymaa.com/articles/stories-proverbs/blessing-in-disguise

Kodak's failure to predict the value of the IP incidentally shows that this value is forward-looking, in the sense that their portfolio of patents related to the personal computing industry had more value than all of its chemistry-related technology, regardless of their 100 years of experience in this area. What mattered was the emerging personal computing industry and Kodak's possible insertion at the time. That never happened.

The point here is that entrepreneurial uncertainty is uninsurable, but that does not render valuation futile. What it means is that valuation is forward looking and speculative. For this reason, risk management must adopt a proactive effort that takes into consideration strategic issues, not only legal ones.

The realities of the contemporary business environment require a robust valuation and risk mitigation effort to realize the upside potential of an organization's intellectual property. This is the essence of a successful IP management strategy. The alternative is being exposed to all sorts of threats arising from the gaps of a legal system that, by nature, is open and never fully certain.

This is why IP risk management involves a high degree of leadership and, above all, vision at the corporate management level, to align the risk management program with the competitive goals sought. That endeavor may involve developing a program framework through publication of policies and standards, reviewing network architecture, and education and training.

From another viewpoint, this strategy is a reaction to the murkiness of the IP system, which undermines legal certainty in technology markets. Companies often have a fragmented IP asset ownership, because knowledge is scattered among them. Also, IP is often left unused; traders do not know where to find the right technology that suits their knowledge production activities, and deals are private. In mature industries, where products integrate different technologies, patent ownership fragmentation across companies may prevent businesses from investing in capital equipment and product development because they may not possess all the necessary technologies. Also, rivals owning close and complementary technologies may sue them for infringement with implied risk of losing sunk capital (Cohen et al. 2000; Reitzig 2004). Hence, due to the diversity of these problems affecting a company's IP asset value, they need to be treated holistically.

In short, risk management is usually understood in a monetary sense, by reference to the value of the underlying intellectual assets that are affected as result of some contingency. However, businesses employ a broader strategy to minimize their risks of diminishing the value of their IP portfolio. This broader plan involves not only valuation of the intellectual assets that would eventually be negotiated in IP markets, but an overall strategy of managing their intellectual assets in a way that takes advantage of the legal protection afforded by courts and government authorities. Usually, such risk management is a strategy that carries several steps: first, to identify what intangible asset is sensitive to risk; second, to allocate available risk resources efficiently; third, to address new and emerging threats to IP; and finally, to achieve compliance in the jurisdiction where these portfolios are managed.

Chapter 7
Government Strategies Towards IP Management

Two Brazilian stories highlight why proper IP management is important for firms to develop a competitive advantage supported on a better use of the IP institutions. The first one involves the licensing of biodegradable chemical technology developed at the Chemistry Institute of Universidad de Campinas (Brazil) successfully licensed to Contech in 2007 by its tech transfer office, Agencia de Innovación Inova Unicamp. The patented technology contributed decisively to ensuring Contech's leadership in the market by giving her time savings, as the production of paper could go on without the need to stop the machine for maintenance. The mechanical system applied biodegradable chemicals for pulp and paper machinery that did not hold up the production process. In return, the licensing agreement increased Inova's budget, in a win-win situation.

On the not-so-bright side, the licensing of Monsanto's Roundup Ready soybean technology in Brazil and Argentina showed the problems of not having a clear intellectual property (IP) management policy. In 2005, the company had decided to leave Argentina because of her disagreement with the government's lenient policy towards unlicensed domestic users, mostly farmers.[1] However, given the comparatively larger size of Brazil's market, the company did not want to leave but rather to push hard to get paid. About 98% of farmers in Rio Grande do Sul had planted biotech soybeans, mostly using Roundup Ready seed smuggled from Argentina. Monsanto adopted a gradual strategy implementing a program designed to charge a fee for the use of its technology, working with producer associations and other groups to reach a private agreement on the amount and method of payment. It took Monsanto years of litigation to obtain redress and to fulfill its strategic goals.

These two cases highlight the different outcomes arising from implementing alternative IP management strategies. Government policies largely shape the content of these plans through their innovation promotion policies, so it is critical to understand how they design them.

[1] Contech – News, http://www.contechbrasil.com/eng/novidades.asp?filtro=9/2014 (accessed December 20, 2016)

I. De Leon, J. Fernandez Donoso, *Innovation, Startups and Intellectual Property Management*, DOI 10.1007/978-3-319-54906-4_7

In the previous chapters, we noted how innovators and entrepreneurs react to their institutional constraints by implementing alternative monetizing strategies that include exchanging them for an up-front fee, a licensing royalty, or investing in a successful litigation strategy, or simply hiding from potential imitators while waiting for a client or partner to arrive. These plans depend on the particular circumstances of time and place that make them comparatively attractive, for example, how accessible and literate courts are to engage in IP litigation trials; how easy it is to find a licensee for the technology involved, and so on. In short, designing IP management strategies is not a step-by-step process; it is usually multi-causal and non-linear; therefore it is bound not to follow a single model. It all depends on the surrounding context where it takes place.

In this chapter, we explore how relevant the innovation ecosystem is and the impact of government policies on the design and execution of IP strategies.

7.1 The Institutional Complexity of Technology Transfer

A useful framework to examine the impact of the institutional setting upon IP management–oriented policies is the Triple Helix model, developed in the 1990s. It is a spiral model of innovation that captures multiple reciprocal relationships at different points in the process of knowledge capitalization.[2]

The Triple Helix model is intended to unravel the complex dynamics of a knowledge-based economy regarding its composing sub-dynamics. This model explains how the participants of the innovation ecosystem relate and interact, and how technology transfer flows among them. The design combines three different dimensions: actors, relational influence and its internal transformation.

First, regarding the agents considered in the model, universities and public science research centers, the business community and governments are interdependent players in the innovation ecosystem; their institutional spheres overlap and take the role of the other. Technology transfer is just the outcome of the interaction among several players in the ecosystem: universities and public science research centers, the business community and governments. In Latin America, the role of these actors

[2] This model follows the systems theory. Leydesdorff explains: "In the Triple Helix model of the knowledge-based economy, the main institutions have first been defined as university, industry, and government (Etzkowitz and Leydesdorff 1995). However, these institutional carriers of an innovation system can be expected to entertain a dually layered network: one layer of institutional relations in which they constrain each other's behavior, and another layer of functional relations in which they shape each other's expectations. For example, the function of university-industry relations can be performed by different institutional arrangements such as transfer offices, spin-off companies, licensing agreements, etc. The institutional relations provide us with network data, but the functions in a knowledge-based economy are to be analyzed in terms of the transformative dynamics. The knowledge base of an economy can be considered as a specific configuration of the structure of expectations which feeds back as a transformation mechanism on the institutional arrangements." See, *The Knowledge-Based Economy and the Triple Helix Model*, http://www.leydesdorff.net/arist09/arist09.pdf (accessed December 20, 2016).

has changed over time; we have been evolving from a model where government's influence encompassed industry and academia to one where none of the three prevail, but rather interact dynamically.

Second, the Triple Helix model conceptualizes a context of multidirectional influence whereby, for example, the government develops an indirect industrial policy instrument in the Bayh-Dole Act of 1980. Given the shape of the two other helixes, the change in the rules assigning IP expanded the scope of technology transfer across universities in the United States. By contrast, in Latin America, a similar rule change could have different effects, in the light of the weight of the other helixes in the system. In particular, the prevalence of government influence in the innovation ecosystem could require additional legal reforms to encourage further innovation before one can expect a effect similar to what has occurred in the United States. That could include, for example, introducing incentives for academia and public science research centers to do more industry-oriented research. Another impact may result in cases where industry develops technologies that influence universities, fore xample, through de facto standards.

Third, the Triple Helix model also represents an internal transformation of each helix, as could be the impact of further incentives to commercialize technologies created by academia, or by rewarding researchers through professional development based on their patenting activity record. Here, one needs to note that in the context of decreasing technology costs, Latin American businesses are expected to increasingly benefit from innovation likely to come from outside of the individual firm through open innovation. This is especially valid in disruptive, or non-incremental innovations (Eţzkowitz 2002). Also, the presence of standard-setting organizations is very important. These organizations eliminate transaction costs in industries featured by interoperability between many components to come together and voluntarily produce consensus technical standards (Hagiu and Yoffie 2013: 50). When these organizations endorse a particular technological standard, participants in the relevant industries typically adopt that measure and agree to cross-license or to pay the required royalties to the owner.

In Latin America, we need to adapt the Triple Helix model to the particular conditions prevailing in the region. In the region, venture capital is negligible (Lerner et al. 2014), and businesses nor governments are usually inclined to invest in R&D, which is merely a 2.6% share of the Total Global R&D spending, among the lowest in the World, as seen in Fig. 7.1.

IP management, also known in a narrower sense as "technology transfer," does not follow a single model. It has different forms and modalities, depending on the context where it takes place, the impact of IP legislation, and the internal capabilities of the authorities to do technology transfer. Monsanto's case mentioned above highlights the complexity of technology transfer processes; in this opportunity, the company's decision to leave Argentina, while remaining in Brazil, was guided almost exclusively by the latter's market size, much bigger and commercially attractive. Monsanto resolved that executing a long-term strategy of engaging directly with those infringing their IP was better than leaving the vast Brazilian market altogether. Market size, rather than any concern about the IP involved, was the deal breaker.

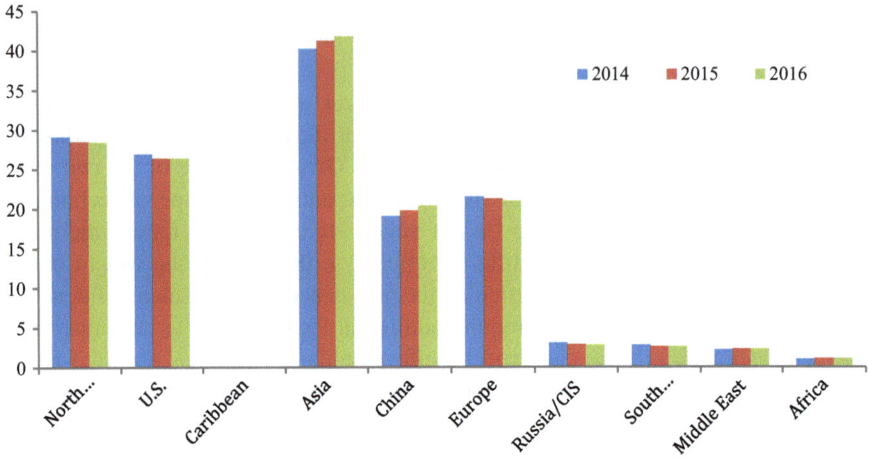

Fig. 7.1 Total Global R&D spending (percent share) (Source: www.rdmag.com)

Designing a government strategy that encourages intelligent IP management thus requires prior understanding of the innovation ecosystem that surrounds its implementation. This context takes consideration of factors such as the maturity of the technology, the receiver's expectations, and the commitment from the receiver. Ingvarsson (2013) identifies the macro level and micro level factors that may influence technology transfer. Macro-level factors are determined at the national level and may be harder to control in the short run. They include openness to FDI and trade; how sophisticated the financial system is; macroeconomic and political risk; availability of inputs (e.g. labor skills, capital, technologies, land); infrastructure; laws and regulations, including patenting and licensing systems; subsidies, taxes and other government incentives; and market conditions. Micro level factors include organization; work culture and ethics; social capital, power balance, activeness of receiving partner in searching for new technology; absorptive capacity and social factors.

Also, timing is critical, because the research must be in a mature enough state and the results from whom the technology is transferred must fit in the receiver's culture and business situation (Gorschek et al. 2006). The interpretative cognition of all the parties involved, again, acquires paramount relevance in deciding on these factors.

IP management also depends on understanding the underlying technology. In the beginning, the commercial value of this technology is not visible, because it has to undergo several stages, from unclear and ambiguous ideas to ideas that industrial processes can use. Therefore, the success of technology transfer depends on the moment in the life cycle the transfer starts. Pioneering ideas without industrial applications will not likely be selected candidates of a tech transfer program.

Moreover, the critical question is at which point the transfer shall start, that is, at which point should the industry be involved? Gorschek et al. (2006) indicate that tech transfer may take many years; this creates coordination problems with product business units, whose time span is shorter since they are driven by current immediate profits. By contrast, it is harder to transfer technology that addresses long-term strategic goals because receiving parties frequently focus their resources on developing capabilities for solving immediate competitiveness problems. Little monetization capacity arising from its long-term design is the reason why pure science is so complicated to be part of IP management programs. Other success factors include continuous communication with the receiving party, demand that an acquiring person is nominated early in the project, that some industry is championing the technology, a clear interest in the technology, and feeling part of the transfer.

Besides the best opportunity to execute IP management, it is interesting also to look at the operational strategies that are needed to be put in place; they highlight how complex this process is, and why planning is of the essence. Patent licensing, for example, involves intensive collaboration, that is, organizing meetings with the potential receiver during the project execution to establish the best option to follow to transfer the technology. These negotiations may involve variations, such as user buy-in, where the intended users advocate the transfer; or management buy-in (involving the opposite). Finally, the parties may decide to do a spin-off company, when the technology idea is strong enough to carry a new business case of its own, even though the technology is not in line with the strategy of the inventing organization, and work on-site. The complexity of the negotiation process involving licensing a technology clearly speaks of why governments are increasingly devoting resources to plan their policies towards increasing IP management strategies.

How do governments design these IP management promotion strategies? What are the policy options they currently pursue? Let us review three concurring policy approaches that governments are increasingly adopting to promote strategic IP management in the international experience. The first strategy focuses on changing the economic incentives through legal reform so that public funds supporting scientific research are funneled into industrially applied technologies. The second strategy rests on the development of effective innovation ecosystems spurred by business incubation. Finally, governments are increasingly supporting IP finance, to overcome cognitive failures that otherwise make it difficult for IP traders to negotiate their assets.

7.2 Changing the Incentives Structure for Technology Transfer

Governments promote a more effective IP management among SMIEs by promoting legal reform that rearranges the incentives that govern the allocation of IP assets and by clearly assigning IPRs among traders in the IP market.

In particular, IP legal reform may be needed to clarify the ownership of intellectual assets funded by public funds. In the U.S., this strategy allowed the federal government to decide what technologies to support, and how much to allocate to them, while leaving the operational details in the hands of licensees at universities, and university spin-offs.

This top-down approach began with the introduction of the Bayh-Dole (BD) Act of 1980 on the patent funding system of the U.S., which set up a standard that many countries later followed. This legislation changed the way public funding would be piped through the innovation ecosystem, by enabling the U.S. federal government to claim ownership of technologies financed through federal funds.

This top-down approach seeks to install financial incentives upon knowledge production centers subsidized by governments. Their goal is to bring a financial stimulus to universities and public scientific research centers by giving them a stake in the intellectual property over the knowledge developed at their labs. Usually, this policy is implemented directly through technology transfer offices (TTO's).

Before BD the ownership of technologies that researchers developed with the support of federal funding contracts and grants would nominally remain in the hands of the federal government. However, since IP ownership remained uncertain—researchers could always claim the IP for themselves—this knowledge produced with the support of public funds would ironically remain away from the public because no one would be interested in its commercial exploitation. Also, there was no uniform policy among federal agencies for the transfer of the technology into the private sector. As a result, in 1978 the U.S. government owned around 28,000 patents but had only licensed less than 4%.

By assigning IP ownership of subsidized technologies, BD gave universities, small businesses, or non-profit institutions the option of deciding whether to pursue ownership of an invention in preference to the government or not. These incentives fostered a functional innovation ecosystem whereby the innovations created by researchers at University labs and federal technology centers found its way to the market by stimulating professors and researchers to incorporate their spin-offs commercializing the technologies they develop through licensing agreements.[3]

Notwithstanding, the Bayh-Dole Act also encouraged universities to collaborate with commercial concerns to promote the utilization of inventions arising from federal funding; it provided guidelines to induce universities to file patents on inventions they elect to own or to give small businesses license to exploit the technology; it also lets non-profits, including universities, and small businesses decide whether to retain title to innovations developed under federally-funded research programs. In turn, the government retained a non-exclusive license to practice the respective patent throughout the world retained march-in rights.

[3]In addition to the Bayn-Dole Act, this ecosystem was reinforced by three key institutional changes. First, in 1982, a specialized appeals court that from the beginning had a pro-patent approach was created. Second, the Antitrust Division of the Justice Department amended its hostile attitude to intellectual property rights, emphasizing the benefits of innovation dynamic versus static monopoly costs. Finally, pharmaceutical, audiovisual and software industries ensured that the US government would link international trade with the strengthening of intellectual property rights. On the effect of Bayn-Dole growth, see Cimoli and Primi (2008: 42).

Boettiger and Bennett (2006) indicate: "fundamentally, Bayh-Dole shifted the incentive structure that governed the research and development path of federally funded inventions by allowing institutions to own inventions resulting from federally sponsored research and to exclusively license those inventions. The Act also requires the institution to establish patent policies for its employees, to actively seek patent protection and to encourage the development of their inventions. Beyond these basic requirements, the legislation leaves a great deal of discretion to the institutions."

The effects of BD on repressed technology were staggering. The Act boosted technology commercialization to unseen levels hitherto. According to Pressman et al. (2012), based on data collected on a survey sponsored by the Association of University Technology Managers, gross licensing income out of U.S. universities doubled between 2004 and 2013, from 1.9 to 2.1 million dollars; also, for the same period, the number of patents filed has increased from 12,347 to 22,206 and patents granted from 3,268 to 5,220, respectively. The total contribution of academic licensors to gross industry output ranges from 199 billion dollars to 836 billion dollars; contributions to GDP range from 86 billion dollars to 338 billion dollars. AUTM estimates the impact from sales of products based on licensed academic research in 2012 totaled $80 billion dollars—that is double the entire federal investment in university research.

However, not everyone shares a rosy opinion about the top-down approach of the BD model. A Brookings Institution's report (2013) highlights how the business model of licensing university patents to the highest bidder is unprofitable for most universities and sometimes even risks alienating the private sector. Only 37 universities have been able to reach the top 20 of licensing revenue any given year over the last decade, thus showing that the highest earners have become a small group.

Moreover, this model has tended to assign federal funds upon universities with the highest success in patenting, which has undermined a more balanced assignment for other universities. Of the 155 universities' reporting licensing data in 2012, those belonging to the top half in terms of research expenditures control about nine out of ten dollars of research funds and of licensing revenue. By contrast, most university TTOs in universities not belonging to this elite club are not worth their cost because they are not self-supporting through patent licensing income. In 2012, a year very much in line with the ten-year trends in this sector, the top 5% of earners (eight universities) took 50% of the total licensing income of the university system; and the top 10% (16 universities) took 70%, nearly three-quarters of the system's income. One hundred thirty universities did not generate enough licensing income in 2012 to cover the wages of their technology transfer staff and the legal costs for the patents they file. What is more, with 84% universities operating technology transfer in deficit, 2012 was a good year because over the last 20 years, on average, 87% did not break even.

Moreover, it may be wrong to judge the outcomes of the BD simply by looking at the increase in patenting activity. Valdivia (2014b) contends that patent registration and licensing is not the only metrics of success in technology transfer activities: "In the search for a proper system of accountability, excessive attention to metrics of technology transfer may undermine the multiplicity of pathways in which research and productive organizations interact by undercutting the importance of modes of transfer for which metrics are elusive. Because we can count patents and add licensing fees, we may fall under the illusion that effective technology transfer is simply adequate management of the university's patent portfolio. By dismissing all modes of technology transfer not governed by patents, we strip our understanding of innovation from nuance and complexity; we may even end with the naïve view that the remit of universities is to produce fundamental research as an input to industry."

According to Masnick (2013), the Act has stifled innovation, because they penalize information sharing among researchers, and has placed them into a competition to patent first, which only takes away valuable information from the innovation ecosystem that needs it critically. Moreover, it induced university tech transfer offices to justify their existence by selling their patents at exorbitant prices, thus failing to understand that the important part of innovation is the execution, not the mere idea embedded in the patent. So, while it is true that the number of patents filed after BD skyrocketed, that did not turn into effective research being transferred into the industry, because the high prices charged by university tech transfer offices priced it out of the market. In fact, it may well have happened that BD's incentives could have promoted the emergence of Non-Practicing Entities (NPEs) like Intellectual Ventures,[4] because these companies may have well spotted the pressure upon the tech transfer offices, and possibly went around from university to university and offered to buy patents in bulk. Desperate tech transfer offices, needing to show some revenue coming in, gobbled up the offers.

Some authors say that the BD model is undergoing a process of exhaustion. Much of the university patent activity at the USPTO today seems to be coming from universities overseas, not from U.S. universities. Leydesdorff and Meyer (2013) and Leydesdorff et al. (2016) maintain that three periods can be distinguished in university patenting at the U.S. Patent and Trade Office (USPTO) since the Bayh-Dole Act of 1980: (1) a first period of exponential increase in university patenting till 1995 (filing date) or 1999 (issuing date); (2) a period of relative decline since 1999; and (3) in most recent years – since 2008 – a linear increase in university patenting is coming from foreign universities that maintain patent portfolios in the US such as Taiwan, Korea, China, and Japan. These patents of new entrants and fast growers are mostly concentrated in electronics, whereas a group of moderately growing, mostly European countries patents are mainly in the bio-medical sectors.

After 35 years of implementation, several adjustments are being called into this legislation, to allow the public a broader share of its benefits. Boettiger and Bennett (2006) criticize what they consider to be excessive focus on bringing federally funded technologies to the market, a condition that requires preempting public access to such research, by means of assigning IP to the universities, and then to researchers via exclusive licensing. Of these, probably the anticommons effect is

[4] http://www.intellectualventures.com/

the most important one, in view that it creates incentives that undermine sharing information that is critical for the innovation ecosystem to disseminate.

They explain as follows:

> Among the impacts of Bayh-Dole that have been widely deliberated and criticized, four main issues stand out that warrant consideration in any future revision or national emulation of Bayh-Dole: first, the need for a practical research exemption to permit the ongoing use of technologies developed with public funds for noncommercial research; second, the lack of a systemic approach to provide broad access to publicly funded upstream inventions and research tools; third, the need for reform to address the 'anticommons' effects that result from fragmented ownership of publicly funded research inventions; and fourth, access to patented, publicly funded technologies for humanitarian purposes.

Notwithstanding the increasing disenchantment with the BD model, this has served as inspiration for the tech transfer top-down policies implemented by other countries, including Brazil, China, Denmark, Finland, Germany, Italy, Japan, Malaysia, Norway, Philippines, Russia, Singapore, South Africa, South Korea and the United Kingdom (AUTM 2016). Some countries have supported the development of networks to dilute the cost of providing technical assistance programs or incubation, providing subsidized marketing technology until they can be economically viable services. This is the model followed in Israel, through the creation of Yozma in 1991. This institution, initially funded by the Government of Israel through subsequently privatized public capital, offered companies tax to foreign risk capital incentives and duplicated any level of investment they made using public funds.

As a result of these efforts, Israeli technology transfer offices seek approximately 400 new patents annually. Only YEDA marketing (OTT Weizmann Institute) produced $28 billion in 2013. Fueled by such deal flow, venture capital multiplied 60 times (from $58 million to $3.3 billion) between 1991 and 2000; the number of Israeli constituted with capital risk companies increased from 100 to 800, and earnings of technology companies grew from $1.6 billion to $12.5 billion in the same period.

In retrospect, BD introduced a positive change in the allocation of property rights over innovations because it clarified the role of universities and public research funded as channels of federal funds. Also, it discouraged scientists' inclination to conduct subsidized pure science research, with disregard of its industrial application. The new model funneled public funds into the production of applied science that served the public, as opposed to pure academic publishing, which only favored researchers.

7.3 Business Incubation and IP Management

The innovation ecosystem is also witnessing the emergence of business incubators, most of them, privately-owned, to supply startups with the tools they need to understand and implement successful IP strategies in the context of their business plans.

There is an increasing pressure towards making the system less focused on the incentives to do tech transfer through specialized offices and to leave that instead to startups created by university researchers, supported by business incubators.

Valdivia (2014a, 2014b) indicates how universities in the United States are moving towards a "nurturing start-ups model" whereby universities license to their start-ups for low or nominal fees, deferring payments to specific capitalization milestones and, at times, taking a minority interest share as part of the licensing contract. Nascent companies can then use their liquidity to cover development costs rather than paying hefty licensing fees. Low-fee licenses further improve the financial leverage of startups because it lowers the maintenance cost of their intangible assets. In developing countries, the need is even more justified in the light of the basic training that startups can hardly obtain from their innovation ecosystems.

Business incubation thus represents a bottom-up approach that fills the needs of startups in two senses: first, it provides startups with business consulting services that usually sprawl beyond the rather narrowly focused tech transfer programs (i.e., patent search, patent draft, IP valuation and IP negotiation), into broader areas of business advice, business plan development, corporate law, business mentoring and networking. Second, business incubation is a practical experience that allows businesses to "learn-by-doing" in shared working spaces, in a business-friendly environment that allows startups to exchange ideas with other startups. Business incubators, in turn, obtain equity in exchange (usually, and depending on the amount of services provided, between 5% and 10% of the equity).

The development of business incubators is even more justified, in the light of the scarcity of resources that the innovation ecosystem furnishes entrepreneurs with, thereby creating the incentives for a "market" of consulting services for startups to flourish. These services constitute the business core of business incubators; they include a provision of working space; networking with other startups; mentoring services; training on IP and business strategies.

Thus, business incubators offer a service portfolio that usually includes shared infrastructure (office space, meeting rooms, telecommunications, and Internet); business advisory (IP management including valuation, business planning, marketing, financial management, and regulatory compliance); financial services (providing seed capital, and access to Crowdfunding); and finally, business networking and mentoring (Khalil and Olafsen 2009).

These services are expensive and difficult to implement. For this reason, it requires a large volume of projects to be marketed, in order to justify the specialized services provided by the ecosystem. According to Pratt (2015), in the United States, venture capital funds invest in a startup per 400 companies analyzed; while Angel investors invest on a per 40 companies analyzed. According to Khalil and Olafsen (2009), business incubators "graduate" on average approximately 15% of the incubated companies.

Business incubation plays an important cognitive role for the agents involved in the innovation ecosystem; it helps them assess more accurately the level of risk involved in commercializing a given technology. Only a handful of startups dealing with technologies potentially protected through patents actually succeed in commercializing their innovation. Not only does one have to consider the hazards related to the nature of the technology itself, its technological viability beyond a proof of concept, into a functional prototype, one has to consider all the business challenges that startups need to overcome in order to commercialize such patents or any other IPR involved. Accordingly, business incubation mechanism is intended to reduce the risk of the innovation ecosystem by limiting the exposure of economic agents to uncertain events accruing from market interactions. By limiting this "commercial risk" through support to offer businesses a more predictable network of complementary capabilities, business network and financial risk assessment, entrepreneurs can isolate and gauge more easily the "technology risk" accruing from the innovation itself, which in turn helps them present their venture to potential investors with higher odds of success.

The systemic risk in the technology transfer process affects them in several levels. First, higher risk limits the number of startup projects to be hatched and favors the use of trade secrets and trademarks, which are less tradable, as means of protecting know-how and business reputation, respectively. A reduction in the number of hatched projects makes financial sustainability harder, and reduces the visibility of projects to venture capital funding, since the technologies involved will become patchier and less complementary thus reducing the value of the portfolio.

Thus, business incubation is intended to support firms obtaining the complementary capabilities they need to bring their innovations out to the market, beyond those strictly confined to the nature and complexity of the technology itself. Incubation creates an institutionalized mechanism that identifies potentially valuable ideas, executed by competent management teams, and connects them with other businesses that give them complementary capabilities that ensure commercialization of their innovations.

As the World has seen a virtual explosion in the creation of startups, also a wide array of incubation services has emerged in their support. Business incubation includes incubators, accelerators, mentorship programs, trainings, and every support the startup needs to help them match their lack of complementary capabilities with service suppliers, mentors, and potential partners, as seen in Fig. 7.2.

Business incubators have become essential institutions in the Triple Helix of the innovation ecosystem. Most business incubators address specific startup audiences as seen in Table 7.1.

What is the current situation of business incubators and accelerators in Latin America? After a modest beginning, Latin American incubators have quickly caught up and today command an increasing growth, in third place after the United States and Europe, as seen in Fig. 7.3. Latin American incubators created more than 12,000 direct and indirect jobs with sales revenue of $1.4 billion (Carnicelli 2015). Business acceleration in Latin America commands a respectful size, compared to other regions. Yet, it still remains about one-third the size of that of the United States and Canada. Latin America only has three incubators in the Global Top 25 University Business Incubators of 2014.

Extension of incubator programs into acceleration ones becomes difficult due to the problems finding a supporting innovation ecosystem. For example,

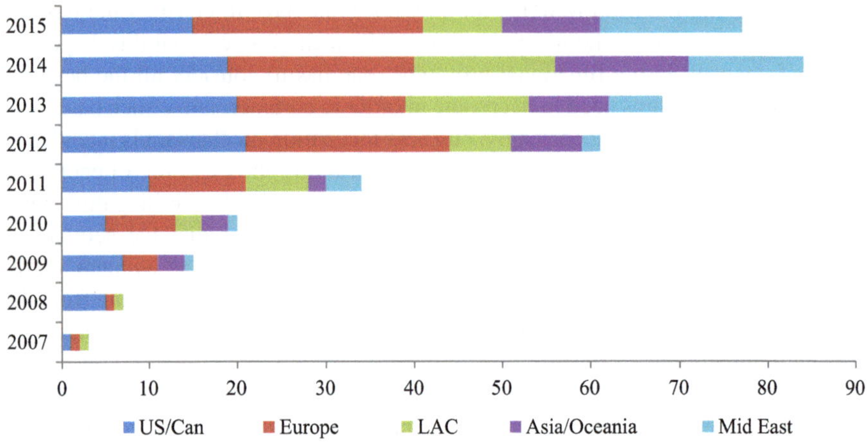

Fig. 7.2 Creation of new incubators (2015) (Source: Gust, Global Accelerator Report 2015)

Table 7.1 Selected Latin American business incubators (2014)

Name	Type	Funding mechanism	Investment sectors	Investment range (USD)	Equity taken
Startup Chile	Govt	Seed, early stage venture and grant investment	E-Commerce, software	40K –early stage	Equity free
Nxtp.Labs	Priv	USD 98.5 M raised Early Stage	E-Commerce, education, finance, venture capital, automotive, mobile	25 K–1 M	2–10%
Wayra	Priv	Debt Financing Investment	E-Commerce Mobile, software	50–100 K	5–10%
Mexican VC	Priv	Seed-stage	Games, telecom, messaging	25 K + 10 K (serv)	5–10%
21,212	Priv	Seed stage	BRA	15 K	5–10%

Source: Fundacity, YoSoyPYME, CrunchBase

Start-Up Chile has faced a shortage of local venture capitalists and has struggled to retain the program's participants in Santiago. "As many as 80% of Start-Up Chile participants leave Santiago after the six month program, a large portion moving on to the United States. Additionally, as much as 85% of the funding Start-Up Chile raised has come from abroad, mainly from the U.S." (Karsten and West 2015).

Business incubators are commercial ventures, therefore they are private for the most part; however, governments also supported them financially in some cases. A case in point is Startup Chile, a government initiative run by CORFO in Chile. This program was intended to bring innovative entrepreneurs from all over the World into

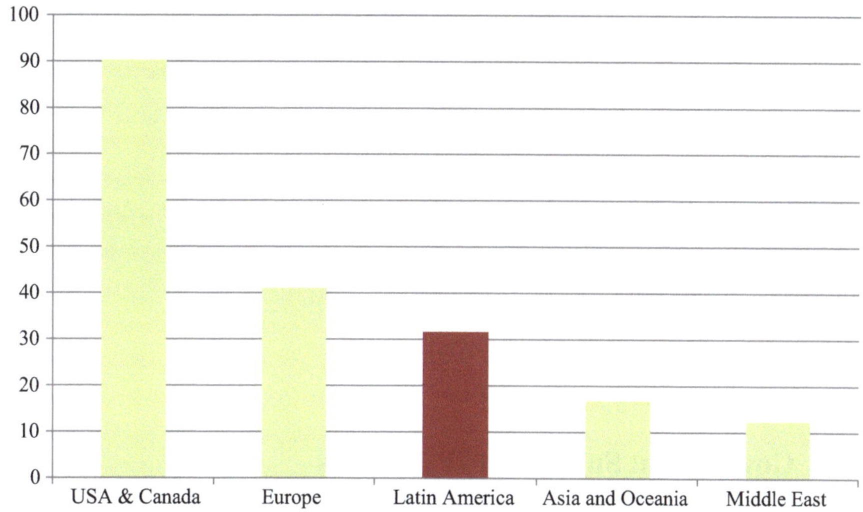

Fig. 7.3 Business incubation by investment (USD M)[5]

the local Chilean innovation ecosystem, thus populating the latter with new tech startups. To create the right incentives, the Chilean government promoted specific immigration rules and equity-free funding to make the program especially appealing to foreign entrepreneurs. Start-Up Chile has designed three incubation programs targeting special audiences: the S Factory is a pre-acceleration program for early concept stage focused on female founders (USD 14,000 and 3 months acceleration) and supports around 60 companies a year; the Seed is an acceleration program with a functional product and early validation (USD 30,000 and 6 months acceleration), and gives support to 200 companies a year; and the Scale is a follow up fund focused on top performers that have traction and are planning to scale (USD 86,000), and supports 60 companies a year. Each participant receives equity-free funding, a one-year temporary visa, office space, and opportunities for mentoring and coaching. In return, the budding startups must earn 4,000 "social capital points" by hosting workshops, mentoring local entrepreneurs, teaching classes, organizing hack-athons – anything to engage the local population in entrepreneurship, tech, and innovation.

Even so, Chile has the most sophisticated incubation/acceleration policy in the region, in terms of investment funds allocated, number of startups served and diversity of programs, as seem in Table 7.2.

Knowing about the current state of business incubators and accelerators in Latin America helps us understand the breadth and scope of technology transfer and IP commercialization in the region. After all, one of the several services provided by these entities is valuation and management of intellectual property.

[5] Data available at Gust Global Accelerator: http://gust.com/global-accelerator-report-2015/.

Table 7.2 Latin American accelerators – top countries by investment (USD M)

	Country investment on acceleration	Number of startups accelerated	Number of accelerator programs
Chile	15,096,929	442	14
Brazil	5524.320	297	26
Uruguay	4,373,900	105	6
Mexico	2,702,592	306	13
Argentina	2,385,700	61	6
Colombia	328,400	67	5
Venezuela	265,000	32	3
Peru	257,000	13	1
Paraguay	20,000	10	1

Source: Gust, Global Accelerator Report (2015)

7.4 Government Support of IP Markets

The adoption of proper incentives to promote IP markets is creating a secondary, but not less important level of IP government measures beyond the introduction of legal changes aimed at adjusting the incentives given to science researchers working under public funding. This second tier of reforms is not aimed at promoting a better use of government funds in the promotion of technology transfer but is intended to solve broader systemic problems undermining the development of IP markets. As seen in the previous chapter, a major challenge to IP management is the inherent risk involved in conducting IP monetization strategies, whether collateralization of IP assets or securitization of its royalties streams.

The systemic risk of the IP markets is associated with the problems of valuing such assets. IP valuation is expensive and cumbersome; there are no uniform standards, but rather a wide array of valuation methodologies whose selection is often unclear. Finally, the reduced level of deal flow is usually low in these countries which makes it hard for markets to sustain the emergence of specialized expert IP valuation firms, guarantors and other financial intermediaries of IP value. According to an OECD report, most SMIEs either do not register enough IP or they do not manage it well. In Australia, for instance, around 45% of SMIEs possess formal IP rights, while within this group 28% rely on secrecy or confidentiality agreements, only 8.2% on patents and 23% on copyrights and trademarks. The situation is even worse in the Latin American region, as seen in detail in Chap. 5. Evidently, without registered IP it is impossible to carry out their valuation.

Moreover, reporting IP value is very difficult to do through the usual financial reporting instruments, such as a corporate balance sheet. Usually, IP developed in-house is marked as an expense, while purchased IP is valued in the transaction (Brassell and King 2013).

In view of these problems, governments interested in promoting stronger IP commercialization are beginning to take decisive action in reducing transaction costs, in an attempt to enable the emergence of the chain of intermediate organizations that the IP market needs to make commercialization happen. This strategy covers the stages following the moment the patent or copyright or other IP title is granted to the point where the title becomes traded, thus monetized. Governments are intervening in support of IP markets in three dimensions: institutional, financial and cognitive.

The institutional dimension is primarily intended to bring support to IP markets by making them more transparent, and active. IP markets suffer from opacity due to the structure of the claims system, as indicated above.[6] That creates an impending problem of assessing the technology quality of the patents. To solve this problem, governments are implementing several measures intended to raise the "quality" of the patents submitted for review. South Korea's Technology Finance Corporation (KIBO), for example, assesses the technological quality of patents used as collateral for commercial lending. KIBO evaluates the future value of technologies and issues a technology certificate of "viability" giving credibility to the proof of concept developed by a startup. That technology financing eases their way into requesting loans from the commercial banks. KIBO has been equipped with technology appraisal infrastructures of technology appraisal specialists, technology appraisal centers, a central technology appraisal institute and above all, an advanced technology appraisal system.

Another set of measures is intended to encourage IP right holders to disclose ownership, transfer and licensing information. The government of Singapore has developed a series of measures aimed at that goal, as part of their program to make the country a "Global Hub for IP" (Singapore IP Steering Committee 2013).

Institutional support of IP markets from governments also includes measures directed towards stirring their activity. The goal is to ease information traffic among potential patentees and licensees, investors, and other interested parties. These measures include programs for developing online IP trading platforms; standardized license contracts; and information about the technology development and stage of the respective application (for instance, Patent Cooperation Treaty; patent applied; patent grant; and so on). A recent example of this type of intervention is the Regional Enterprise Asset Commercialization Hub (REACH), a program implemented in the Caribbean since 2014 by the Inter-American Development Bank and the University of the West Indies.

The financial dimension is intended to reduce the risk involved in IP transactions. Government intervention in this area focuses on creating risk-sharing mechanisms of IP-based financial instruments. These measures cover an extensive set of measures that include subsidizing interest rates applied to IP based loans, or guaranteeing eligible firms seeking bank lending. An example of this is Malaysia's provision of a 2% subsidy, as well as a guarantee of 50% of the loan. Also, development banks in some countries take IP as collateral for loans. This is the case of Brazil's Development Bank, the Beijing Branch of the Chinese Bank of Communications, the Thais SME Bank and the Development Bank of Japan (OECD 2015).

[5] See Sect. 1.3.

Table 7.3 Government support of IP financing offers in selected Asian countries

	IP valuation experts	Guarantors	Financial intermediaries	Companies
Singapore	Appointed by the IP Office of Singapore	Singapore government partial underwriting Also, partial subsidy of IP valuation costs	AFC Merchant Bank DBS Bank Ltd. Oversea-Chinese Banking Corporation (OCBC) Ltd. United Overseas Bank (UOB) Ltd	2-year $70 m IP financing scheme on patents (extended by 2 years and also covering trademarks and copyrights)
Malaysia	Panel of 7 stated-endorsed experts	Government guarantee of 50% of the loan Also subsidy (2% of interest)	MDV- Malaysian Debt Ventures Financing up to $2.22 million or 80% of valued IP, whichever is lower	$8.5 m in 5 IP-backed loan in a year
Korea	Government's certified IP valuation agency (KIPA) 60–80% of IP valuation is funded by the Korean IP Office	Korea Credit Guarantee Fund	Commercial Bank	$35 m in 29 companies in a year
China	Non-available			>$15 bn deployed since 2008

Source: Nguyen-Dinh (2016) and personal data

Another area of government IP financial support involves supporting IP risk insurance programs. IP insurance is very limited and costly, due to the lack of sufficient dealflow. This is the reason why governments are beginning to subsidize this service. For example, South Korea's Credit Guarantee Fund subsidizes up to 70% of the insurance premium with SMIEs. In Europe, IP risk insurance development is stalled due to the limited size of national markets. The awaited creation of a Unified Patent Court system will likely develop the deal flow needed for this industry to bloom (EC 2015: 72) (Table 7.3).

Finally, the cognitive dimension is aimed at promoting better awareness of IP among its users. This dimension touches upon the cognitive problems raised throughout this book.

The case of Ruta N of Medellin, Colombia, is eloquent. Ruta N is a regional government program created in 2009 by the Mayor of Medellin, to foster an innovation ecosystem in that city. This organization has a dozen programs to build capacity among entrepreneurs on the use of intellectual property, among others, assessment of technologies, strategic management (commercial) intellectual property (Patent N), implementing innovative concepts to life daily, capacity in internationalization, which allows companies with products or services based on know-how and technology services to access international markets (Passport N), and others.

These endeavors are addressing the "systemic" nature of the changes needed. Given our emphasis on the cognitive factor, it follows that these changes involve dissemination of information to the players to learn to use the system, as much as legal reform. For example, Inova Unicamp carries out a policy to explain to the university community the importance of protecting intellectual property, as well as providing advice on how to prepare and submit national and international patent applications, negotiate agreements on technology licensing, and manage the nursery at the University.

Other initiatives in the same direction are the methodology "Step by Step" National Intellectual Property Institute of Chile (INAPI) and the Institute for the Defense of Competition and Intellectual Property of Peru (INDECOPI). These institutions also offer accompaniment ("coaching") Legal Free. In the case of Peru, in 2014 it increased the number of applications for university patents by 51% and around 20% of total applications, just in the year in which the system implemented coaching. However, it is difficult to discern whether the effect is due to the introduction of "coach" or campaigns to disseminate the benefits of patents to innovators (e.g. national convention patents, patent inventors competition, dissemination of books and other Peruvian inventions, Indecopi has done campaigns for 2014). In the case of Chile, she has not experienced a boom in the number of applications, despite having reformed their institutions, disseminating information and having a system of "coaching".

One initiative to develop a regional technology transfer network is the Innovanet Network. This initiative represents a network group of TTO networks, which integrate intellectual property authorities and technology transfer offices. It facilitates continuous dialogue and exchange of best practices among member states of the OAS, under the Regional Dialogue of the High Authority of startups to contribute to its strengthening as a hemispheric forum for policy and strategy development startups linked to the commercialization of intellectual property, among others.[7]

7.5 Technology Transfer in Latin America: The Current Debate

Government failure to carry out IP monetization successfully has negatively impacted the development of innovation markets in developing countries. In Latin America this is particularly severe. According to the World Bank (2014), companies in the region are 20% less likely to introduce a new product than those countries with medium in Europe and Central Asia income; this percentage is even lower in Caribbean countries where the likelihood of introducing new products decreases to

[7] http://www.redinnovanet.org/drupal/

less than half of comparable businesses in other regions. Similarly, the average R&D as a percentage of GDP in the five largest economies in Latin America is barely a third that of China; the situation worsens if one compares the other economies of the region, where it does not reach a tenth.[8]

It has taken much toil for governments in the region, to grasp that IP management is essentially a private driven activity, for which success depends on setting the right systemic conditions around innovative SMIEs. Governments are not well equipped to deal with an enabling, non-intrusive role, perhaps due to the nature of government tradition in the region.

Today's startups are amidst a profound structural change caused by the revolution from an Industrial Society to a Knowledge Society. That has impacted the economic structure of society, very quickly, and the policies intended to support innovation. While innovation ecosystems are still largely dominated by the presence of governments trying to bring systemic risks down to a minimum, the kaleidoscopic structure of the IP system makes it difficult, even inconvenient, to achieve full certainty about how intangible capital should be structured in society in order to eliminate systemic capital misalignment completely. Indeed, that would be an impossible task; after all, intellectual assets are by-products of innovation, which is uncertain by nature.

The recent emergence of a startup culture around universities and private incubators is increasingly causing a shift in the organizational structure of the innovation ecosystem. From the previous dominant role of government funded technology transfer offices leading the dissemination of publicly funded technology, innovation ecosystems are increasingly relying upon market innovation mechanisms, mainly driven by business incubators. These entities operate under a wider portfolio of services compared to a narrower approach of technology transfer offices, usually confined to IP management. By contrast, private incubators focus on the broader business aspects of entrepreneurial endeavors, better suited to the nature of problems found by startups during their first years of existence.

Perhaps this is the most evident feature that differentiates the emphasis of innovation policies in Latin America and many developing countries, focused around the activity of government-funded public research centers, on the one hand; and the United States and other developed countries on the other hand, where the bulk of innovation rests on the private sector and academic centers (Greenstone and Looney 2011). In the former case, governments directly support the research activity, and in many cases guide the direction of research programs; whereas in the latter, governments take an arm's length approach, financially supporting through incentives (such as Bayh-Dole) but leaving the specific direction of research to private

[8]Another study by the OECD (2013: 26) also indicates that the growth of innovation in Latin America and the Caribbean is slower than in OECD countries. While in Latin America, investment in R + D + i grew on average 0.5% (2004) of GDP to 0.63% (2009), in OECD countries it grew from 2.2% to 2.4% for the same period. Countries with relatively larger markets like Brazil, Mexico or Argentina tend to concentrate the bulk of innovation produced in the region. Brazil accounts for 50% of patents filed by companies resident in a country of the region, but even in this case, the net income from patent licensing is negative.

businesses or academic centers, with notable exceptions.[9] Whereas in the former IP commercialization is mainly conducted by business incubators, in the latter, universities play a paramount role in conducting these services.

It comes as no surprise that the legislation in either case reflects the underlying policy approach. The legal instruments aiding intellectual property transfer in Latin America usually are scant, patchy and uncertain. There are no certain policy standards in place regarding technology transfer activities. Until recently, technology transfer has been almost unheard of, and confined to the elite of specialized top-level law firms.

The adoption of a modern approach in Latin America has been delayed by cultural factors as well. The negative ideological perception towards intellectual property among many Latin American policymakers (e.g., Venezuela, Ecuador, and Argentina) still mars the innovation debate. That perception has changed in recent times, thanks to a combination of several factors. Perhaps the most important of these is the impact created by the implementation of technology transfer in the United States that, in the context of globalization, has impacted the inbound flows of knowledge into Latin America through licensing and sale of technology.

The lack of uniform policies applied regarding the allocation of intellectual property rights arising out of innovations developed with public funds is a central concern of multilateral agencies, who share the top-down approach of developing innovation ecosystems. They emphasize the weak links between the academia, public research institutes, and the industry, and how the academic research agendas are not in touch with the needs of the economy. Thus, there is little experience trading technologies produced in university labs or public research institutes. According to Almeida et al. (2012), only 6% of surveyed companies had cooperation agreements with universities and about 5% had done so with public research institutes.

Lasagabaster and Reddy (2010) summarize these problems as follows:

> Leading universities in Latin America have started to build TTOs to interact with the productive sector, but most of them are not yet performing at international levels. The main problems include uncertainties in the incentive structure applied by some universities; lack of commercial focus by some TTOs; insufficient skills in intellectual property management and licensing; limited networks of contacts internationally; and inadequate funding which affects their staffing and access to legal services and necessary contacts. There is a need to rapidly develop effective networks of TTOs and upgrade the quality of services provided by the existing TTOs in LAC. A few initiatives are already underway in the region.

Thus, Latin American universities are still stuck in the ranks. According to the Times Higher Education World University Rankings 2015–2016 the highest ranked university from Latin America is situated at a distant tier 201–250; Under the Best Global Universities rank, the highest ranked university in Latin America is placed 111th in the rank.

---

[9] Among those exceptions one can identify the Defense Advanced Research Projects Agency (DARPA). This U.S. government agency targets technologies with high innovative capacity, that is, transformational innovations, as opposed to incremental innovations.

Table 7.4 Technology transfer by selected countries (2015)

	University–industry collaboration		PCT patent applications/million inhabitants	
	Rank/140	Score (max 7)	Rank	Score
Argentina	66	3.6	65	1.3
Brazil	54	3.8	51	3.5
Chile	39	4.2	43	7.1
Colombia	49	3.9	63	1.4
Costa Rica	33	4.4	64	1.4
Mexico	43	4.0	57	1.9
Peru	108	3.1	84	0.3
Venezuela	106	3.1	89	0.3
India	50	3.9	61	1.6
China	32	4.4	32	13.4
Israel	7	5.5	5	239.1
United States	2	5.8	11	160.3
Korea	26	4.6	7	220.7

Source: WEF Global Competitiveness Report (2015)

Given their leading role in the innovation ecosystem of Latin America it may be helpful to focus our attention into the governance, policies towards commercialization of their research, and institutional capabilities of universities, as the analysis of this microcosm could shed light on the challenges to implement a successful and widespread technology transfer mechanism.

Government funding of research in Latin America had emphasized the generation of conceptual knowledge but had been less efficient at energizing technological innovation such as the production of patents; also, they noted that collaboration between industry and universities was limited, hindering the transformation of new knowledge into innovation. That situation has changed little, as seen in Table 7.4.

Academic collaboration between Latin American scholars and scholars from overseas clearly adds value to domestic research: 22.8% of all the academic research published between 2010 and 2014 was the result of international collaboration; Latin American scholars fare well above this benchmark: Argentina, 44%; Chile, 60%; Colombia, 50%; Peru, 78% and Venezuela, 50%. However, international citations of patents developed by Latin American researchers is very low: on average, Mexico and Brazil receive 4.7 per each R&D project, compared to the United States (21), and Germany (17).

Moreover, collaboration increases opportunities for collaboration with the industry. An analysis of firm-level data from Chile finds that collaboration with universities increases the chances of a private enterprise being involved in patenting by 35%. However, as Thorn and Soo (2006) note linkages between universities and private companies are weak because of the entrepreneurial distrust towards the alignment of the academic curricula to the commercial priorities dictated by the industry dynamics, as well as the low quality of university education and the lack of capacity of local firms to absorb knowledge.

Aside from the lack of a policy promoting collaboration between academic scholars and the industry, the flaws in the university and public research governance is perhaps even more critical. Usually, public universities in the region are funded through budgetary allocations from the Ministry of Education or a similar entity. Naturally, criteria used to determine the allocation of resources, the student admission policy, the content of curricula, and the promotion policies are at odds with the search or economic efficiency, much less any commercial considerations. Some countries even require existing universities to issue a recommendation whenever a new university applies for a new license.

Pure science research is encouraged; no incentives or rewards are given to scholars who develop patents; hiring and promotion rules are based upon publishing research, which may well run against the commercial needs of confidentiality required by a patent protected knowledge.

Successful technology transfer policy in Latin America requires reform in three areas: institutional or legal, operational, and cultural. First, institutional reforms require increased flexibility in university and public science center management, to align institutional incentives to the social needs of bringing technologies developed in these centers to the market as fast as possible. That requires changes in the management rules of these institutions, promoting linkages with foreign peer institutions, and ensuring non-governmental funding, to break with the government budget dependence.

However, until now, Mexico seems to be the only country moving positively towards a more effective use of IP management strategies, as indicated in Table 7.5, which evaluates the net income received from technology transfer.

Finally, creating a commercially driven technology transfer ecosystem is a process that combines various elements staged concurrently and simultaneously. But

Table 7.5 Net income received from patent licensing – balance of payments – in selected Latin American countries vs. US, China and South Korea

Country	2005	2010	2014	Percent change (2005–2014)
Argentina	−599,560,000	−1,465,095,439	−1,799,931,177	−200.2
Brazil	−1,302,834,000	−2,453,035,436	−5,547,557,408	−325.8
Chile	−293,500,000	−662,199,282	−1,461,942,942	−398.1
Colombia	−108,151,470	−305,917,073	−444,214,529	−310.7
Costa Rica	−56,773,080	−56,079,039	−133,969,000	−136.0
Mexico	−1,863,840,830	−570,289,200	−368,270,751	80.2
Peru	−79,842,000	−193,711,615	−263,472,181	−230.0
China	−5,163,852,077	−12,209,062,645	−21,937,418,858	−324.8
Korea, Rep.	−2,684,400,000	−5,994,500,000	−5,378,900,000	−100.4
United States	48,871,000,000	74,971,000,000	88,237,000,000	80.6

Source: World Bank (2015)

perhaps the most important of these elements is cultural, or one could even say, ideological: the social conviction that embraces excellence, pragmatism, and social utility of the innovation system, which in Latin America translates into excellence at the sources of research, namely, public universities and public science research centers. Obvious as it sounds it is not necessarily the case in LAC, where pragmatism and common sense is often overshadowed by ideology and resentment. To evidence this, here is a quote taken from a Latin American scholar, summarizing his iconoclastic views on the role of the university in the region.

> Latin American institutions of higher education should not allocate human nor economic resources to the exclusive objective of appearing among schools ranked worldwide. Not only is this objective erroneous, but it also distorts all the accomplishments attained by university scholars in nearly one thousand years.
>
> World rankings measure the qualifications of only one type of university, so for that reason it's unfortunate that academics have given so much importance to these top ten listings; the Academic Ranking of World Universities (created by Jiao Tong University in Shanghai) and the World University Ranking (published by the Times Higher Education in London) measure a first-world concept of quality; they measure, in summary, the university's fame and its capacity of becoming well-known around the world, which is again a marketing strategy… Trying to imitate Harvard without taking into account our economic, cultural, and socio-political conditions is a reflective notion that may derive in new manifestations of mental colonialism.[10]

Fortunately, this view does not represent the majority. In fact, a practical perspective is gaining ground, one that conceives a "third mission" for universities, that is, commercializing her knowledge, the other two missions being research and teaching.

In this line of thinking, universities are quickly implementing technology transfer offices. Some countries are more advanced than others on this road. For example, in Brazil, the Inova Unicamp Innovation Agency is the first technology transfer office created in a Brazilian university. Founded in 2003, Inova has more than 50 employees whose task is to guide the university community on using the intellectual property system. In 2008 alone, Inova filed 51 applications with INPI and 12 international applications through the Patent Cooperation Treaty (PCT), they registered 13 trademarks and authored ten computer programs, licenses were granted to industry for three of its technological innovations, and they concluded more than 30 collaborative research agreements with Brazilian companies and institutions that are entrusted to provide some 8 million reais (just under $5 million) in investment to Unicamp. In late 2008, five Unicamp laboratory technologies were sold in Brazil, which generated revenues for the University of BRL at a total of 900,000 in royalties.

Technology transfer programs like this are beginning to spread across the region. There is a clear interest in developing partnerships between government, academia and private sector to induce better awareness and knowledge on how to value intellectual property, how to find potential licensees of their technologies, and how to integrate it in their business plans.

[10] In this paragraph one could hear the overtones of Miguel de Unamuno's sentence "let them be the ones to invent", who clearly was wrong in his appraisal about the roots of innovation and industrial growth (De Leon 2016).

Chapter 8
Conclusions

Movie piracy across Latin America is usual business, but nowhere like in the streets of Caracas. There, you will find movie stores that sell pirated blockbusters from the Box Office on demand, with the highest customer service quality, in the open. Ask these solicitous shop owners for any movie on any given day, no matter how vintage or special it may be, and they will deliver it the next day. They offer the widest selection of films you can think of, in well-organized catalogs that could turn Netflix or Amazon pale.

Interestingly, these little shops no longer sell through street peddlers in traffic-jammed highways at rush hours as they used to a few years ago; they are now legally incorporated, being located in the modern shopping malls of the wealthy quarters of Caracas's South East. Yet despite their increasing well-to-do, they still sell illegal merchandise. In fact, the owners of some of these shops proudly vouch for the quality of their illegal stock by stamping each of these illegal DVDs with their brand.

This is the sort of contradictory perception that underlies IP institutions in developing countries, where the boundaries of what is legal and what is not is blurred by social preferences. They highlight the evanescence of the legislation formally declared through official channels, coexisting side by side, often rather schizophrenically with institutions that emasculate the very purpose of legal mandates, creating a perception among users that laws forbid them from behavior that is irrelevant or plainly idiotic—therefore, why bother.

Informality highlights a clash between the official law and the real customs and practices of those subject to the law. Under closer inspection, such divorce creates a real, underlying, parallel legal order that is imposed over the official one, which then becomes irrelevant or worse, a nuisance, to those who would prefer to conduct their businesses according to alternative rule making. At the micro level, the use of an alternative, custom-based legal order seems better adapted to the real needs of the people (De Soto 2000) and usually takes precedence in the world of ordinary transactions across the region.

I. De Leon, J. Fernandez Donoso, *Innovation, Startups and Intellectual Property Management*, DOI 10.1007/978-3-319-54906-4_8

This peculiar set of ownership rules can be extended beyond real estate markets, into other segments of the economy. In the market of foodstuffs, for example, it is quite usual to see how these goods disappear from the market when they are subjected to price controls and other forms of transaction costs, just to reappear in black markets. Taxis are subject to regulations, but "pirate taxis" are everywhere offering their transportation services at higher prices, often reflected in the comparatively poor quality of the services paid. Intellectual assets are governed by similar rules: they are traded in the market if transaction costs are low; but if transaction costs are high they may decrease in the open, but still are conducted in the shadows at higher prices (i.e., of searching and negotiating with the right partner to trade with).

De Soto (2000) explained how society's unawareness of the wealth creation impact of aligning to "official" markets and property law undermines asset capitalization. He showed that physical infrastructure couldn't be capitalized as valuable tangible assets because they cannot be exchanged or otherwise traded in the real estate market. The same logic applies to intellectual assets, which fail to become tradable capital due to their lack of official protection through intellectual property because of innovators' unawareness, especially among startups and SMEs. In other words, regardless of their physical or intangible nature, these assets become "capital" as long as they serve some particular purpose in the business plan of some entrepreneur; this can only be "verified" through their capacity to be traded, i.e., exchanged. Paraphrasing the words of Oscar Wilde, herein is the importance of being aware of the challenges (hence, possibilities) that the patent system complexity presents to us.

Speaking of culture at the macro level disguises what happens at the micro-level of cognitive awareness. The fact that many SMEs all over the world share a different set of beliefs towards IP makes a huge difference. They believe that there is no problem in piracy because they do associate the potential value of developing a solid distributorship chain, but concentrate on the immediate cash out received from piracy. No investments are made on improving the institutional setting by which movies, music or works of art can be made profitable.

However, the coexistence of informality with the legal order comes at the cost of legal fragmentation. The lack of a centralizing authority declaring the law to everyone creates obvious knowledge gaps on people, who do not know with certainty the scope of their rights and accordingly, their capacity to trade them. The negative effects of informality are readily visible in an extended order of undercapitalized assets that become main objects of market exchanges: half-used plots of land; half-built, weary buildings in shantytowns; street markets, as opposed to shopping malls and main street stores; and a faulty use of intellectual property.

Informality, legal fragmentation, and the emergence of black markets, also pervades IP markets. Here, informality manifests itself as unawareness of the existence of legal rules protecting innovations or lack of understanding of their capitalization potential over their intellectual assets. Being aware of the actions potentially viable from other market agents, as construed under the mandate of legal or customary rules, is a question of subjective expectations entertained by market participants. This is a very important trait of market interactions that is often buried under the math of conventional economic models, more concerned with drawing the logical implications of their premises, rather than understanding the mindset of market participants, their motives and reasons.

Put it differently, social perceptions and beliefs constitute the backbone of the institutional maze where economic progress rests; but seldom has the literature of economic science made this connection. The nature of perceptions is cognitive, and cognition is taken to belong to a realm of knowledge aside from conventional economic science, namely, that of social psychology, not applied mathematics.

Adam Smith (1776) explained that the extent of the division of labor is limited by scope of the market; this book shows that Smith begged the question of what exactly he meant by speaking of the scope of the market. In our view, the scope of the market is limited by the awareness of its participants. Culture is a critical factor underlying the wealth of countries because it sets forth the boundaries of awareness that ultimately allows individuals to perceive profit opportunities, thereby inducing them to trade. IP markets are no exception to this rule.

8.1 Cognitive Perceptions Drive IP Management

IPRs effectively do not exist if society is not aware of their existence, or if the cost of use is such that they no longer serve the purpose of cheaply conveying information. This cost tends to be particularly high to startups, whose most urgent priorities are focused on making the business and its technology operational and differentiated from her competitors. Faced with the costs of registering and protecting their IP, many startups choose to rely on alternative means such as lead time, secrecy, confidentiality, and product complexity. That leads startups to assign a lower priority to invest in learning about IP and its strategic use, with potentially disastrous consequences.

Walt Disney's story highlights this point. After many years struggling to keep his cartoonist company alive, in 1926 Disney's company was asked by his distributor Charles Mintz to develop a new cartoon character for Universal Studios that would compete with the popular "Felix the Cat" and "Krazy Cat". Disney signed a contract where he committed his company to sell the new character to Universal.

Disney put his team of cartoonists into developing "personality animation," in which cartoon characters were defined as individuals not just by their design but by their movements, mannerisms and acting. As he said: "I want the characters to be somebody. I don't want them just to be a drawing." His innovative techniques emulated human behavior in his new cartoon.[1] Thus "Oswald the Lucky Rabbit" was

[1] Disney put his full creative ingenuity to make his Oswald cartoons look "real," thus turning away from the styles of Felix the Cat, Koko the Clown and Krazy Kat and instead emulating the camera angles, effects and editing of live-action films. To learn how to base gags on personality and how to build comic routines, rather than heaping one gag after another, he studied Laurel and Hardy, Harold Lloyd, Charlie Chaplin and Buster Keaton. In order to stir emotion in an audience, Disney studied and scrutinized the shadow effects, cross-cutting and staging of action in films featuring Douglas Fairbanks and Lon Chaney (Canemaker 1994).

born, and immediately became a smashing success. However, Walt's happiness would be short-lived. In 1927, after a strained discussion with Mintz about renegotiating his company's fees with him, Disney discovered that his distributor had gone behind his back offering his cartoonists better contracts to work directly for him. At that moment, Disney realized his error of yielding his copyrights over "Oswald the Lucky Rabbit" to Universal, a client over which he had no leverage, and whose relationship Mintz completely controlled.

Even though in hindsight we know that this sad moment in Disney's life would be the turning point of his career, as it led him into giving birth to Mickey Mouse in 1927, it teaches us, as much as it did to Disney, that creativity is worth nothing if it is unprotected through IP, in the absence of alternative means such as lead time or product complexity.

In the context of the digital economy we live in today, featured by increasing returns, control over strategic dynamic capabilities through non-tradable assets is more critical than in the 1920s. Today, increasing returns determine the payoff to strategic behavior and amplify the importance of timing and responsiveness resulting from effective dynamic capabilities.

At a macro level, Disney's story highlights the relevance of controlling non-tradable assets, as a means to create competitive capabilities. Control over non-tradable features is a natural reaction of firms seeking to preserve their competitive dynamic capabilities in the context of real or perceived ineffective IP law enforcement. Yet, in the context of perceived or real ineffective IP law enforcement, a natural business reaction of firms seeking to preserve their competitive dynamic capabilities is to take valuable non-tradable assets away from the market.

How can public policy prevent this outcome to happen, thus enabling as many IP transactions as possible?

8.2 Governments Need to Creatively Address Awareness

In the knowledge economy era we now live, featured by technological cost reductions and nimble corporate structures, startups have become the beacon of innovation. Innovation no longer takes place exclusively in the well-furnished R&D labs of large corporations; in many cases open innovation carried out by creative startups takes precedence today. However, this paradigmatic shift in the structure of business corporations is stifled by the resilience of an IP system that suffers from institutional breakdowns and lack of awareness.

Thus, awareness is a cognitive problem that public policy should underscore, as much as building the institutional framework. Individuals' perceptions are critical to induce them to trade IPRs or abstaining from doing so. This has profound public policy implications. If the problem of using the IP system is not simply one of incentives, instrumented through legal reform and institutional capacity building to execute these rules, then we have to switch our attention to the users of the system, increasing their awareness and capacity to use the system effectively. Here lies the importance of emphasizing the development of business incubators and accelerators, as part of a policy directed towards bringing know-how into the IP system users, on how to design and execute their IP competitive strategies effectively.

Trade affects intangible assets as much as physical ones, and this trading is more difficult and affected by the degree of institutional uncertainty, due to knowledge's incorporeal nature. The previous chapters emphasize how trust is a key component for the success of the IP system in supporting intellectual assets capitalization, through the creation of a functional market for the exchange of IP. Thus, in the same line of thinking of Hernando de Soto (2000), who noted how the value of physical assets in developing countries diminishes due to legal hurdles, we show the impact of costly legal rules on the development of IP markets. However, we go one step further, by emphasizing how these hurdles are rooted in the cognitive perception of entrepreneurs, which dims their awareness and trust on the institutional mechanisms otherwise enabling them a better, i.e. profitable use, of the IP system.

They highlighted that Latin American innovators abstain from using the system, thereby decreasing their chances to increase their wealth through higher exposure to technological partners and clients. In the same line advanced by Adam Smith (1776) who argued that specialization is limited by the extent of the market, Latin American entrepreneurs undervalue their intellectual assets by taking them away from the trade flows.

Entrepreneurs' cognitive perception is influenced by the very nature of the IP system, which is inevitably open. Given that the system must allow some degree of flexibility, the obvious question is how can public policy ensure a proper degree of flexibility, such that trust in the system will not be undermined? Here the role of empowering the system user is again critical. So far the efforts to overcome this problem have focused on the supply of legal services, either by developing IP legislation that balances the interests of innovators and the public domain, or by increasing the resources available to IP offices to better administer the rules. We advocate improving the capacity of users to understand the system and to use it to their advantage.

8.3 In Closing

In medieval times alchemists used to claim special powers to transform the base metals into gold, the discovery of a universal cure for disease, and the discovery of a means of indefinitely prolonging life. Alchemists played a significant role in early modern science (particularly chemistry and medicine). Islamic and European alchemists developed a structure of basic laboratory techniques, theory, terminology, and experimental method, some of which are still in use today. However, they continued antiquity's belief in four elements and guarded their work in secrecy including cyphers and cryptic symbolism.

Today, institutions like intellectual property fulfill a similar role to that of alchemists, transforming mere ideas into valuable assets. Like alchemy, institutions embody a set of basic techniques, and protocols that help firms to do the magic: creating wealth out of nothing.

The convoluted nature of IP markets makes it difficult for innovators to commercialize their knowledge; this complex nature is inherent in the way the patent system is built. Naturally, this negatively affects innovators in general, but it especially affects SMEs due to their relative financial weakness.

Policy strategies designed to overcome the structural flaws in the IP system have primarily focused on providing patent offices with financial and technical resources to improve their capacity to administer and enforce IP laws. Governments have funneled resources to enhance patent authorities' effectiveness to review patent claims. This approach has emphasized improvements on the provision (i.e., supply) of IP services, as opposed to making IP users (i.e., demand) aware of strategic uses of their IP. While it is true that some countries have perceived the relevance of addressing the systemic risk involved in the use of the IP system,[2] these interventions do not address directly the cognitive problem that underlies the startups' decision not to use the IP system strategically. Instead, these policy measures are incentives intended to stir changes in the innovators' behavior.

Yet, these cognitive shortcomings largely drive the behavior of the IP system users, both innovators and entrepreneurs interested in the technologies arising from it. Profit opportunities are usually thought to be the result of creative products being traded in the market; yet, as we propose in this book, the causality also runs in the opposite direction: profit opportunities help innovators to devise solutions through creative innovations that become valuable because they can solve market needs.

Of course, this is not to say that money making drives creative processes; rather it implies that IP markets (i.e. demand as much as supply) are needed to materialize innovations. If no one wants a technology, because it does not address a particular need, it is unlikely that the innovation will see the light of day. As seen above, the proportion of patented technologies that remain unused is much higher than that of those effectively used. Therefore, awareness of potentially valuable commercial opportunities is a critical element of the innovation process.

IPRs help innovators perceive the commercial relevance of their innovations, as it represents a measuring rod of such market needs. Once a technology license is priced, or a patent sold, or a copyright litigation settled, innovators can obtain a clearer idea of how well received (i.e., valued) their creative endeavors are. If no IPRs existed, innovators would have no way of establishing if they should put more brains and perseverance into products or know-how that ultimately would end in the dustbin. IPRs are thus important, because they convey useful information about the value markets attach to a particular innovation.

[2] For example, the South Korean government assumes the cost of funding litigation where the ownership of companies in this country is questioned (Ghafele and Gibert 2012: 18).

At a macro level, the fact that markets drive innovation possibilities reverses the causality conventionally assumed, whereby innovation levels (measured by the number of patent applications or R&D investment) results in mature IP markets. This is an important finding. As Kim et al. (2012) note the patents and other IPRs may have different effects depending on the level of economic growth of the country involved. Patent protection enhances innovation and economic growth in countries where the capacity to conduct innovative research exists, and innovation ecosystems are mature. Patent protection is an important determinant of innovation and patentable innovations contribute to economic growth in developed countries, but not necessarily in developing ones, where lesser forms of IP such as utility models may be better suited to adapt to the current level of innovation in these countries. Thus, IPRs are not only tailored to the particular type of intellectual protection sought, but also, to the particular complexity and level of economic development of the country involved.

This book showed the alchemy of wealth: how to develop valuable IP assets knowledge is as important as IP itself.

Bibliography

Aberdeen JA (2005) The Edison Movie Monopoly: The Motion Picture Patents Company vs. the Independent Outlaws. http://www.cobbles.com/simpp_archive/edison_trust.htm

Albanesius C (2011) Every place Samsung and Apple are suing each other. PC Magazine (Ziff Davis), Sept 14. Retrieved 11 Aug 2012

Almeida M, de Mello JMC, Etzkowitz H (2012) Social innovation in a developing country: invention and diffusion of the Brazilian cooperative incubator. Int J Technol Glob 6(3):206–224

Anson W (2007) The intangible assets handbook. American Bar Association, Washington, DC

Anson W (2015) Alternate approaches to the valuation of intellectual property. IPWatchdog, 11 Feb 2015

Anton JJ, Yao DA (2004) Little patents and big secrets: managing intellectual property. RAND J Econ 35(1):1–22

Arrow K (1962) Economic welfare and the allocation of resources for invention. In: The Rate and Direction of Inventive Activity: Economic and Social Factors. Princeton, Princeton University Press, pp 609–626

Arundel A (2001) The relative effectiveness of patents and secrecy for appropriation. Res Policy 30:611–624

Arundel A (2003) Patents in the knowledge-based economy, report of the KNOW survey. MERIT, University of Maastricht, Maastricht

Augier M, Teece DJ (2008) Strategy as evolution with design: the foundations of dynamic capabilities and the role of managers in the economic system. Organization Studies 29:1187–1208

AUTM (2016) Bayh-Dole Act Landmark Law Helped Universities Lead the Way. https://www.autm.net/advocacy-topics/government-issues/bayh-dole-act/. Retrieved 20 Dec 2016

Ayyagari D-K, Maksimovic (2011) Small vs. young firms across the world: contribution to employment, job creation, and growth. Policy research working paper 5631. Development Research Group, Finance and Private Sector Development Team, Washington, DC, World Bank

Bader MA, Gassmann O, Jha P, Liegler F, Maicher L, Posselt T, Preissler S, Rüther F, Tonisson L, Wabra S (2012) Creating an organised IP rights market in Europe. Intellectual Asset Manage Mag 26:33–38

Bansal AK, Koradia V (2005) The role of reverse engineering in the development of generic formulations. Pharm Technol 29(8):50

Barzel Y (1997) Economic analysis of property rights. Cambridge University Press, Cambridge

Belleflamme P (2006) Patents and incentives to innovate: some theoretical and empirical economic evidence. Ethical Perspect J Eur Ethics Netw 13(2):267–288

Ben-Aaron D, Pohjanpalo K (2011) Nokia Wins Apple Patent-License Deal Cash, Settles Lawsuits. Bloomberg Technology, July 14. http://www.dingding.tv/bbs/read.php?tid=5623. Retrieved 19 Dec 2016

I. De Leon, J. Fernandez Donoso, *Innovation, Startups and Intellectual Property Management*, DOI 10.1007/978-3-319-54906-4

Benavente JM, Goya D (2012) The economics of IP in the context of a middle income country. Economia y negocios, Depto de Economia, SDT 350, Santiago de Chile

Benjamin J (2010) The other side of the debate over patent trolls. IP Watchdog, 10 Dec 2013. http://www.ipwatchdog.com/2013/12/10/the-other-side-of-the-debate-over-patent-trolls/id=46671/

Bergson H (1910) Time and free will: an essay on the immediate data of consciousness. George Allen Unwin, London

Besen SM (1998) Intellectual property. In: Newman P (ed) The new Palgrave dictionary of economics and the law, vol 2. Macmillan, London, pp 348–352

Besen SM, Raskind LJ (1991) An introduction to the law and economics of intellectual property. J Econ Perspect 5(1):3–27

Bessen J (2002) Technology adoption costs and productivity growth: the transition to information technology. Rev Econ Dyn 5(2):443–469

Bessen J, Meurer MJ (2012) The private costs of patent litigation. JL Econ & Pol'y 9:59

Bessen JE, Ford JL, Meurer MJ (2012) The private and social costs of patent trolls. Regulation 34(4):26–35

Bilir K (2014) Patent laws, product lifecycle lengths, and multinational activity. Am Econ Rev 104(7):1979–2013

Blind K, Thumm N (2006) Intellectual property protection and standardization. In: Advanced topics in information technology standards and standardization research, vol 1. IGI Global, pp 166–182

Blind K, Edler J, Frietsch R, Schmoch U (2006) Motives to patent: empirical evidence from Germany. Res Policy 35(5):655–672

Boettiger S, Bennett AB (2006) Bayh-Dole: if we knew then what we know now. Nat Biotechnol 24:320–323

Boger JW, Ziegler KE (2012) The IPXI: an alternative to the license agreement? Maybe! Legal and Regulatory, Oct. http://www.hrfmlaw.com/wp-content/uploads/2015/05/The_IPXI_An_Alternative_to_the_License_Agreement_Maybe__article_265805.pdf. Retrieved 19 Dec 2016

Boldrin M, Levine D (2012) The case against patents. Working paper 2012-035, Federal Reserve Bank of St. Louis, Research Division. http://research.stlouisfed.org/wp/2012/2012-035.pdf

Botella C, Suárez I (2012) Innovación para el desarrollo en América Latina: Una aproximación desde la cooperación internacional. Serie Avances de Investigación n° 78, Fundacion Carolina, Madrid, mayo

Boyle J (2008) The public domain. Yale University Press, New Haven

Brachmann S (2016) The Four Consequential Patent Trends of 2016, IP Watchdog, 30 Dec 2016. http://www.ipwatchdog.com/2016/12/30/patent-trends-2016/id=76356/. Retrieved 31 Dec 2016

Brassell M, King K (2013) Banking on IP?: The role of intellectual property and intangible assets in facilitating business finance. Published by The Intellectual Property Office of the United Kingdom. https://www.gov.uk/government/uploads/system/uploads/attachment_data/file/312008/ipresearch-bankingip.pdf. Accessed Jan 2017

Brunsvold BG, Patrick O'Reilley D, Brian Kacedon D (2012) Drafting patent license agreements, 7th edn. Bloomberg BNA, Bethesda

Brynjolfsson E, Hitt LM, Yang S (2002) Intangible assets: computers and organizational capital. Brookings Papers on Economic Activity 1:137–198

Buchanan J, Vanberg VJ (1991) The market as a creative process. Economics and Philosophy 7:167–186

Bueno R (2009) La historia del éxito de Inova: transferencia de tecnología en el Brasil, Revista de la OMPI, Nov. http://www.wipo.int/wipo_magazine/es/2009/06/article_0009.html

Burton BW, Bienias E, Quinn CK (2014) Financing alternatives for companies: using intellectual property as collateral, SRR. http://www.srr.com/assets/pdf/financing-alternatives-companiesusing-ip-collateral.pdf. Retrieved 27 Sept 2016

Canemaker J (1994) Life before Mickey. The New York Times, July 10. Retrieved 23 July 2016

Cardullo MW (undated) Intellectual property – the basis for venture capital investments. World Intellectual Property Organization. http://www.wipo.int/export/sites/www/sme/en/documents/pdf/venture_capital_investments.pdf
Carnicelli L (2015) South American business incubators – facts & figures. Ubi Global, Blog, Apr 10. http://ubi-global.com/south-american-incubators/
Casino JM, Kasdan MJ, Amster R, Ebenstein, with Intellectual Property and Technology (2015) Patent litigation: mapping a global strategy. http://www.arelaw.com/downloads/ARElaw_PatLit_Mapping_PracticeNote.pdf
Cattaneo C (2001 [1861]) Del Pensiero come Principia d'Economia Publica, Libri Scheiwiller, Milano
Cho K, Kim C, Shin J (2015) Differential effects of intellectual property rights on innovation and economic performance: a cross-industry investigation. Sci Public Policy 42(6):827–840, first published online April 8, 2015
Cimoli M, Primi A (2007) Technology and intellectual property: a taxonomy of contemporary markets for knowledge and their implications for development. CEPAL/GTZ, Santiago de Chile
Cimoli M, Primi A (2008) Propiedad Intelectual y desarrollo: una interpretación de los (nuevos) mercados del conocimiento. In: Piva JMM (ed) Generación y protección del conocimiento: propiedad intelectual, innovación y desarrollo económico. CEPAL, México
Cloodt M, Hagedoorn J, Roijakkers N (2006) Trends and patterns in interfirm R&D networks in the global computer industry: an analysis of major developments, 1970–1999. Bus Hist Rev 80(4):725–746
Closson K (2009) Patent pools: are they right for your business? SPIE Professional. https://spie.org/membership/spie-professional-magazine/spie-professional-archives-and-special-content/oct2009-spie-professional/patent-pools
Coase RH (1937) The nature of the firm. Economica 4(16):386–405
Coase RH (1960) The problem of the social cost. J Law Econ 3:1–44
Coase RH (1988) The firm, the market, and the law. The University of Chicago Press, Chicago
Cockburn IM, Kortum S, Stern S (2002) Are all patent examiners equal? The impact of characteristics on patent statistics and litigation outcomes. Working paper 8980, National Bureau of Economic Research Paper Series at http://www.nber.org/papers/w8980.pdf
Cohen W, Levinthal RN, Walsh JP (2000) Protecting their intellectual assets: appropriability conditions and why US manufacturing firms patent (or not). NBER, working paper, 7552, Feb 2000
Colson T (2007) Protecting your intellectual property with patent alternatives. IndustryWeek, 3 Oct 2007. Available at: http://www.industryweek.com/regulations/protecting-your-intellectual-property-patent-alternatives
Colson T. Protecting your intellectual property with patent alternatives there are myriad methods for protecting innovation and intellectual property. http://www.industryweek.com/regulations/protecting-your-intellectual-property-patent-alternatives. Retrieved 16 Dec 2016
Contreras JL, Reichman JH (2015) Sharing by design: data and decentralized commons. Science 350(6266):1312–1314
CREATE (2012) Trade secret theft: managing the growing threat in supply chains. Create.org, Washington, DC
Crespi G, Steiner E, Fernandez E (2014) Rethinking productive development, development in the Americas. BID, Washington, DC
Crouch D (2015) Inspector general: USPTO needs to strengthen patent quality assurance practices, Apr 15. http://patentlyo.com/patent/2015/04/strengthen-assurance-practices.html
Dam K (1993) The economic underpinnings of patent law. John Olin law and economics working paper, no. 19, 2nd series. University of Chicago Press, Chicago
De Faria P, Lima F, Santos R (2010) Cooperation in innovation activities: the importance of partners. Res Policy 39(8):1082–1092
De Leon I (2016) Que inventen ellos: El Mal dia de Don Miguel de Unamuno. In: Blog Puntos sobre la i. BID, Washington, DC

De León IL, Donoso JF (2015) El Costo de uso de los sistemas de propiedad intelectual para pequeñas empresas innovadoras: el caso de Chile, Colombia y México. Documento para la Discusión IDB-DP-373, BID, Washington, DC

De Leon I, Donoso JF (2016) The cost of using formal intellectual property rights: a survey on small innovative enterprises in Latin America. Inter-American Development Bank, discussion paper N° IDB-DP-482

De Soto H (2000) The mystery of capital: why capitalism triumphs in the west and fails everywhere else. Basic Books, New York

Dent JR, Victor MB (2004) The role of risk analysis in dispute and litigation management. Paper presented on October 6, 2004 at the American Bar Association, Sheraton Wall Centre Hotel, Vancouver

Derwent (2000) Dismantling the barriers: a Pan-European survey on the use of patents and patent information by small and medium-sized enterprises. Unpublished Manuscript

Dilger DE (2014) iPhone IP Wars: Nokia vs Apple vs HTC, Motorola & Samsung. Apple Insider, Mar 27. http://appleinsider.com/articles/14/03/27/iphone-ip-wars-nokia-vs-apple-vs-htc-motorola-samsung

Dimech-DeBono J (2016) Creating value through IP asset management and valuation. Interview at Financier Worldwide Magazine, Jan 2016

Elmer MC (2010) Where to win: patent-fiendly courts revealed. Managing Intellectual Property, Sept 2010

Etzkowitz H (2002) The triple helix of university-industry-government: implications for policy and evaluation. Swedish Institute for Studies in Education and Research, Stockholm

Etzkowitz H, Leydesdorff L (1995) The Triple Helix – University-industry-government relations: a laboratory for knowledge based economic development. EASST Rev 14:14

European Commission (2006) Study on evaluating the knowledge economy what are patents actually worth? The value of patents for today's economy and society, Tender n° MARKT/2004/09/E, Lot 2, 23 July 2006. http://ec.europa.eu/internal_market/indprop/docs/patent/studies/tech_report_lot2_en.pdf

European Commission (2015) A single market strategy for Europe – analysis and evidence. Commission Staff Working Document, SWD(2015) 202 final, Brussels, 28 Oct 2015. http://ec.europa.eu/DocsRoom/documents/14012?locale=fr

European Commission (2015) Communuication from the commission to the European Parliament, the Council, the European Economic and Social committee and the committee of the regions. Upgrading the Single Market: more opportunities for people and business," Brussels, 28.10.2015. Available at: https://ec.europa.eu/transparency/regdoc/rep/1/2015/EN/1-2015-550-EN-F1-1.PDF

Eurostat (2016) Community Innovation Surveys (CIS4) available online at: http://ec.europa.eu/eurostat/web/microdata/community-innovation-survey. Site last visited on 21 July 2016

Executive Office of the President of the U.S. (White House Report) (2013) Patent assertion and U.S. innovation. President's Council of Economic Advisers, the National Economic Council, and the Office of Science & Technology Policy, Washington, DC, June

Faye J (2014) Copenhagen interpretation of quantum mechanics. In: Zalta EN (ed) The Stanford encyclopedia of philosophy, Fall 2014 Edition. http://plato.stanford.edu/archives/fall2014/entries/qm-copenhagen

Feder BJ (2002) Business; patent donations are novel corporate gift. The New York Times, 17 Nov 2002. Available at: http://www.nytimes.com/2002/11/17/business/business-patent-donations-are-novel-corporategift.html

Fernandez Donoso J (2014) Do complex inventions need less international patent protection? Econ Lett 125:278–281

Fernandez Donoso J (2017) A simple index of innovation with complexity. J Informet 11:1–17

Festinger L (1957) A theory of cognitive bias. Stanford University Press, Stanford

Fisher WW III, Oberholzer-Gee F (2013) Strategic management of intellectual property. Calif Manag Rev 55(4):157–183

Frontier Economics (2011) Estimating the global economic and social impacts of counterfeiting and piracy, Feb 2011. Frontier Economics Ltd., London. http://www.iccwbo.org/Advocacy-

Codes-and-Rules/BASCAP/BASCAP-Research/Economic-impact/Global-Impacts-Study/. Retrieved 1 Oct 2016
Gans JS, Hsu DH, Stern S (2008) The impact of uncertain intellectual property rights on the market for ideas: evidence from patent grant delays. Manag Sci 54(5):982–997
GEM (2016) The Leveraging Entrepreneurial Ambition and Innovation report. http://www.gem-consortium.org/report
Ghafele R, Gibert B (2012) Promoting intellectual property monetization in developing countries. Policy research working paper 6143. The World Bank, Washington, DC
Giedion S (1948) Mechanization takes command. Oxford University Press, Oxford
Gilbert RJ, Newbery DMG (1982) Preemptive patenting and the persistence of monopoly. Am Econ Rev 72:514–526
Global IP Project, LLC (2015) Trends in global patent litigation. Available at: http://globalpatent-metrics.com/wpcontent/uploads/2015/01/Significant-Trends-Slides-25-Jan-2015.pdf
Gollin M (2008) Driving innovation: intellectual property strategies for a dynamic world. Cambridge University Press, New York
Gorschek T, Garre P, Larsson S, Wohlin C (2006) A model for technology transfer in practice. IEEE Softw 23(6):88–95
Greenstone M, Looney A (2011) A dozen economic facts about innovation. The Hamilton Project, Policy Memo, August 2011, Brookings Institute. https://www.brookings.edu/wp-content/uploads/2016/06/08_innovation_greenstone_looney.pdf. Retrieved 3 Jan 2017
Grimes P (2016) Jenny Yoo files suit against David's Bridal. The Fashion Law, 12 Apr 2016. http://www.thefashionlaw.com/home/bridal-designer-jenny-yoo-files-trade-dress-patent-suit-against-davids-bridal. Retrieved 25 Dec 2016
Hagiu A, Yoffie DB (2013) The new patent intermediaries: platforms, defensive aggregators, and super-aggregators. J Econ Perspect 27(1):45–66
Hall B, Helmers C, Rogers M, Sena V (2014) The choice between formal and informal intellectual property: a review. J Econ Lit 52(2):375–423
Haltiwanger J, Jarmin RS, Miranda J (2013) Who creates jobs? Small versus large versus young. Rev Econ Stat 95(2):347–361
Harabi N (1995) Appropriability of technical innovations an empirical analysis. Res Policy 24(6):981–992
Hargreaves I (2011) Digital opportunity: a review of intellectual property and growth. http://webarchive.nationalarchives.gov.uk/20140603093549/http:/www.ipo.gov.uk/ipreview-finalreport.pdf
Harper MA (1994) International protection of intellectual property rights in the 1990s: will trade barriers and pirating practices in the audiovisual industry continue. Calif West Int Law J 25:153
Harper D (1996) Entrepreneurship and the market process: an enquiry into the growth of knowledge. Routledge, London
Harper D (2012) Property as a complex adaptive system: how entrepreneurship transforms intellectual property structures, New York University. J Evol Econ 24(2):335–355, 2014
Harper DA (2014) Property rights as a complex adaptive system: how entrepreneurship transforms intellectual property structures. J Evol Econ 24(2):335–355
Harper D (2015) Intellectual property as a complex adaptive system. In: Pyka A, Foster J (eds) The evolution of economic and innovation systems. Springer International Publishing, Cham
Hart OD (1988) Incomplete contracts and the theory of the firm. J Law Econ Org 4(1):119–139
Hassett KA, Shapiro R (2008) What ideas are worth: the value of intellectual capital and intangible assets in the American economy. SONECON. http://www.sonecon.com/docs/studies/Value_of_Intellectual_Capital_in_American_Economy.pdf
Hayek F (1948a) The use of knowledge in society. In: Individualism and economic order. Chicago University Press, Chicago, pp 77–91
Hayek FA (1948b) 'Economics and knowledge', in his individualism and economic order. Chicago University Press, Chicago, pp 33–56
Henkel J, Pangerl S (2008) Defensive publishing: an empirical study. DRUID working paper no 08-04. http://www3.druid.dk/wp/20080004.pdf

Hilgevoord J, Uffink J (2016) The uncertainty principle. In: Zalta EN (ed) The Stanford encyclopedia of philosophy, Winter edn. Forthcoming URL = https://plato.stanford.edu/archives/win2016/entries/qt-uncertainty/

Hill L (2015) How to manage for collecting creativity, Ted Talks business, ted.com, 13 Mar 2015. Retrieved 23 Dec 2012

Hsu DH, Ziedonis RH (2008) Patents as quality signals for entrepreneurial ventures. Academy of Management Proceedings, vol. 2008. no. 1. Academy of Management.

Huang KG-L (2016) Uncertain intellectual property conditions and knowledge appropriation strategies: evidence from the genomics industry. Industrial and corporate change, 24 Dec 2015, pp 1–31. Available at SSRN: https://ssrn.com/abstract=2773266

Hughes A, Mina A (2010) The impact of the patent system on SMEs, Centre for Business Research, University of Cambridge, Working paper no 411

Hunshell DA (1984) From the American system to mass production, 1900–1932: the development of manufacturing technology in the United States. Johns Hopkins University, Baltimore

Industrial Research Institute (2016) Global R&D funding forecast. R&D Magazine, Winter 2016

Ingvarsson M (2013) North–South and South–South technology transfer: a conceptual framework. Working paper 02/2013, Business Investment Technology Services, UNIDO

Ip G (2016) Economic drag: few big ideas. Wall Street J 7:A1

Isaacson W (2011) Steve Jobs. Simon & Schuster Paperbacks, New York, 10020

Isaacson W (2014) The innovators: how a group of hackers, geniuses, and geeks created the digital revolution. Simon & Schuster, New York

Jaffe AB, Lerner J (2004) Innovation and its discontents. Princeton University Press, Princeton

Johnson MW (2010) Seizing the white space: business model innovation for growth and renewal. Harvard Business Press, Boston

Johnson EE (2012) Intellectual property and the incentive fallacy. Fla State Univ Law Review 39:623–679

Karsten J, West DM (2015) Start-Up Chile: a “start-up for start-ups” in Chilecon Valley, Brookings Institute, TechTank, August 19. http://www.brookings.edu/blogs/techtank/posts/2015/08/19-startup-chile-chilecon-valley. Reviewed 28 July 2016

Keynes JM (1936) The general theory of employment, money and interest. Macmillan, London

Khalil MA, Olafsen E (2009) Enabling innovative entrepreneurship through business incubation. In: Claros AL (ed) The innovation for development report 2009–2010. Palgrave Mcmillan, London

Khan BZ (2013) Trolls and other patent inventions: economic history and the patent controversy in the twenty-first century. Working paper, National Bureau of Economic Research, Draft of September 2013. http://cpip.gmu.edu/wp-content/uploads/2013/09/Khan-Zorina-Patent-Controversy-in-the-21st-Century.pdf

Kim T, Yoo JJ-E, Lee G (2011) The HOINCAP scale: measuring intellectual capital in the hotel industry. Serv Ind J 31(13):2243–2272

Kim YK, Lee K, Part W, Choo K (2012) Appropriate intellectual property protection and economic growth in countries at different levels of development. Res Policy 41:358–375

Kirzner IM (1997) Entrepreneurial discovery and the competitive market process: an Austrian approach. J Econ Lit 35(1):60–85

Kitch EW (1977) The nature and function of the patent system. J Law Econ 20(2):265–290

Kitching J, Blackburn R (1999) Management training and networking in small and medium-sized enterprises in three European regions: implications for business support. Environ Plann C: Gov Policy 17(5):621–635

Knight FH (1921) Risk, uncertainty and profit. Hart, Schaffner and Marx, New York

Kwoh L (2012) You call that innovation? The Wall Street Journal, 23 May 2012

Lachmann LM (1943) The role of expectations in economics as a social science. Economica 10(37):12–23

Lachmann L (1977) Professor Shackle on the economic significance of time. In: Capital, expectations and the market process: essays on the theory of the market economy, Institute for Humane Studies. Sheed Andrews and McMeel, Inc., Kansas City
Lachmann L (1994) In: Lavoie D (ed) Expectations and the meaning of institutions: essays in economics. Routledge, London
Lamoreaux NR, Sokoloff K (2003) Intermediaries in the U.S. market for technology, 1870–1920. In: Engerman SL, Hoffman PT, Rosenthal J-L, Sokoloff KL (eds) Finance, intermediaries and economic development. Cambridge University Press, Cambridge, pp 209–246
Lamoreaux NR, Sokoloff K, Sutthiphisal D (2013) Patent alchemy: the market for technology in US history. http://www.hbs.edu/businesshistory/Documents/BHR870102.pdf
Lasagabaster E, Reddy R (2010) Supporting innovation in Latin America and the Caribbean: successful examples of technology transfer promotion, 164 En Breve, November
Lawton C, Chopping D (2011) Nokia, Apple make up iPhone maker to pay royalties under license agreement. The Wall Street Journal, 15 June 2011. http://www.wsj.com/articles/SB10001424052702303714704576384783542753682. Retrieved 28 Dec 2016
Lederman D, Messina J, Pienknagura S, Rigolini J (2014) Latin American entrepreneurs: many firms but little innovation. The World Bank, Washington, DC
Léger A (2007) Intellectual property rights and innovation around the world: evidence from panel data. Social Science Open Access Repository (SSOAR), IV, p 29. http://www.ssoar.info/ssoar/handle/document/11071
Lekachman R, Keynes JM (1964) Keynes' general theory; reports of three decades. St. Martin Press, New York
Lemney MA, Shapiro C (2005) Probabilistic patents. Journal of Economic Perspectives 19(75):75
Lerner J, Leamon A, Tighe J, Garcia-Robles S (2014) Adding value through venture capital in Latin America and the Caribbean, Working Paper, Harvard Business School
Levin RC, Klevorick AK, Nelson R, Winter SG (1987) Appropriating the returns from industrial research and development. Brook Pap Econ Act 3:242–279
Lewin P (1994) The economics of Ludwig M. Lachmann: attempting a new perspective. Adv Austrian Econ 1:233–256
Leydesdorff L, Meyer M (2010) Technology transfer and the end of the Bayh-dole effect: patents as an analytical lens on university-industry-government relations. Scientometrics, Jan 2010
Leydesdorff L, Meyer M (2013) A reply to Etzkowitz' comments to Leydesdorff and Martin (2010): technology transfer and the end of the Bayh–Dole effect. Scientometrics 97(3):927–934
Leydesdorff L, Etzkowitz H, Kushnir D (2016) Globalization and growth of US university patenting (2009–2014). Ind High Educ 30(4):257–266
Loasby B (1989) The working of a competitive economy: G. B. Richardson's post-Marshallian analysis. In: The mind and method of the economist. Edward Elgar, Aldershot
Loasby B (2004) Cognitivism and innovation in economics: two lectures. Working paper series, no 77, May 2004, Department of Economics, University of Milan – Bicocca
Loasby B (2005) Making connections. Symposium on information and knowledge in economics. Econ J Watch 2(1), April 2005, pp 56–65
Lohr S (2009) Patent auctions offer protections to inventors. N.Y. Times, Sept 20. http://www.nytimes.com/2009/09/21/technology/21patent.html?_r=0
Machlup F (1958) An economic review of the patent system. No. 15. US Government Printing Office, Washington, DC
Macneil IR (1978) Contracts: adjustment of long-term economic relations under classical, neoclassical, and relational contract law. Northwest Univ Law Rev 72:854–905
Marco AC (2005) The value of certainty in intellectual property rights: stock market reactions to patent litigation. Vassar College economics working paper #82
Marketwire (2015) U.S. Chamber of Commerce Presents Masimo CEO Joe Kiani With Intellectual Property Champion Award. Marketwired, 20 Apr 2015. http://www.marketwired.com/press-

release/us-chamber-commerce-presents-masimo-ceo-joe-kiani-with-intellectual-property-champion-nasdaq-masi-2011503.htm

Martin S, Scott JT (2000) 29 Research Policy, pp 437–447

Masnick M (2013) Patenting university research has been a dismal failure, enabling patent trolling. It'stimetostop,www.techdirt.comathttps://www.techdirt.com/articles/20131122/01322825335/patenting-university-research-has-been-dismal-failure-enabling-patent-trolling-its-time-to-stop.shtml

Mc Donald S (2003) Bearing the burden: small firms and the patent system. J Inf Law Technol 1:3

Melo A (2001) Innovation systems in Latin America. Inter-American Development Bank, Washington, DC

Mercurio B (2014) The Trans-Pacific partnership: suddenly a 'game changer'. World Econ 37(11):1558–1574

Merges RP, Nelson RR (1990) On the complex economics of patent scope. 90 Colum. L Rev 839

Merton RK (1957) Priorities in scientific discovery: a chapter in the sociology of science. Am Sociol Rev 22(6):635–659

Merton RK (1963) Resistance to the systematic study of multiple discoveries in science. Eur J Sociol 4(2):237–282

Millien R, Laurie R (2009) A survey of established and evolving IP monetization models, 984 PLI/PAT 1033, 1038

Milstein S (2002) New economy; many midsize companies find that 'defensive publishing' is a quick and cheap way to protect intellectual property. NYTimes.com, 18 Feb 2002

Mises L (1949) Human action: a treatise on economics. William Hodge and Co. Ltd., London

Moore G (1965) Cramming more components onto integrated circuits. Electronics Magazine 38(8)

Moulin A (2005) Intellectual property rights and Nordic SMEs-a study of IPR practices in the IT and biotech sectors. Digitala Vetenskapigla Arkivet. http://www.diva-portal.org/smash/record.jsf?dswid=-6419&pid=diva2%3A707078

Mueller F (2012) Apple seeks $2.5 billion in damages from Samsung, offers half a cent per standard-essential patent. FOSS Patents, July 24. Retrieved 28 July 2012

Mullin J (2016) Trolls made 2015 one of the biggest years ever for patent lawsuits. Law and Disorder, Civilization and Discontents, 5 Jan 2016. http://arstechnica.com/tech-policy/2016/01/despite-law-changes-2015-saw-a-heap-of-patent-troll-lawsuits/

Nazer D (2014) Watch Out Trolls: Supreme Court Expands Fee Shifting in Patent Cases, Electronic Frontier Foundation. https://www.eff.org/deeplinks/2014/04/watch-out-trolls-supreme-court-expands-fee-shifting-patent-cases. Retrieved 1 Oct 2016

Neiger C (2016) Jawbone and Fitbit's Lawsuit: everything you need to know. The Motley Fool, 15 July 2016. http://www.fool.com/investing/2016/07/15/jawbone-and-fitbits-lawsuit-everything-you-need-to.aspx. Retrieved 25 Dec 2016

Newton J (1987) Uncommon friends: life with Thomas Edison, Henry Ford, Harvey Firestone, Alexis Carrel & Charles Lindbergh. Houghton Miffln Harcourt Publishing Co, New York

Nguyen-Dinh L (2016) IP finance and securitisation: the development of IP financing offers. Presentation given at the European Union, Brussels, 14 June 2016. https://ec.europa.eu/jrc/sites/jrcsh/files/20160616-ipexchangeandfinance-nguyendinh_en.pdf. Retrieved 3 Jan 2017

O'Driscoll G, Rizzo M (1985) The economics of time and ignorance. Routledge, London

OCDE (2013) Startup America Latina: Promoviendo la Innovación en la región; Estudios del Centro de Desarrollo, OCDE, Paris

Ocean Tomo (2015) Annual study of intangible asset market value from Ocean Tomo, LLC, 5 Mar 2015. http://www.oceantomo.com/2015/03/04/2015-intangible-asset-market-value-study/. Retrieved 2 Oct 2016

OECD (2011) New sources of growth: intangible assets. http://www.oecd.org/sti/inno/46349020.pdf

OECD (2013) Innovation in Latin America. OECD Observer No 296 Q3 2013 en. http://www.oecdobserver.org/news/fullstory.php/aid/4231/Innovation_in_Latin_America.html

OECD (2015) Enquiries into intellectual Property's economic impact. OECD, Paris

OHIM (2015) Intellectual property rights and firm performance in Europe: an economic analysis. Firm-level analysis report
OMPI (2008) Introducción a la financiación basada en la propiedad intelectual. Revista de la OMPI, (Septiembre). http://www.wipo.int/wipo_magazine/es/2008/05/article_0001.html
Orr JR (2013) Patent aggregation: models, harms, and the limited role of antitrust. Berkeley Technol Law J 28(4):525–568. http://scholarship.law.berkeley.edu/btlj/vol28/iss4/8
Osawa J (2016) Patents drive Chinese phone push. Wall Street J 21:B1
Palfrey JG (2012) Intellectual property strategy. MIT Press, Cambridge, MA
Parchomovsky G, Polk Wagner R (2005) Patent portfolios. Univ Pa Law Rev 154(1):1–77
Park WG (2008) International patent protection: 1960–2005. Res Policy 37:761–766
Paul JC, Kacedon DB (2012) Membership in a defensive patent-aggregation service may provide a plausible basis for alleging pre-suit knowledge of a patent for a claim of willful infringement. LES insights, Sept 24. http://www.finnegan.com/resources/articles/articlesdetail.aspx?news=28f22c0e-5826-4e8a-8357-3690f00b38fc. Retrieved 24 July 2016
Pelletier P (2016) What to know about patent reform bills heading into 2016. Law 360. http://www.law360.com/articles/740947/what-to-know-about-patent-reform-bills-heading-into-2016. Retrieved 1 Oct 2016
Perdue G (2004) Understanding the economic value of trade secrets, American Bar Association, Intellectual Property Litigation Committee, 28 Mar 2014. http://apps.americanbar.org/litigation/committees/intellectual/articles/spring2014-0314-calculating-economic-value-trade-secrets.html
Perez de Anton F (2002) Memorial de Cocinas y Batallas. Aguilar, Guatemala Ciudad
Pistor K, Xu C (2003) Incomplete law. Int Law Pol 35:931–1013
Polanyi M (1958) Personal knowledge. University of Chicago Press, Chicago
Polonenko, Daniel and Alaka Chatterjee (2011) A shift in commercialization strategies: from closed to open innovation, June 28. http://www.lexology.com/library/detail.aspx?g=6f5f7725-c5db-4862-89cc-a248747c1141. Retrieved 23 July 2016
Pratt MR (2015) New venture finance: startup funding for entrepreneurs. University of Maryland, Coursera. https://class.coursera.org/venturefinance-005
Pressman L, Roessner D, Bond J, Okubo S, Planting M (2012) The economic contribution of university/nonprofit inventions in the United States: 1996–2010. Biotechnology Industry Organization. https://www.bio.org/sites/default/files/Biopercent20Economicpercent20Impactpercent202012percent20Junepercent2020.pdf
PricewaterhouseCoopers (PWC) (2015) Global Annual Review 2015. Available at: http://www.pwc.com/gx/en/about-pwc/global-annual-review-2015/campaign-site/pwc-global-annual-review-2015.pdf
PricewaterhouseCoopers (PWC) (2016) Global Annual Review 2016. Available at: https://www.pwc.com/gx/en/annual-review/2016/pwc-global-annual-review.pdf
Quian Y (2007) Do national patent laws stimulate domestic innovation in a global patenting environment? A cross-country analysis of pharmaceutical patent protection 1978–2002. Rev Econ Stat 89(3):436
Quinn G (2015) Biased report chastises USPTO for insufficient quality control. IP Watchdog, Apr 15. http://www.ipwatchdog.com/2015/04/15/biased-report-chastises-uspto-for-insufficient-quality-control/id=56851/
Rader R (2011) The state of patent litigation. E.D. Texas Judicial Conference. http://patentlyo.com/media/docs/2011/09/raderstateofpatentlit.pdf
Randazo S (2016) Litigation attracts wave of investors. The Wall Street Journal, 16 May 2016
Rantanen J (2015) The malleability of patent rights. Michigan State Law Review, 895
Reichelt KM (2007). University technology transfer and national innovation policy: success stories from Brazil, Colombia and South Africa
Reisinger D (2016) Samsung wins appeal in $120M patent fight with Apple. Forbes, Feb 26
Reitzig M (2004) The private values of ‘thickets’ and ‘fences’, towards an updated picture of the use of patents across industries. Econ Innov New Technol 13:457–476

Relan P. 90 percent of incubators and accelerators will fail and that's just fine for America and the world. Techcrunch.com. https://techcrunch.com/2012/10/14/90-of-incubators-and-accelerators-will-fail-and-why-thats-just-fine-for-america-and-the-world/. Posted 14 Oct 2012; Retrieved 7 Dec 2016

Richardson GB (1960) Information and investment. Oxford University Press, London

Richardson GB (1972/1996) The organization of industry. In: Buckley P, Michie J (eds) Firms, organizations and contracts. Oxford University Press, Oxford

Rizzo M (1996) Real time and relative indeterminacy in economic theory, New York University, paper presented at the Austrian Economics Colloquium, Department of Economics, New York University, November

Rodriguez M, Dunwoody W (2014) The sword and the shield: building an offensive and defensive IP portfolio. Inside Counsel, May 6. http://www.insidecounsel.com/2014/05/06/the-sword-and-the-shield-building-an-offensive-and

Sada MJ (2016) Brothers bringing habanero sauces to U.S. since 1989 ready to turn up the heat, published in Fox News Latino. http://latino.foxnews.com/latino/money/2016/07/28/brothers-bringing-habanero-sauces-to-us-since-18-ready-to-turn-up-heat/

Schutz RJ (1999) Strategies for patent holders contemplating litigation, Sept 21. http://www.robinskaplan.com/resources/articles/strategies-for-patent-holders-contemplating-litigation

Schwab K (2016) The fourth industrial revolution. World Economic Forum, 11 Jan 2016

Seah J (2012) Some in Asia see Bian in US. Apple Veredict, The Asian Lawyer, Sept 3, 2012

Shapiro C (2001) Navigating the patent thicket: cross licenses, patent pools, and standard-setting (PDF). In: Jaffe AB et al (eds) Innovation policy and the economy, vol I. MIT Press, Cambridge, pp 119–150

Simon HA (1962) New developments in the theory of the firm. Am Econ Rev 52(2):1–15

Singapore IP Steering Committee (2013) Intellectual Property (IP) Hub Master Plan: Developing Singapore as a Global IP Hub in Asia, Apr. https://www.ipos.gov.sg/Portals/0/Press%20Release/IP%20HUB%20MASTER%20PLAN%20REPORT%202%20APR%202013.pdf. Retrieved 4 Jan 2017

Smith A (1776) The Wealth of Nations, Metalibri. https://www.ibiblio.org/ml/libri/s/SmithA_WealthNations_p.pdf

Taleb NN (2007) The black swan. Penguin Books, London

Tavoletti E (2013) Business incubators: effective infrastructures or waste of public money? Looking for a theoretical framework, guidelines and criteria. J Knowl Econ 4(4):423–443

Taylor B (2013) Stop me before I "innovate" again! Harvard Business Review, Dec 6. https://hbr.org/2013/12/stop-me-before-i-innovate-again/. Reviewed 24 July 2016

Teece D (1986) Profiting from technological innovation: innovation for integration, collaboration, licensing and public policy. Res Policy 15:285–315

Teece D (1998) Capturing value from knowledge assets: the new economy, markets for know-how, and intangible assets. Calif Manag Rev 40(3):55–79

Teece D (2000) Managing intellectual capital: organizational, strategic, and policy dimensions. Oxford University Press, New York

The Fashion Law (2016) Carolina Herrera Sues Oscar de la Renta Over Monse Founder, Laura Kim, Dec 23, 2016. http://www.thefashionlaw.com/home/carolina-herrera-sues-oscar-de-la-renta-over-monse-founder-laura-kim. Retrieved 25 Dec 2016

The World Bank, World Development Indicators (2015) Retrieved from: http://data.worldbank.org/

Thomsen E (1992) Prices and knowledge. Routledge, London

Thorn K, Soo M (2006) Latin American universities and the third mission: trends, Challenges and policy options, World Bank policy research working paper 4002, World Bank, Washington, DC

Times Higher Education World University Rankings 2015–2016. https://www.timeshighereducation.com/

U.S. Federal Bureau of Investigation (2010) Former paint manufacturing chemist pleads guilty to stealing trade secrets valued up to $20 million. https://archives.fbi.gov/archives/chicago/press-releases/2010/cg090110-1.htm
U.S. Federal Trade Commission (2016) Patent assertion entity activity: an FTC study, Washington, DC, 16 Oct 2016. https://www.ftc.gov/reports/patent-assertion-entity-activity-ftc-study. Retrieved 31 Dec 2016
UK Intellectual Property Office (2012) From ideas to growth: helping SMEs get value from their intellectual property, London. https://www.gov.uk/government/uploads/system/uploads/attachment_data/file/316116/ip4b-sme.pdf
UK Intellectual Property Office (2015) UK Intellectual Property Awareness Survey 2015. https://www.gov.uk/government/uploads/system/uploads/attachment_data/file/500211/IP_awareness_survey_2015.pdf
Un CA, Cuervo-Cazurra A, Asakawa K (2010) R&D collaborations and product innovation. J Prod Innov Manag 27:673–689
UNESCO (2013) Creative economy report: widening local development pathways. UNDP, New York
Unified Patents (2015) Patent dispute report. Unified Patents, 31 Dec 2015. https://www.unified-patents.com/news/2016/5/30/2015-patent-dispute-report. Retrieved 30 Sept 2016
United Nations (2011) Intellectual property commercialization: policy options and practical instruments. United Nations Economic Commission for Europe, New York
University of Dublin (2001) Enforcing small firms patent rights. European Commission, Enterprise DG, Luxemburg
USNEWS (2016) Best Global Universities rank. http://www.usnews.com/education/best-global-universities/rankings
USPTO (2016) Intellectual property and the U.S. economy: 2016 update, USPTO, Washington, DC. http://www.uspto.gov/sites/default/files/documents/IPandtheUSEconomySept2016.pdf. Retrieved 2 Oct 2016
Valdivia W (2013) University start-ups: critical for improving technology transfer, Brookings. http://www.brookings.edu/research/papers/2013/11/university-start-ups-technology-transfer-valdivia
Valdivia W (2014a), Technology transfer: highly dependent on university resources. TechTank, Improving Technology Policy, Brooking, 4 Mar 2014
Valdivia W (2014b) Tech transfer in the groves of academe. Innovation 12(1). http://www.innovation-america.org/tech-transfer-groves-academe
Wacker P-A (2013) Key considerations in transnational patent litigation. IP Value, IAM, Kuhnen & Wacker. https://www.kuhnen-wacker.com/kuhnen-wacker/documents/paw_transnational-patent-litigation.pdf
Walker J (2014) The real patent crisis is stifling innovation. Forbes, 18 June 2014. http://www.forbes.com/sites/danielfisher/2014/06/18/13633/#412ced894183. Retrieved 16 Dec 2016
Wanamakert M (2003) The First Studios. http://free-culture.cc/notes/12.pdf\\
Wang AW (2010) Rise of the patent intermediaries. Berkeley Technol Law J 25(1):159–200
Weingust S (2016) Q&A: creating value through IP asset management and valuation. Financer Worldwide Magazine, Jan 2016
Wicksteed PH (1967 [1910]) The common sense of political economy, vol 1. Augustus M. Kelly, New York
Wolfe RM (2016) Business research and development and innovation: 2013. National Science Foundation, National Center for Science and Engineering Statistics. Available at: https://www.nsf.gov/statistics/2016/nsf16313/pdf/nsf16313.pdf
World Bank (2006) Where is the wealth of nations? The World Bank, Washington, DC
World Bank (2014) World development report 2015: risk and opportunity – managing risk for development. World Bank, Washington, DC

World Intellectual Property Indicators (2014) World Intellectual Property Organization. Available at: http://www.wipo.int/edocs/pubdocs/en/wipo_pub_941_2014.pdf

World Intellectual Property Indicators (2015) World Intellectual Property Organization. Available at: http://www.wipo.int/edocs/pubdocs/en/wipo_pub_941_2015.pdf

World Intellectual Property Organization (WIPO) (2010) WIPO Magazine. IP litigation costs special edition. Geneva, Feb 2010, No. 1. Available at: http://www.wipo.int/export/sites/www/wipo_magazine/en/pdf/2010/wipo_pub_121_2010_01.pdf

Yarow J (2012) How Apple really lost its lead in the '80s. Business Insider, 9 Dec 2012. http://www.businessinsider.com/how-apple-really-lost-its-lead-in-the-80s-2012-12. Retrieved 23 Dec 2016

Young A (1928) Increasing returns and economic progress. Econ J 38(152):527–542

Yudkowsdy E (2008) Cognitive biases potentially affecting judgment of global risks; machine intelligence research institute. In: Bostrom N, Ćirković MM (eds) Global catastrophic risks. Oxford University Press, New York, pp 91–119

Ziedonis RH (2004) Don't fence me in: fragmented markets for technology and the patent acquisition strategies of firms. Manag Sci 50(6):804–820

Zimmerman E (2013) Assessing the impact of business incubators. The New York Times, 12 Aug 2013. http://boss.blogs.nytimes.com/2013/08/12/assessing-the-impact-of-business-incubators/?_r=0. Retrieved 7 Dec 2016

Zucoloto G (2013) Propriedade Intelectual em Debate. presentado en Conferência Internacional LALICS 2013 "Sistemas Nacionais de Inovação e Políticas de CTI para um Desenvolvimento Inclusivo e Sustentável", 11–12 de Noviembre de 2013, Rio de Janeiro

MIX
Papier aus verantwortungsvollen Quellen
Paper from responsible sources
FSC® C105338

If you have any concerns about our products,
you can contact us on
ProductSafety@springernature.com

In case Publisher is established outside the EU,
the EU authorized representative is:
Springer Nature Customer Service Center GmbH
Europaplatz 3, 69115 Heidelberg, Germany

Printed by Libri Plureos GmbH
in Hamburg, Germany